workers' li

reason in revolt ✓

Contents

Subscription information page 120

Workers' Liberty Volume 2 no. 2

Published March 2002 by the Alliance for Workers' Liberty

Editor: Sean Matgamna
Assistant Editors: Cathy Nugent, Martin Thomas
Design: Cath Fletcher, Duncan Morrison
Business Manager: Alan McArthur

ISBN: 0-9531864-2-3

What is Workers' Liberty?

The Alliance for Workers' Liberty organises to fight the class struggle on all levels — trade union and social battles, politics and the combat of ideas. We are active in workplaces, in trade unions, in the Socialist Alliance and in the Labour Party, in single-issue campaigns, in student unions, and in debates and discussions on the left. We aim to integrate all these activities into a coherent effort for socialism.

If you want to know more about the Alliance for Workers' Liberty, write to: PO Box 823, London SE15 4NA, phone 020 7207 3997, or email office@workersliberty.org

www.workersliberty.org

EDITORIAL

The rule of greed and deceit

"**A**N UNHOLY convergence of greed, incompetence and deceit" is how the *Financial Times* describes the events leading to the collapse of Enron, once the USA's seventh largest company, now the biggest bankruptcy ever declared.

Enron boasted of being "asset light". It traded. It didn't produce anything. It generated "virtual wealth through virtual companies". It created 3,500 affiliates and "off-balance-sheet" partnerships, many managed by Enron executives. At its height, $27 billion of its $60 billion assets were off-balance-sheet. It used those side-companies in various ways, to draw in outside investors, to inflate seeming profitability, and to hide losses.

For example, it would make deals with off-balance-sheet partners at the end of each financial quarter which increased its paper income, and then cancel them at the beginning of the next quarter.

With long-term energy contracts, it would book as current income money that might not be realised for ten years, and seriously underestimate commodity costs to itself in the later years of a contract. These practices are described by the former Enron accountant as "skirting the edges" of legality.

Enron also avoided taxes during the period when its stock was riding high. Between 1996 and 2000, when its pre-tax profits totalled $1.79 billion, it received $381 million in US federal tax rebates and only once paid tax — $17 million in 1997.

All these practices were well known to Enron's partners, including most of the big players in world finance, Citigroup, CIBC, Deutsche Bank, Dresdner Bank. JP Morgan Chase actively advised on the fiddles. As the *FT* points out, "The fancy manoeuvring was surely not practised by Enron alone."

Now thousands of employees and pensioners have lost their jobs and their savings in the collapse — 60% of the Enron employee retirement plan was held in now-worthless Enron stock — while the top executives have made hundreds of millions of dollars personally by selling their shares before Enron's collapse became public knowledge.

And still the IMF, the World Bank, the World Trade Organisation, and the governments, big corporations and banks behind them, tell us that "the market" is the only rational and efficient system for coordinating economic life – impersonal, impartial, robust.

In fact, the rule of "the market" means clearing the way for the rich to get richer by greed and deceit, just as the Enron bosses got rich. When governments talk of bringing "market discipline" into public services, it means that global capitalism is on the rampage and public services are the main target, the new "dark continent" to be opened up for exploitation. New Labour accepting Enron's "cash for access" is a small thing compared to their planned dismembering of what is left of our public services – handing them over to the Enron clones and aspirant clones.

The Pakistani socialists' stand against war and fundamentalism

By Farooq Tariq, general secretary of the Labour Party of Pakistan

THE Labour Party of Pakistan has nothing to do with the policies of the Labour Party of Britain. The Labour Party of Britain is on the side of the dictators, on the side of the fundamentalists, on the side of the bombings; and we are just on the opposite side — on the side of the socialists and Marxists, and the side of those who want to promote peace and human rights with the active participation of the working class.

We see fundamentalists as a new sort of fascists who have to be opposed. There is nothing progressive, there is nothing anti-imperialist in the strategy of the fundamentalists against America. We have seen in practice that the fundamentalists are an outrightly extreme right wing, suppressive, anti-democratic force who have nothing in common with progressive ideas.

Some left groups say that we should side with the fundamentalists because they are opposing American imperialism. But we in Pakistan have learned this lesson through hard realities.

We have seen what happened in the Iranian revolution when the Tudeh Party, the Communist Party of Iran, made an alliance with Khomeini's fundamentalists against the Shah of Iran. The Tudeh Party played an important part in the mass movement, but, with the defeat of the Shah, when Khomeini took over, the first thing he did was to hang the General Secretary of the Tudeh Party. Hundreds of activists were hanged.

We saw a total collapse of those forces of the left who thought that maybe for the time being we can align with those forces among the fundamentalists who seem to be anti-imperialist and who are making a lot of noise against imperialism.

We have also seen something similar in Pakistan. In 1977, when there was a movement against Bhutto, sections of the Stalinists aligned with Jamat al-Islami to launch a movement against him. The Stalinists argued that Bhutto was a fascist and that we should join hands with fundamentalists to liberalise Pakistan and to get rid of him. The result was that the military took over and those left forces were put into jail by Zia.

We have also seen the example of Afghanistan. During the Najibullah period, most of his opponents within the party collaborated with the mujahedeen. They hoped that they could have an alliance with the mujahedeen — with the fundamentalists — and once they had defeated Najibullah together that they could deal with the mujahedeen. In 1992 the mujahedeen took over — and the Najibullah party was totally finished.

So, when the war against Afghanistan started, we condemned the terrorist action, but we also said that war is no way to stop terrorism. In our weekly paper, *Workers' Struggle*, we said "No Terrorism against Terrorism". But we also said, no alliance with fundamentalists.

That was nothing new for us. Since the LPP came into existence in 1997 we have said we will never have any alliance with the fundamentalists, or with any section of the religious parties. There have been many offers to us, in the trade union field and in the political field. Some of the fundamentalists said, we are against privatisation, let's get together and fight against the privatisation of the railways.

Our response was to say: if we look at your philosophy, you are in favour of private property, you are in favour of feudalism, you are in favour of capitalism – how can you fight privatisation? We won't go along with your demagogy. The only reason you say you are against privatisation is the pressure of the working class who do not want privatisation. They are forcing you to take this initiative so that you can have some social base in the working class.

The Pakistani fundamentalists and Arab fundamentalists who went to Afghanistan to fight with the Taliban were massacred, whereas the local Pashtun Taliban left the jihad and just became Pashtun. They made a compromise with Karzai. Omar and Osama left the foreign fundamentalists to be massacred by the Northern Alliance and the American army. Most of the Taliban leadership were not killed. They made a compromise – maybe with the approval of American imperialism – and they escaped to safety. Karzai will be able to use them in the future if there is tension between Uzbeks and Hazaras and Tajiks and so on.

When it came to their own necks, they forgot about the jihad and their slogans that they would fight until death. It was only to Kandahar that they fought! Then they ran away on motor bikes. That has left a very bad taste in Pakistan because the Pakistani Taliban did not escape.

There is some feeling in the West that if Osama is alive, or Omar, the Taliban could regenerate. But I think that the Taliban are finished. They are totally exposed. There will be new leaders, with different forms of fundamentalism, but this current is finished.

I will just say a few words on the role of the LPP. The first demonstration we organised was on 27 September, before the attacks of American imperialism on Afghanistan, with over 500 women activists from the Women Workers' Helpline. They took the initiative to launch the first peace demonstration – and it made headlines across the country that women had come out for peace in Pakistan.

It brought an alternative view in the country. Before that, every day the fundamentalists were on the streets with their slogans that Osama was the hero of the Muslim world . There were not in general many on their demonstrations, but there was a general feeling of support for what the fanatics were saying, which is not surprising given what American imperialism has done to Third World countries. When the events of September 11 took place, many in Pakistan supported them – the majority of the working class in Pakistan sympathised with the terrorists.

That first action of ours on September 27 was very much a minority position. But then on October 15 in Lahore, over 1000 party activists rallied at the same time as the fundamentalists called a General Strike. The police pressured us to cancel our action, but we said no, you're not telling the fundamentalists to cancel their action, why should we be the ones to back down?

Over 1000 came, of whom about 400 were women, and we had a very militant demonstration against the war and against the fundamentalists. We said that we totally opposed American imperialism but that we would not support Osama and Mullah Omar, who have attacked women's rights. At the same time, we exposed the hypocrisy of American imperialism and their new-found support for women's rights. As one of our women activists said that day: "They are killing women in Kabul. How can they defend the rights of women?"

On November 6, over 8000 people demonstrated in Rawalpindi on our initiative, and the majority of them were women. Some NGOs who were involved wanted to use the demonstration just against the fundamentalists, and maybe in favour of the army. We made sure that the main slogan and the main tone of that demonstration was against imperialism, against the bombing and so on, but we also condemned fundamentalism on the same demonstration. That demonstration really changed the mood in many organisations. It really gave courage to people to come out against both American imperialism and the fundamentalists.

Then on 10 December we had another demonstration in Lahore of 2000. On December 31 we had brought 2000 activists to the border with India, and we had slogans on both sides of the border opposing war.

For you it is probably normal to celebrate New Year. But the fundamentalists have made this big thing to prevent it. In Lahore particularly they roam around the streets in gangs on New Year's night. If someone has had a drink, or there is a party going on, they will attack and try to disperse people. The police will just stand by and watch while they do that.

The LPP announced in the press that we would go onto the main road to celebrate New Year's night as a Peace Night. Thirty of us went there. We saw hundreds of police waiting for us, and we were really afraid that we would be arrested. Actually, when we got there they said, at least someone has dared to come to this place to celebrate the New Year. They wished us Happy New Year. It was a very good initiative by the Labour Party. Thousands of people waved to us. For the first time in maybe 25 years, there was a little demonstration on the main street in Lahore to celebrate New Year's night openly and publicly. It was very symbolic — symbolic that someone had dared fight against fundamentalism — and it gained us publicity in all the newspapers.

● *Farooq Tariq, general secretary of the Labour Party of Pakistan, spoke in London on Friday 25 January 2002, at a meeting organised by the International Socialist Group.*

The politics of globalisation and imperialism today

By Colin Foster

S INCE the 1990s new patterns have emerged in world capitalism. Their immediate roots go back to the 1970s. In 1973, the major oil-producing states
forced a big increase in oil prices. Among the big capitalist powers, the oil
price rise hit the US less hard than others. It even made some of the US's own new
oilfields profitable. Britain, too, would gain from the oil price rise, when North Sea
oil production boomed in the early 1980s. But in essence the increase was one of
the signals of the end of the colonial era.

In 1975, Portugal's African colonies − Angola, Mozambique, Guinea-Bissau −
at last won their independence. Over the previous three decades, the great colonial
empires of West European states like Britain, France, and the Netherlands, which
long dominated the globe, had bit by bit been liquidated. India, Indochina,
Indonesia, Egypt, Algeria, Nigeria had become independent.

In 1973 states like Iran, Iraq, Libya, Venezuela and even Saudi Arabia − some
once colonies or semi-colonies, others long very subaltern and pliant partners of
the big capitalist states − showed that they had their own capitalist ambitions.
They were no longer willing just to serve as platforms for the ambitions of US or
British oil companies.

Oil-producing states stashed a lot of their vast new revenues with the international banks, who in turn lent the cash to industrialising ex-colonial states. When
the big capitalist economies lurched into slump after 1979-80, trade contracted,
interest rates rose, and credit got tighter: those borrower states could no longer pay
yesterday's debts from today's profits and new loans. In 1982, Mexico's failure to
meet debt repayments signalled the start of a global debt crunch. The capitalists of
the less-industrial states had put large slices of the loan money into safe US or
European property or bank accounts, and now they co-operated with the banks in
making the workers and peasants pay the cost of the crisis, on a scale which made
British Tory austerity look gentle.

The crunch was not just a sudden crisis. The capitalists and governments of the
poorer countries did not respond to the debt squeeze by shifting into their old
mode of having their own national states as the main financiers for development,
as some of them had when they became unable to meet debt payments in the
1930s. They made a new permanent regime out of heavy indebtedness, sharpened
austerity and a drive for exports to cover the costs of debt. Their industrial development had reached a level requiring substantial imports − and thus international credit − to continue. Some of the costs of keeping internationally creditworthy
were irksome to the ex-colonial wealthy, but most of those costs they could offload
onto the workers and peasants − and most of the benefits of the borrowing they
could pocket for themselves.

The USA and other big economies recovered after 1983. Though the recovery
was sluggish, and interrupted by new crises in 1990-2 and 2001, it provided sufficient markets for the ex-colonial capitalists to pursue their new strategy − at least
until they got well locked into it. In the 1980s, the ex-colonial states, in total, started to export more manufactured goods to the US than it imported from there.

As the ex-colonial states sweated to make debt payments, they took on new loans. Their debt burden often increased. In 1999, debt-service took 76% of Argentina's export income, 33% of India's, 30% of Indonesia's, between 22 and 26% for each of Brazil, Chile, Mexico, and South Korea.

Tariffs fell. Under the "Uruguay round" of trade negotiations, average advanced country tariffs on manufactured imports are to be cut to less than 4%. Tariffs of ex-colonial states are set to fall from 34% (in 1984-7) to 14%. Brazil's weighted mean tariffs have fallen from 32% in 1989 to 13% in 1999; China's, from 33% to 16%; India's, from 50% to 30%; the USA's, from 4% to 3%.

World merchandise exports increased 137% between 1987 and 1997 — much faster than world output — and the merchandise exports of countries classified by the World Bank as "low and medium income" almost tripled, increasing by 187%. The ratio of trade (imports plus exports) to output (GDP) doubled for "low and medium income" countries between 1970 and 1997. It increased from 18% to 40% in low-income countries and from 25% to 50% in medium-income.

Investment in ex-colonial countries by companies which buy or construct facilities there (called foreign direct investment, as distinct from just buying shares or making bank loans) sagged in the 1980s but increased fast in the 1990s.

Local private capitalists also figured more largely, often displacing the ex-colonial states from their previous centrality in capital investment. Even states still run by "Communist Parties", like Vietnam, Cuba and, most spectacularly, China, sought foreign investment and encouraged private enterprise. Telecoms, other utilities and basic industries were privatised in many countries. The Chilean state started privatising in 1973, and has sold off 95% of its state-owned enterprises. Mexico sold off or shut down 80% of its 1,500 state-owned enterprises between 1982 and the end of 1992, cutting 200,000 jobs in the process. South Korea started a new wave of privatisations in 1987, following previous sell-offs in 1962-66 and the early 1980s. In Pakistan, which started privatising in 1991, 43% of workers in the sold-off enterprises were laid off within the first year after privatisation, and many workers elsewhere have lost jobs, or job security, through privatisation.

In many countries, tariff reductions, a drive to make exports and attract foreign investment, and privatisation were tied together with cuts in whatever minimal welfare provision existed — such as food price subsidies — through "Structural Adjustment Programs" negotiated with the IMF or the World Bank as the price for further loans. Fifty-five countries borrowed from the IMF under Structural Adjustment Facilities between 1986 and April 1998.

This was "globalisation". It has brought an increase in inequality both within and between nations. Millions have been pauperised. Whole populations, especially in sub-Saharan Africa, have been marginalised and left as "basket cases" by the onrush of world-market capitalism. Since 1960, the gap between the richest and the poorest fifth of nations has doubled.

Yet the development of an industrial base in the ex-colonial world continues. Power production increased in "low income" countries 170% between 1960 and 1990, and 189% between 1990 and 1998; in "middle income" countries, 370% 1960-90, 204% 1990-98. The number of telephone lines, the amount of paved roads, the extent of drinking-water supply and irrigated land, have also increased fairly fast. Between 1990 and 1997, manufacturing production increased 49% in "low income" countries, 57% in "middle income" countries (and 15% in "high income" countries). Countries like Korea, Taiwan, Singapore, Malaysia, Thailand, Mexico and Brazil now export relatively high-tech goods. Even in the poorest ex-colonial countries, there is generally some increase in the preconditions for industrial production, even if that increase is outpaced by a parallel rise in misery and poverty. The proportion of illiterates dropped fairly fast between 1980 and 1995 — from 30.5% to 22.6% — though the world's total illiterate population increased from 877 million to 885 million.

Trade has changed in structure as well as increased. Manufacturing as a percentage of the exports of "low and middle income" countries increased from 20% in 1960 to over 50% in 1990 and over 60% in 1999. Within the reduced share of world trade due to agriculture, a new pattern has emerged where the South specialises in export of labour-intensive luxury crops and the North (especially the USA) in export of capital-intensive "low-value" bulk foods.

John Pilger, in his book *Hidden Agendas*, puts a widespread view when he contends that the increase in inequality and poverty, and the increased role of big multinational companies and international banks, make globalisation really a euphemism for US reconquest of the ex-colonial world. But capitalist development can bring huge misery and inequality without having to be compounded with colonialism. And that is what is happening now.

The "globalist" path has been followed by virtually all governments, not only those pushed into it because their debt burden obliges them to do the bidding of the IMF or the World Bank. Although no doubt the governments would prefer to be able to choose their own tempo rather than obey the international bankers, the basic strategy suits their class interests. They impose the welfare-cutting, privatising, foreign-investment-seeking plans primarily because they are capitalist governments, not because they lack national independence. They queue up to join the IMF, while in the 19th century the peoples of Africa and Asia often fought hard to avoid "joining" colonial empires. The IMF today (2001) has 183 members, as against 130 in 1975.

Despite the rapid rise of foreign direct investment in the 1990s, the economies of most ex-colonial countries today are dominated by local capitalists. Those ex-colonial states able to provide infrastructure and educated labour for enterprises competitive in world manufacturing and services – and they include some with vast hinterlands of absolute poverty, like India and Indonesia – are doing so not because their states have been weakened, but because they have been strengthened – because they are now established capitalist states, with local capitalist classes behind them of some substance and bulk, rather than what they often were, proto-capitalist states run by a thin middle class layer anxious to use all the levers of state protectionism to build a base and ward off big outside capital. Globalisation depends on the states of newly-industrialising countries being stronger, not weaker.

"Transnational capital may be more effective than was the old-style military imperialism in penetrating every corner of the world, but it tends to accomplish this through the medium of local capital and national states... it depends on many local jurisdictions – on, say, the Indian or Chinese state – to maintain the conditions of economic stability and labour discipline which are the conditions of profitable investment" (Ellen Wood).

Full-fledged capitalism has spread much more widely than ever before. As the gleaming skyscrapers reach upwards in the cities of the ex-colonial states, the grim shanty towns spread outwards. Hundreds of millions of people suffer hideously – peasants pushed out of subsistence farming by the drive towards higher-priced world-market cash-crops; workers who lose their jobs in privatisations or debt crises; the urban poor, hit by cuts in food subsidies and increases in public transport fares and utility charges; and whole peoples in those ex-colonial countries still dependent on bulk raw material exports.

The pillage of the workers and peasants of the ex-colonial countries continues, but in a different form – the urbane international banker replacing the colonial soldier and tax collector. The difference of form is not just a "formality". Far from it. Today's "imperialism of free trade" is a domination of rich over poor, and richer nations over poorer nations, achieved primarily, to use a phrase from Marx, by "the dull compulsion of economic relations... Direct force, outside economic conditions, is of course still used, but only exceptionally".

Historians have called British imperialism in the early and middle 19th century, "the imperialism of free trade". In South America, for example, Britain did not need to establish its own colonial rule in place of Spain's. The competitive supremacy of its industry gave it economic dominance, and with that political influence. A new, more multi-faceted, more universal, "imperialism of free trade" is the main form today.

It is not "purely economic", purely a matter of the anonymous and automatic workings of the market. The capitalist market economy, despite having "the dull compulsion of economic relations" at the core of its relations of exploitation, requires far more police, military establishment, and machinery of government than pre-feudal or tribute-paying economies. The deliberate, semi-political or political, actions of IMF and World Bank officials, of World Trade Organisation negotiators, of the big business executives who fly around the world requesting and giving bribes, and of the metropolitan administrators of military and economic aid programmes, all count for much.

But the basic mechanism is the pursuit by the big multinationals and banks of a world open to the free flow of their products and their capital, the drive towards such a world by the biggest capitalist states, and the compulsion on the weaker capitalist states either to join in such a world, with all its disadvantages to them, or be excluded, with even greater disadvantages.

Three distinct epochs of modern imperialism can now be distinguished.

● Between the 1870s and the end of the Second World War, "imperialism" meant a world divided up into rival colonial empires. Each of the big capitalist states ruled over vast millions of less-capitalistically-developed peoples, using their territories as controlled sources of industrial raw-materials, captive markets for manufactured exports, and sites where capital could be safely exported (mainly for extractive industries and infrastructure) to win dividends, interest and profits. They used colonial or semi-colonial rule because they could do at manageable cost; in order to give them advantage in rivalry with other big powers; and often because without direct metropolitan power no cooperative local machinery of government could be established strong enough to drive the population into the world-market economy, squeezing out raw materials and pushing in metropolitan exports.

● In the epoch from the Second World War to 1989, the USSR practised an ultra-monopolistic imperialism in its sphere of influence, and the USA deliberately promoted an "imperialism of free trade" as its main counter.

In its "backyard", Central America, until the 1960s at least, it maintained a system of semi-colonialism, under which the Marines could be sent in against any large reformist threat to the super-profits of the big American corporations which dominated whole countries based on the export of a few raw materials.

But even in Central America, the pattern began to shift in the 1970s. And elsewhere, steadily but effectively, the USA favoured the break-up of the old colonial empires held by Britain, France and other European powers. It did that because it knew that its capital could dominate on the basis of free trade, and because otherwise the colonial independence movements would be pushed towards seeking alliance with the USSR.

If any country "went communist" or threatened to do so — Vietnam 1965-75, Cuba in the 1960s, Nicaragua after 1979 — then the USA would certainly not rely on automatic economic mechanisms to stop this. The USA would use direct, murderous, often huge military force to police the frontiers of its sphere of influence. If US strategists saw a military dictator as offering more stable and compliant local rule than a democratic or reforming alternative — if the dictator would be "a son-of-a-bitch, but our son-of-a-bitch", in the phrase coined by F D Roosevelt for Trujillo in the Dominican Republic and found so apt that later US leaders repeated it for Somoza in Nicaragua and Batista in Cuba — then the USA would deploy its might to make that dictator a pillar of what it called "the free world". That happened much further away than in Central America — in Chile with Pinochet, in Iran with the Shah, in Indonesia with Suharto.

There was still a difference from the old European colonial empires. The USA did not want governor-generals, except to a limited degree in Central America. It did not want trade blocs tying particular poorer countries exclusively to its economy. It could and did tolerate nationalisations and protective tariffs enacted by the ex-colonial governments, so long as they remained broadly within its sphere.

South Korea, for example, was kept within the US sphere of influence at the cost of a large war against Stalinist North Korea (1950-53). It was heavily dependent for its startling industrial growth on its position as a supply base for the US war effort in Vietnam. Yet it had a markedly "nationalist" industrial policy, largely based on local ownership, and with more Japanese than US capital among the foreign owners of its enterprises. Its position in the US "imperialism of free trade" was markedly different from its position before World War Two in the Japanese colonial empire.

● Since 1989-91, the USSR has no longer existed as a superpower. The old Stalinist bloc has collapsed. The USA has been able to push for a whole world based on the "imperialism of free trade". It can do this in an environment where communication and transport costs have been radically reduced; where manufacturing, especially of a great variety of less bulky goods, spreads wider and wider; and where a greater number of poorer countries have both the state-power and infrastructural preconditions for becoming sites for world-market industry.

A structure is emerging which Toni Negri and Michael Hardt, in their recent influential book, call "Empire". Not an empire, not the empire, not the US empire, either, but simply "empire". It is not the work of the USA alone, not by any means. Other capitalist powers, big and small, have joined in, because, once the push is underway, joining in gives fewer disadvantages than staying out. International bodies like the WTO, the IMF, the European Union, and even the UN have seen their weight substantially increased, although we are qualitatively distant from a "world government". The pressures towards a world of three big trade blocs (Americas, Europe, Japan-centred Asia) have been contained and subordinated to a more general "globalisation".

The shift towards an "imperialism of free trade" has come partly because the great metropolitan capitalist interests can afford it. For example, exclusive control by their "own" nation-state over sources of raw materials is less important to modern big capitalist concerns — often organised in transnational companies with substantial operations in many countries outside their home country, and with several alternative sources for most raw materials — than to the big capitalist classes of earlier eras.

Historically the central reason, however, was nothing to do with the metropolitan profiteers "mellowing". The social and political awakening of the peoples of Africa, Asia and Latin America, their transformation from populations with dispersed and illiterate peasant majorities into nations with big cities, substantial working classes, autonomous bourgeois classes and some industry of their own, made the risk and expense of colonial or semi-colonial rule generally far too great for the metropolitan powers.

Ever since the liquidation of the old colonial empires became an unmistakable trend, Marxists have argued about "the end of imperialism". However, all the theories of the "end of imperialism" have been as confusing as their mirror-images, the schools of thought insisting that the differences between the imperialism of today and that of, say, 1916, when Lenin wrote his famous pamphlet entitled *Imperialism*, are only superficial and secondary.

This is best seen by reviewing those various theories.

In his writings around 1916, Lenin argued — against others in the Bolshevik Party, such as Bukharin and Pyatakov, who claimed that the political independence of small nations was an utter impossibility in an imperialist epoch — that imperialism in the sense of the world dominion of finance capital and monopoly capital centred in the most powerful nations could quite possibly continue even with political independence of the ex-colonies. No Marxist, therefore, has ever said straight out that the end of colonial empires is the end of imperialism.

The first version of the "end-of-imperialism" came from Michael Kidron of the SWP (then IS), though the SWP has since flipped over from his views to something much more like a standardised Stalinised-Leninism. Kidron based himself on the idea, drawn from selected passages of Lenin, that the essence of imperialism was the export of capital.

In some circles, that idea had led to the conclusion that decolonisation would mean metropolitan capitalism choking to death on its uninvestible riches. Kidron used the same assumptions to argue that the post-1950 metropolitan capitalist prosperity meant the end of imperialism. Imperialism had been the "highest stage but one" of capitalism.

Arms spending was draining away the glut of capital, so the basic economic mechanism of imperialism no longer operated. The demand created by the state through the "permanent arms economy" filled the "underconsumptionist gap" supposedly caused by workers not being able to consume enough. Export of capital was no longer needed to provide a "drain" for excess capital from the advanced countries. The Third World was also less and less important to the advanced capitalist countries as a source of raw materials, because of new technologies, use of substitutes, etc.

In short, imperialist exploitation of the Third World was no longer necessary for the West, and that explained decolonisation. However, Third World countries were left crushed and battered in the world of military competition between nation-states. "The societies maimed and shattered by the imperialist explosion of the last century are again being maimed and shattered — by the growing economic isolationism of the west (an imperialist implosion as it were)..."

Kidron's argument fell down on several grounds. Firstly, imperialism is not fundamentally about providing a "drain" for superfluous capital. Secondly, the "functionalist" argument that economic activities must happen if they are "necessary for capitalism", and not happen if they are not "necessary for capitalism", is false in general. A capitalist world is shaped by capitalists acting on capitalist interests — with deflections and detours imposed by workers pursuing workers' interests — not by some superhuman force called "the needs of the system".

Kidron's argument also fell down on straightforward factual grounds. The major trend has been "globalisation", or at least internationalisation, of capital, rather than "growing economic isolationism", and capitalist development in the ex-colonial states has not been squeezed into nothingness.

So drastic was the factual falsity of Kidron's argument that another "end of imperialism" argument soon developed which was its exact contrary. For Kidron, imperialism had ended because of "not enough" capital in the Third World; for Bill Warren, because of "too much" capital there.

Warren was a member of the British Communist Party and then of a Stalinist-Kautskyist sect, the British and Irish Communist Organisation. His first article, in 1973, presenting facts on industrial development, was an important blow in forcing Marxists to re-think their "conventional wisdom" of the time about the supposed impossibility of serious capitalist development in the ex-colonies. But Warren's further theorisations became a simple inversion of the "orthodoxy" he was arguing against, that of the supposedly inexorable and uniform "development of underdevelopment".

Where the 1960s radical orthodoxy said that colonialism hindered the development of the colonies, also that the removal of formal colonial rule had not removed those hindrances. Warren replied that colonialism helped the development of the colonies — and that the end of colonialism helped even more! Where the radical orthodoxy attacked the social and cultural effects of colonialism and imperialism, Warren responded with a vigorous defence of the historically progressive role of bourgeois culture — yet had little but scorn for a major example of that progressive role, the self-assertion of the ex-colonial peoples through bourgeois national struggles.

Where the radical orthodoxy held that imperialism generates underdevelopment — using "underdevelopment" as a term to cover both lack of capitalist industry, and unevenness of industrial development, and mass misery within that development. Warren replied that imperialism generates development — meaning growth of capitalism, and increasing evenness of development, and increased social welfare.

Warren came to paint the development of capitalism in the most glowing colours, not only recognising it (as Marxists must) but effectively praising and advocating it. Everything that pointed to capitalist progress in the Third World was played up, the other side of the picture played down. One example: Warren noted briefly that "Agriculture has failed..." in the ex-colonial countries — but rapidly moved on to speculations about favourable prospects for the future.

If you read closely, Warren offered qualifications and reservations. But the main drift of his argument was that the world is moving towards more even development, with relations of economic domination weakened. In fact capitalist development has become more uneven. The economic domination of big states, international banks, and transnational corporations has sharpened, not weakened.

A third and more recent theory about the "end of imperialism" is, so to speak, neither "not enough" capital in the Third World, nor "too much" there, but rather "too much" capital *nowhere in particular*.

This argument acknowledges the continuing or growing power of multinational banks and corporations, indeed highlights it, but argues that they have become increasingly footloose, increasingly free of ties to particular states, and so the actions of the big capitalist states are increasingly "uncoupled from" and secondary to the actions of particular capitalist interests. Since (so the argument goes) imperialism means actions by big capitalist states to impose the interests of their "own" particular capitalists on other states, it is obsolete. So argue such writers as David Becker and his colleagues in their book *Postimperialism*, and David Lockwood in the Australian Marxist journal *Reconstruction*.

In the first place, most imperialist state actions in the heyday of "high imperialism" were not directly linked with the interests of a particular business, either. In an influential polemic against what he understands as "Marxist theory of imperialism", D K Fieldhouse writes that the theory "alleges that partition [of the world] was due to economic necessity. The industrialisation of continental Europe and the revived protectionism of the last quarter of the century made tropical colonies necessary as never before to provide markets for manufactures, fields for the investment of surplus capital, and an assured source of raw materials. Colonies were deliberately acquired to fill those needs." In fact, "remarkably few colonies were annexed as the result of a deliberate assessment of their economic potential by an imperial power... In short, the modern empires lacked rationality and purpose: they were the chance products of complex historical circumstances."

Everything is a "product of complex historical circumstances"! Kautsky, Luxemburg and Hilferding had demonstrated the roots of colonial conquest in the logic of capitalist exploitation in the colonies, not just in a "rationality" of metropolitan-capitalist deliberations. And Lenin pointed to politically or ideologically motivated colony-grabbing and "the conquest of territor[ies], not so much directly for themselves as to weaken the adversary..."

It is true that world capitalism's new "regime" since the late 1980s has combined great accumulations of highly mobile capital with more-or-less free trade, and that in this regime imperialist interventions, whether by the IMF in Indonesia or Brazil or by the US military in the Gulf, are on the whole more likely to be about securing the general conditions for profit-making by the big transnational capitalist interests than to resemble the mid-century "sending in the Marines" by the USA to keep small Central American countries safe for the United Fruit Corporation. But, overall, the "post-imperialist" writers exaggerate the "uncoupling".

And anyway, what conceptual precision is gained by insisting that the Gulf War, or the actions of the IMF, are not imperialist? The argument that "imperialism" is defined by (some rehash or other of) Lenin's picture of the world in 1916 is no better when used to claim that the world today is not imperialist than when used to insist that, being imperialist, it must correspond to that "Leninist" picture.

Imperialism has seen many forms, and it is pedantic dogmatism to claim that the modern "imperialism of free trade", led by the IMF, the World Bank, the big commercial banks, the transnational corporations and the military power of the US and NATO, is not a form of imperialism.

It still destroys and oppresses, and maybe on a larger global scale than its forerunners. It is a system which conveys the choicest fruits of the world's labour to the billionaires in "highly concentrated command points in the organisation of the world economy... a new type of city... the global city... New York, London, Los Angeles, Tokyo... The more globalised the economy becomes, the higher the agglomeration of central functions in a relatively few sites, that is, the global cities" (Saskia Sassen). Despite all the relative capitalist advance in the ex-colonial world, and some significant advance in commerce within Latin America, the proportion of "low and middle income" countries' trade done with the "high income" countries, rather than with each other, increased between 1987 and 1997. The producers of the ex-colonial world still mostly have to do their haggling in trade with bigger, richer, more powerful concentrations of capital, centred in the rich countries. Yet the difference of form has immense political significance.

In Marxist documents of the era of "high" imperialism, the era dominated by great rival colonial empires, the term "imperialism" was often used not to designate the system, but as a shorthand or pejorative alternative name for "the colonial or semi-colonial power". Imperialism designated a person, or at least a definite social grouping, as in "the plans of imperialism" or "the aims of imperialism". And the Marxists could write about battles to "drive imperialism out" of a country, or to wrest a country from "the grip of imperialism". No great confusion resulted. They meant the struggle for national independence.

To continue that usage in today's epoch of the "imperialism of free trade" is confusing.

Battles to "regain" or "increase" national independence are today generally a snare. The ex-colonial states mostly have as much political independence as they can have in a dog-eat-dog capitalist world. No extra measure of "independence" can undo economic dominance arising from the fact that the international banks have the dollars needed for international trade, and the big transnational corporations the technologies needed for world-competitive production. To "wrest a country from the grip of" the "imperialism of free trade" is only to wall it off from the world market — the one alternative, in today's world, even worse and more destructive than integrating it into the world market.

Imperialism can be fought only by working-class struggle, which must tackle the local capitalist classes as the most immediate enemy. If those capitalist classes, or factions of them, call on the workers and peasants to rally behind them in the cause of "anti-imperialism" or "national independence", generally they are lying, or promoting downright chauvinism.

Time was when "imperialism" could be used as shorthand for "the advanced capitalist states", without great confusion. To do that today is essentially to use the word "imperialist" as a way of branding advanced capitalism as a particularly bad form of capitalism. But the evil in advanced capitalism is capitalism, not advance!

Capitalism develops unevenly on a world scale, and with a tendency for the unevenness to increase and compound itself. Some countries become sites for modern infrastructure, advanced industries and services, major finance capital, the headquarters of multinational companies, and heavy investment, while others remain with few industries (often primary-product or low-technology), operated by low-wage labour, with low investment and widespread pauperism. Capitalism is in its very essence a system of ruthless competition, where the rich and the strong do down the poor and the weak, and the richer capitalist states, and the banks and multinationals based in them, dominate over poorer countries.

This system is as predatory as ever. But it is predatory because of the logic of capital, not because of the special ill-will or arbitrary propensities to tyranny of the US or any other particular government. The states which police it are as vicious as ever. But there is no way to "fight imperialism" of this sort by upholding the weaker predators against the stronger.

Against political domination we fight for the right to self-determination of all nations and for consistent democracy. Against the impositions of the IMF on poorer countries, we support the struggles of workers and peasants in those countries. Against the depredations of international capital, we fight for social ownership and for the planned use of the world's resources and technology to get rid of poverty. This fight against imperialism is a part of our fight against capitalism, not something superseding and overriding it.

Old-style military-conquest imperialism is practised today most often not by the big powers, whose capitalist classes find the "dull compulsion of economic relations" cheapest and most effective, but by smaller "sub-imperialist" powers who have to resort to such risky methods for lack of economic strength. The term "sub-imperialist" was coined in the 1970s by Ruy Mauro Marini, for Brazil. Brazilian capital has acquired its share of what Saskia Sassen calls "command points" largely by economic-based means. But it is not so easy for smaller states.

The last of the European colonial powers to relinquish their empires were the economically weakest, Portugal (in 1975) and Russia (in 1989-91). Today some ex-colonial or ex-semi-colonial countries have some military means to dominate their neighbours, but relatively little economic clout. They use the methods of the old imperialism, "paleo-imperialism", as it might be called — Turkey in Kurdistan and Cyprus, Serbia in Kosova, Iraq in Kurdistan and Kuwait, Indonesia in East Timor, Morocco in the Western Sahara, Libya in Chad, Ethiopia in Eritrea, Argentina in the Falklands...

This "paleo-imperialism" is a small-scale parody of the high imperialism of the late 19th century. It is not anti-imperialist. It is not a progressive alternative to the economic domination of the big powers.

It may clash with the modern "imperialism of free trade", and with the USA as the chief policeman of that new order — or cooperate with it as a junior partner. But even when it clashes with the USA, the "paleo-imperialism" does not represent liberation or progress. It does not show a way out of underdevelopment, or towards a fairer and more equal world.

Only independent working class struggle can do that. And the working class which can wage that struggle is growing in numbers, and often in organisation, all across the ex-colonial world.

Afghanistan and the shape of the 20th century

By Sean Matgamna

"Two conditions, at least, are necessary for a victorious social revolution — highly developed productive forces and a proletariat adequately prepared for it. But in 1871 both of these conditions were lacking. French capitalism was still poorly developed, and France was at that time mainly a petty-bourgeois country (artisans, peasants, shopkeepers, etc.). On the other hand, there was no workers' party; the working class had not gone through a long school of struggle and was unprepared, and for the most part did not even clearly visualise its tasks and the methods of fulfilling them. There was no serious political organisation of the proletariat, nor were there strong trade unions and co-operative societies..."

V I Lenin, *In Memory of the Commune*, April 1911

"The predominating type among the present 'communist' bureaucrats is the political careerist, and in consequence the polar opposite of the revolutionist. Their ideal is to attain in their own countries the same position that the Kremlin oligarchy gained in the USSR. They are not the revolutionary leaders of the proletariat but aspirants to totalitarian rule. They dream of gaining success with the aid of this same Soviet bureaucracy and its GPU. They view with admiration and envy the invasion of Poland, Finland, the Baltic states, Bessarabia by the Red Army, because these invasions immediately bring about the transfer of power into the hands of the local Stalinist candidates for totalitarian rule".

Leon Trotsky, *The Comintern and the GPU*, August 1940.

"Comrade Taraki had appraised the Afghan society on a scientific basis and had intimated [to] the party since the 1973 [Daud] coup that it was possible in Afghanistan to wrest... political power through a shortcut, [inasmuch] as the classical way in which the productive forces undergo different stages to build a society based on scientific socialism would take a long time. This shortcut could be utilised by working extensively in the armed forces. Previously the army was considered as the tool of dictatorship and despotism of the ruling class and it was not imaginable to use it before toppling its employer. However, Comrade Taraki suggested this too should be wrested in order to topple the ruling class."

From the official biography of Noor Mohammed Taraki, a leader of the People's Democratic Party of Afghanistan, published in August 1978.

ALL the horrors that engulfed the peoples of Afghanistan in the last quarter of the twentieth century were called down on them by the Stalinist "Great Saur Revolution" of 27 April 1978. It triggered the bloody 23 year cycle that ended with the fall of the Taliban regime in December 2001. A new cycle now opens with an uneasy coalition of warlords installed as the government in Kabul.

The "Great Saur Revolution" — "Saur" means April — was in fact a military-Stalinist coup d'etat. It put a very tiny Stalinist party, the People's Democratic

Party of Afghanistan, which may have numbered only three to four thousand members, subdivided into two groups murderously at odds with each other, in a position to attempt to make a "revolution from above".

In some of its features the "Great Saur Revolution" was unique. The PDPA had first won over the decisive layers of airforce and army officers and then seized the state. There was considerable bloodshed in the April 1978, but it was inflicted by one section of the old state on another, in a conflict involving only the military.

Nonetheless, in its essentials, what happened in Afghanistan between April 1978 and the Russian invasion of Christmas 1979 reprised, in a concentrated and intensified way, the experience that, together with the convulsions of world capitalism, shaped the history of the 20th century — the many attempts to make anti-capitalist revolutions from above in unripe societies.

Afghanistan's Great Saur Revolution was the last of the 20th century Stalinist revolutions from above* — at one and the same time the epitome, caricature, and reductio ad absurdum of all the others, in Eastern Europe, China and elsewhere. It was all the 20th century revolutions from above summed up, reprised, and pushed to conclusions truly terrible for the people of Afghanistan.

What happened in Afghanistan cannot be understood outside of Afghanistan's close relationship with the USSR from the 1950s onwards, and the symbiotic relationship that developed between sections of the Afghan elite and the bureaucratic ruling class in the USSR. The war of colonial conquest into which Russia was drawn in Afghanistan in turn helped bring about the collapse of Stalinism in the USSR.

What follows is an attempt to analyse the "Great Saur Revolution" in its connection with the international experience of Stalinism and the problems posed to Marxist socialists by Stalinism, and an account of what happened afterwards in Afghanistan, from April 1978 to the fall of the Taliban.

First we need to examine the pattern of Stalinist revolution from above, of which the Great Saur Revolution was part.

Revolution from above in the 20th century

THE dichotomy, "revolution from above", or revolution from below, stood, for anti-Stalinist revolutionary socialists from the 1940s onwards, at the heart of a cluster of vexed questions about the nature of Stalinism. What was its relationship to the working class? Its place in history? Its relationship to the Marxist conception of the "shape" of history? The appearance of Stalinist states in backward countries, in the first place the USSR, seemingly finding their own unexpected non-capitalist route to modernisation and development, had thrown that conception into disarray.

From above or from below? That way of posing the difference between Marxists and Stalinist anti-capitalists was the pressing into new usage of an old dispute between anarchistic and "statist" socialists. The anarchists emphasised the anti-state element in revolution, the Marxists insisted that the state could not be dispensed with and that a workers' state would play a positive role in the emancipation of the proletariat.

It was also the pressing into use, for understanding the 20th century, of the experience of the 19th century European bourgeoisie. After the abortive 1848 revolutions in Europe, as Frederick Engels would later summarise it: "The period

---

* Nicaragua, where the quasi-Stalinist Sandinista National Liberation Front led a popular revolution against the Somoza family in 1979, does not count here. The Sandinistas neither established a totalitarian state, nor attempted to transform society by forcible imposition from above of a preconceived model.

of revolutions from below was concluded for the time being; there followed a period of revolutions from above" (*Introduction to The Class Struggles in France*, 1895). He had in mind the way that the state under Bismarck in Germany, had pushed through essentially the same bourgeois transformation as was worked by people's revolutions in France and England, but had done it "from above", from within the existing power structures.

For socialists in the mid 20th century, "from above" or "from below" was really too abstract a way of posing the issue. Pro-Stalinists posed it like that, because it left the question begging: what was it that was done "from above"? Was it really the same, in essence, as what a working-class revolution would do "from below"? Those Marxists, the best known of whom was Isaac Deutscher, who insisted that the working class too could make progress by way of (Stalinist) "revolution from above", implied that, just as Bismarck's reforms in Germany had worked a variant of bourgeois social revolution, so also what the Stalinists made was some variant of working-class social revolution.

That was the view reluctantly accepted by the big majority of revolutionary Marxists, or Trotskyists. It was the point of the phrase "revolution from above" used by such as Deutscher. The revolutionaries in the Marxist tradition who now used the old anarchistic emphasis on revolution from below did so as a means of insisting on such ABC principles as that expressed in Karl Marx's dictum that the task of emancipating the proletariat belongs to the working class itself.

"Revolution from below" meant simply what "the socialist revolution" used to mean — the self-liberation of the working class at the head of other working plebeian layers of the population; replacing the rule of a minority bourgeois class by consistent democracy in society and the economy. "The emancipation of the working class is the task of the working class itself."

"Revolution from above" was what the Stalinists did, in different ways but according to one basic pattern. In more or less backward countries — societies far from what Marx or Lenin would have recognised as having outgrown capitalism, and some of them mainly pre-capitalist — closed-in elite formations, varying in their origin and in their degree of mass support, seized the state power or destroyed it and set up their own state power, entrenching themselves as a new exploiting upper class. Working from inside a totalitarian state, they used immense concentrations of force and power to reshape society "from above". The totalitarian state became the owner of everything in society. But who owned the state? As Trotsky put it (*The Revolution Betrayed*, 1936), while the means of production belonged to the state, "the state, so to speak, 'belongs' to the bureaucracy", organised as a collectivist elite.

The Stalinists said this was working-class rule, but everywhere it was the rule of an exploiting bureaucratic class who subordinated everything to economic development. Their special technique of development was the intense exploitation and super-exploitation of the proletariat and other working people, who stood defenceless before the totalitarian state which deprived them of the right to trade unions, political parties, free assembly and free speech.

By 27 April 1978, when the People's Democratic Party of Afghanistan embarked on its own "revolution", using the armed forces as its instrument, "revolution from above" had already taken a rich variety of forms.

In the USSR at the close of 1928, the Stalinist bureaucracy, having effectively suppressed the Bolshevik party and politically expropriated the working class, embarked on Stalin's "Second Revolution". The whole population was driven by a mixture of terror and totalitarian-millenarian propaganda out of the old society, which was deliberately uprooted and overturned by decision of a state grown gigantic in relation to society.

Over 100 million peasants were driven into collective farms. New state industries were created with tremendous speed, human cost and recklessness. Isaac Deutscher, an inveterate apologist for the Stalinist system and incorrigible romancer about what it was and would become, described what had happened vividly in his 1949 biography, _Stalin_:

"The whole experiment seemed to be a piece of prodigious insanity, in which all rules of logic and principles of economics were turned upside down. It was as if a whole nation had suddenly abandoned and destroyed its houses and huts, which, though obsolete and decaying, existed in reality, and moved, lock, stock and barrel, into some illusory buildings, for which not more than a hint of scaffolding had in reality been prepared; as if that nation had only after this crazy migration set out to make the bricks for the walls of its new dwellings and then found that even the straw for the bricks was lacking; and as if then that whole nation, hungry, dirty, shivering with cold and riddled with disease, had begun a feverish search for the straw, the bricks, the stones, the builders, and the masons, so that, by assembling these, they could at last start building homes incomparably more spacious and healthy than were the hastily abandoned slum dwellings of the past. Imagine that nation numbered 160 million people; and that it was lured, prodded, whipped, and shepherded into that surrealistic enterprise by... a man who established himself in the role of super-judge and super-architect, in the role of a modern super-Pharaoh. Such, roughly, was now the strange scene of Russian life, full of torment and hope, full of pathos and of the grotesque..."

This radical overturning of existing society by an all-powerful state, driving and coaxing the people and then exploiting them mercilessly, is what happened in varying degrees in all the Stalinist revolutions-from above. In Maoist China, to give another example, the "Great Leap Forward" of 1958-61 turned the country upside down, and perhaps thirty million people died in the economic disruption, chaos and famine that followed.

The Stalinist revolutions-from-above outside the USSR came in two basic varieties*:

1. Where an indigenous Stalinist formation took power without dependence on outside help − in Yugoslavia (1943-5), China (the Chinese Stalinists held power in backward parts of China from the 30s; they took control of China in the civil war of 1946-9), Vietnam (1954 and then 1975), Cambodia (1975).

2. By military conquest and annexation to an existing Stalinist state. The USSR thus conquered, and transformed in its own image, 10 countries (Latvia, Lithuania, Estonia, Poland, Czechoslovakia, Hungary, Romania, Bulgaria, Albania and East Germany) in Eastern Europe. China extended its control to Tibet, formally in 1950, in substance from 1959 onwards, in a savage still-continuing war.

The "agencies" of the revolutions-from-above in Russian-occupied Eastern Europe were Stalinist parties acting as the nucleus around which were grouped splinters of other parties and elements of the old state personnel (including, for example, in Hungary, pre-1945 fascists), fused together under pressure to create

---

* A third category, or a hybrid, is Cuba. There was only one Cuba, but in the mid 1970s it seemed as if Cuba would be the pattern for countries such as Angola and Ethiopia.
In Cuba, in contrast to China, the old state power was conquered and destroyed (in 1958-9) by an armed insurrectionary force, the 26 July Movement, that was not Stalinist, though some Stalinists and Stalinist sympathisers were part of it. The official Cuban Communist Party was bitterly opposed to the revolution until its very last stages. Once in power the revolutionary leaders came into conflict with the USA, which was crudely defending the interests of US companies in Cuba, and moved into the orbit of the USSR. The 26 July Movement was only transformed into a Stalinist state apparatus after it had taken power.
In the African states which Russia in the 1970s expected to follow "the Cuban road" it was, the agency was, in Ethiopia, sections of the old state (through an army officers' coup) and, in Angola, a victorious non-Stalinist anti-colonial movement. Essentially Afghanistan had more in common with Ethiopia than with either Cuba or Angola.

replicas of the USSR.

With the exception of Czechoslovakia and perhaps East Germany, all the East European and Balkan Stalinist states were economically and socially underdeveloped. The Communist Parties in the Eastern European states "structurally assimilated" to the USSR after 1944 were typically tiny and unrepresentative. The purging of elements in the Stalinist organisations unsuited to their new role was a feature of the early life of most of the new Stalinist states. The general pattern was that CP leaders who had been in the underground at home — Poland's Gomulka or Hungary's Rajk and Nagy, for example — were purged at Russia's behest as unreliable and nationalistic, to be replaced by those who had spent the war years in Russia and came back beside the Russian Army with, as the saying went, "pipes in their mouths", that is, as Russian puppets, aping Stalin's style and manner.

In this way, from Communist Parties and other parties, from elements of the old state and the old owners and managers, and from elements of the working class and old labour movements, the new ruling class was selected and fused together in a hierarchical, bureaucratic discipline, misleadingly called a party, centred on the state.

Where Stalinist revolutions were made by forces that did not depend on the Russian state, they were made by militarised army-parties based on the peasantry and led mainly by declassed intellectuals and some declassed workers. Thus Yugoslavia, China, Vietnam*.

These "revolutions from above" pitted entrenched militarised states of varying origins against the people and against "organic" social development. The arbitrary bureaucratic craziness — Trotsky, in the early 1930s, called the social theory of the Stalinists "bureaucratic raving" — which Deutscher describes during the forced collectivisation in the USSR had countless smaller manifestations in all the Stalinist states. The degree of consent and of concern with moving and mobilising the people by way of millenarian propaganda varied from case to case and from time to time, but the reserve power of coercion, adroit or crude, select or all-pervasive, was there always. Thus were created societies modelled after that created by Stalin's "Second Revolution" in the USSR — decreed from above, from the heights of authoritarian and totalitarian state power.

That was essential to the project because what characterised all of the societies thus transformed was that they were underdeveloped and backward, sometimes very backward, and unripe for any large collectivisation of industry and agriculture other than that imposed from above as a special form of organisation for totalitarian state exploitation.

In almost all poor countries, in the second half of the 20th century, state enterprise "from above" was a major driving force in industrial and economic devel-

---

* Czechoslovakia has some of the appearances of yet another distinct type — a genuine working-class revolution that nonetheless created a Stalinist state. In fact it was not. There was no working-class revolution. The Russian army, having in 1945 occupied Czechoslovakia and put the Czech Stalinists in control of key elements of the state (the police, etc), then withdrew. By 1948 the period of pseudo-"coalition" governments in the satellites was over in Eastern Europe and full Stalinist regimes were being imposed everywhere. In Czechoslovakia the Stalinist coup (February 1948) took the form of a parody of a working-class revolution, with mass working-class demonstrations. The coup was carried out not only in the name of but seemingly by the working class.

The Communist Party of Czechoslovakia had been a mass party before World War Two. It was still a genuine mass party in 1948, more akin to the French or Italian CPs then than to the Polish or the Romanian. In fact, however, since the Stalinists already controlled the Czech state, the events of February 1948 were only a matter of tightening the bands and screws, an affair of a regimented working-class stage army and not of working-class self-emancipation. The working-class demonstrations that clothed the essential police action by the Stalinists entrenched in the state machine were the signal for the final loss of all freedom of thought, organisation, expression, and social movement, by the working class of Czechoslovakia.

opment. Development was driven by bureaucratic, military or even aristocratic elite groups, spurred on by foreign example, pressure and competition, rather than by a bourgeoisie which grew up "organically", in the interstices of the old pre-capitalist order. Even early in the century, Trotsky remarked that capitalism emerged in Tsarist Russia as a creation of the state.

That sort of development had many variants: what made it a "reformism from above", in contradistinction to the Stalinist "revolutions from above", was that it was the work of the old ruling circles (or a decisive section of them), rather than of a new force which broke up the old state (or at least its top layers) and installed its own totalitarian power instead. Afghanistan in the 20th century would see both "reformists from above" – notably King Amanullah, in the 1920s, and Mohammed Daud, in the 1950s and the 1970s – and then a unique and extreme, indeed caricatural, form of attempted Stalinist "revolution from above".

A mature socialist society that has grown out of developed capitalism; one where the productive forces have been liberated by a working-class revolution from the limitations imposed on them by private ownership; where labour productivity has been raised higher than capitalism can attain – such a *socialist* society would be able to guarantee a high standard of living impossible under private industry. The level of productivity attained by working-class democratic collectivism would be such that the breaking up of the integrated, collectivised economic system would mean social decline (an analogy would be to collapse the present levels of labour productivity, created by market capitalism, back into its historical antecedent, feudalism). Stalinist collectivism in underdeveloped economies is the opposite of that. Its primitive collectivism is not the organisation of a level of labour productivity unattainable to privately-organised industry, but a historically specific form of exploitation of the producers.

Socialism, understood as working-class self-rule, comes out of advanced capitalism; its collectivism is the logical and necessary organic culmination of mature capitalism's tendency to socialise production; it is made and sustained by the working class. Stalinist "socialism", by contrast, comes by way of more-or-less arbitrary. revolution from above. The collectivism it imposes is a primitive, bureaucratic collectivism, forced on societies unripe for democratic collectivism (and sometimes unripe even for large-scale capitalism). It has to be set up and sustained by force, not only or primarily against the old ruling class, but against those whose interests it purports to serve. The state power is its strength, not popular support, though it may at times enjoy popular support. Even after great complexes of collectivism have been created, the entrenched state power, standing above society, remains essential to its continuation. Totalitarian state power is the lynch-pin without which the system falls apart.

Afghan society

N O society was less "ripe" for revolution – even bureaucratic Stalinist revolution – than Afghanistan in the 1970s. It was one of the most backward pre-capitalist societies on earth.

Ahmed Rashid, author of Taliban, quotes this mythic traditional description of Afghanistan.

"When Allah had made the rest of the world, he saw that there was a lot of rubbish left over, bits and pieces and things that did not fit anywhere else. He collected them all together than threw them down on the earth. That was Afghanistan".

Afghanistan's borders are artificial in relation to the population, and they cut through the ethnic groups. The territory of the state was determined by the farthest points reached by its neighbours rather than by the natural limits of anything in Afghanistan itself. British India, the Tsarist Empire, Iran and China, but decisively Russia and British India, formed the matrix inside which was held a conglomerate of ethnic groups, incipient nations. There was no integrated Afghan society, no intermeshing Afghan economy.

There are scores of languages in Afghanistan. Pashtu is the native language of about half the people. The other widely used language is Afghan Persian, Dari. There are perhaps eight million of the Afghan Pashtuns, the biggest ethnic group and the dominant one. They are subdivided into two basic tribal confederations, Ghilzais and Durranis, and those in turn are sub-divided.

Except for a nine-month interlude in 1929, and a four year period between the fall of Najibullah in 1992 and the Taliban capture of Kabul in 1996, Durrani Pashtuns have ruled for over 200 years. Afghan originally meant Pashtun. Other ethnic groups, Tajiks, Uzbeks, etc., tend to refer to themselves by these names and to Pashtuns as Afghans.

Tajiks are the second biggest ethnic group, three to four million strong. Far less tightly enmeshed tribally than Pashtuns, they form a disproportionate part of the town population as traders and administrators. There are about one million Uzbeks, who have tended to be merchants and artisans. Hazaras (descendants of Mongol invaders), Kirghiz, Aimaqs, Turkomans, and Baluchis are the most important of the many other ethnic groups. Some "nationalities" in the Eastern mountains are said to be only a few hundred strong.

Three quarters of the Afghan people have tribal kin across one or other of the borders. There are as many Pashtuns and more Baluchis in Pakistan than in Afghanistan. The USSR had, and its Central Asian successor states have, far larger populations of Turkomans, Tajiks, Kirghiz and Uzbeks than Afghanistan. For a long time the borders of Afghanistan were of no significance to its peoples. Afghanistan's only natural border, separating separate peoples, is its 40km border with China. These people prized the self-respecting independence of the American Indian tribesmen we read about in James Fenimore Cooper and the Scottish clans depicted by Walter Scott. Many of them were habitually armed. Traditionally they regulated their lives by the Islamic code (Shari'a), by tribal custom and by decisions of the community or tribal assembly (Jirga). The latter was absolutely binding: there were no "minority rights". Decisions of Kabul government were filtered through the Shari'a, tribal custom and decisions of the assembly. Where disobedience to Kabul was indicated, they disobeyed.

Common ethnicity, even where it exists, is anyway no more than the raw material of nations. A nation is formed and knit together economically, linguistically and culturally through a historical process. Nothing like that happened in Afghanistan. The state emerged in the 1740s as a loose empire under Ahmed Shah Khan known, after the dominant sub-section of the Pashtuns, as the Durrani Empire. In 1818 the Empire collapsed into a series of principalities: Herat, Kandahar, Kabul, Peshawar, corresponding to ethnic divisions. Unification of sorts was again achieved in the mid 19th century under Dost Mohammed (1826-63), around the Kabul principality.

In the first British-Afghan war (1838-42) the British failed to extend their Indian Empire northwards. In January 1842, 16,500 British troops and their camp followers were forced to leave Kabul; only one man made it to Jalalabad a week later. In the second British-Afghan war (1878-80) Britain also failed to prevail, but succeeded in reducing Afghanistan to the level of a protectorate whose foreign affairs were controlled by Britain. In a third war with Britain, forty years later (1919), the new emir or king, Amanullah Khan, defeated another British invasion and re-established Afghanistan's full independence. In that war fighting erupted in British India too, Pashtuns supporting Pashtuns in Afghanistan.

From that point on, Afghanistan began to come under Russian influence — initially that of the Russia ruled by the Bolsheviks. Afghanistan and Russia gave each other mutual recognition in the dangerous year 1919, and Lenin and Amanullah exchanged ceremonial greetings.

In the 19th and 20th centuries Afghanistan had stood on the fringes of the civilised world. It was "bits and pieces" in terms of ethnic groups, and also "bits and pieces" of different civilisations, different eras of civilisation and different levels of development. Hundreds of years of historical development separated the towns from the countryside.

In early medieval feudal Europe, the towns become oases of the merchant bourgeoisie and of handicrafts, and places of refuge for fleeing serfs — the first shoots of a new bourgeois world that would take centuries to grow to dominance over the antagonistic countryside. As wide a gap and a similar antagonism existed between the towns of Afghanistan and the countryside. And almost as large a span of time and development separated the towns from their equivalent in more advanced countries.

In terms of its levels of development, Afghanistan was on the very edge of the modern and modernising world — and yet it was inexorably pulled into that world's orbit. It faced unsuccessful intrusion and attempted conquest by the armies of the most advanced society on earth in the 1840s, partially successful invasion in the 1880s, defeated invasion and the winning of full independence in 1919. Inevitably over time it was impressed on those who ran the state and on a section of the urban elite that they had to learn from the outside world and acquire as much as possible of its military technology.

Ideas of modernisation and of economic development found roots — shallow roots — in the urban crevices of Afghanistan. To keep up with the rest of humanity, Afghanistan needed to develop its forces of production beyond nomad herding (which was how about two million of its people still lived in 1980), big landlordism and debt-ridden peasants, tribal sub-division, merchant capitalism in the towns, and handicraft production.

In terms of its own social forces and processes, Afghanistan was very far from such development. State initiatives and outside resources therefore came to seem to successive layers of the elite and of those who controlled the state to be the only way Afghanistan could develop. The condition of Afghan society placed the onus of reform on the state. Reform and revolution from above are the central themes of Afghan history in the 20th century.

Elite groups looked for outside patterns and models. Repeatedly they failed in their initiatives. Naturally the reforming emirs saw the strengthening and modernisation of the state itself, that is of their own power vis-a-vis society, as the key to everything else. Standing against them were the structures of an archaic tribal-feudal society where power lay in the ethnic groups, the nobility, and the priests.

The economy developed, but very slowly and very unevenly. The territory came nowhere near to the prerequisite of a capitalist state — being knitted together economically. Weak modernisers met with defeat. The pattern was repeated, again and again, feeble or strong but unmistakably the same, from the emir Abdul Rahman Khan, who tried to modernise under the stimulus of Afghanistan's partial defeat in the second Afghan-British war, right through to the blundering Stalinists after the Saur (April) Revolution of 1978.

Abdul Rahman, who ruled from 1880 to 1901, created a standing army, with British subsidies, and attempt to raise the central state above society. He fought internal wars of conquest on which the claims of Kabul in the 20th century to rule Afghanistan were erected. He set up colonies of rebellious Pashtuns among hostile peoples in the North and massacred non-Pashtuns.

Over the decades, the state was strengthened — the state of the 1970s was not the state of the 1880s — but the Afghan state never attained the sort of power vis-a-vis society that the different types of European state have had for centuries.

King Amanullah (1919–29)

AMANULLAH, the king who exchanged greetings with Lenin in 1919, continued Abdul Rahman's work. He had had links during his father's reign with a modernising movement called "Young Afghanistan". He enacted serious reforms in the early 1920s.

He abolished slavery and the slave trade; tried to create a modern secular legal system to replace Islamic Shari'a law and the multiplicity of tribal and clerical jurisdictions; proclaimed equality before the law; encouraged the opening of an academy for girls in Kabul. However, his writ did not run far. Amanullah was a feudal king, an enlightened despot, presiding over a weak central state, with little power to reshape society when he did not have the consent of those who ruled in all the layers of Afghan society and of the Jirgas (councils), feudal assemblies of Khans, priests and "estates" at different levels up to the Loya Jirga (grand council).

Already in the 1920s, links with the USSR were important. Russia would become Afghanistan's main trading partner; and the USSR already did such things for Afghanistan as set up a telegraph line, cotton processing plant and an electric power station. In the mid 1920s the Soviet Union already provided not only teachers but pilots for the modernising king in putting down tribal revolts.

King Amanullah paid a two-week visit to the USSR in 1928, part of an eight-month tour outside Afghanistan, on the eve of Stalin's second revolution. He also visited Iran and Turkey. Inspired by what he saw of the achievements of the Ataturk regime which had reconstructed and begun to modernise Turkey, when he returned to Afghanistan he embarked on a vigorous new drive for reform and modernisation.

What happened then prefigured what would happen fifty years later, after the Stalinist Saur revolution. The revolutionising, enlightened monarch Amanullah attempted to strengthen the central state by putting the feudal-tribal leaders and the priests under government control. It was what was done in England under Henry VII in the late fifteenth century and early sixteenth century, and in France under Louis XIV in the late seventeenth century. He proposed to create a modern army, a conscript army to which no-one would be allowed to send substitutes. The king's dilemma was that in order to proceed he needed first to make the state strong enough to overcome resistance to change. Fatally, he tried to proceed without first having adequately built up a central state capable of imposing the king's will against the tribal leaders and the priests.

In October 1928, Amanullah proposed the setting-up of joint schools for boys and girls. Women were freed from purdah (limits on when they could leave their homes, and the obligation to be heavily covered up when they did). A minimum age was decreed for marriage — that is, for when girls could be taken as sexual partners. Amanullah tried to create a political instrument to carry out this revolution. He set up a revolutionary party, called "Independence and Revolution".

Amanullah reflected the interests and desires of some merchants and intellectuals, but he and they had too narrow a base of support to carry through even this revolution. Perhaps most importantly, Amanullah, like the PDPA fifty years later, had no support among the farmers. Unlike the PDPA, Amanullah offered them nothing. The poor peasants had endured a 45% rise in land tax in 1924 and had nothing to gain from Amanullah's "bourgeois" reforms.

This was an attempt at a bourgeois reform-from-above where the bourgeoisie was feeble and divorced from the countryside. The Afghan merchant bourgeoisie, with their "enlightened despot", the weak king ruling a weak feudal state, were still far weaker than their English or French equivalents had been in the Middle Ages.

A broad anti-Amanullah coalition was formed. At its core were the religious leaders. They rallied the tribal khans, and behind them the entire rural population, including the peasants. By November 1928, after Pashtun tribes in the eastern provinces had raised the standard of revolt, rebellion was spreading quickly throughout the country. Amanullah simply had no forces with which to attempt to defeat it. In January 1929 he abdicated in favour of his brother Inayatullah Khan.

The country was in uproar. On 15 January Tajik rebel forces took Kabul. Their low-born, illiterate peasant-bandit leader Habibullah, nicknamed Bacha-I-Saquo ("son of a watercarrier"), was proclaimed Emir of Afghanistan, as Habibullah Khan.

For the first time in nearly 200 years, Pashtuns did not rule. But this was no plebeian revolution. Habibullah was a reactionary and traditionalist, albeit a usurping, part of the feudal counter-revolution. Amanullah's reforms were annulled — the department of justice was closed down, law remained exclusively a matter for the religious courts, and the schools were closed. The possibility of economic modernisation through the state was greatly weakened*.

Anti-Pashtun revolution and social counter-revolution had briefly been fused, but Habibullah did not last out the year. With the help of the British rulers in India, Mohammed Nadir Khan organised an expeditionary force of 12,000 men — Pashtuns — and united the tribes against the usurper. They took Kabul on 15 October 1929. The presumptuous non-Pashtun Emir surrendered and was shot. Nadir Khan became Emir. He would be assassinated in 1933. His son, Mohammed Zahir Shah — the old man now in Rome — would be king until his first cousin

---

* According to one account, in 1919 a small expeditionary force of the Red Army, consisting of central Asian citizens of the USSR and a few Afghan students, and led by a former Afghan ambassador to the USSR, Ghulam Nabi Charkhi, entered Afghanistan during the disturbances. After some successes it withdrew to Soviet Central Asia. Charkhi returned to Afghanistan in 1931, pledging loyalty to the new king. In 1932, in the royal palace, the king beat him with a rifle and then had him killed.

and brother-in-law, Mohammed Daud, organised a coup and declared a Republic 40 years later, in 1973.

In the story of Amanullah the basic pattern of modern Afghanistan is there in full: outside prodding by example, stimulation, aggression and painful contrast leads the elite or segments of it to attempt to modernise and develop Afghanistan. The central state is too weak to override the conservative forces and the forces of reaction. Those pushing for change are socially weak and are unable to resist, still less defeat, the powerful forces of reaction which they stir up.

At the core of the situation is the weakness of the bourgeoisie and of the tiny working class. The bourgeoisie was a weak merchant class. Under Amanullah in the mid 1920s, merchants increased their influence and power in society at the expense of the landlords, but they remained weak. So did the central state which sought to aid them and which, by modernising, would have strengthened them. The merchants traded mainly with the USSR. The working class was still rudimentary. A few factories, and many small workshops, produced a numerically and socially weak working class. There were no big enterprises, such as there had been in Tsarist Russia, which would concentrate proletarians and give them the social and political weight to affect what happened. When, by the 1960s, workers engaged in strikes, they were politically hegemonised by the Stalinists.

Modernisation or revolution from above was impossible; movements from below were movements of religious and social reaction, even regression. They followed traditional leaders and traditional ideas, and were locked for the most part into traditional social structures. Amanullah was an Ataturk that failed: so, in the 1950s and 1970s, would be the initially more successful Mohammed Daud, the most important of all the reforming royals; so too would be those who made — or rather failed to make — the Saur revolution after April 1978.

Aspirations to modernisation after Amanullah (1929–53)

After the fall of Amanullah, trade relations with Russia remained close and grew. Russia imported Afghan luxury agricultural goods and provided "modern world" things for Afghanistan — helping, for example, to create a cotton processing industry. Agitation for modernisation, and essentially for Amanullah's programme, would go on among tiny segments of the Afghan elite, but it had no way forward. Either the state would pioneer a transformation, or no forces in Afghanistan could. After Amanullah, for a generation, no-one at the centre tried to.

Supporters of Young Afghanistan organised terrorism in the early 30s. One of them killed the king in 1933. The terrorism reflected the weakness of what they represented — essentially, what Amanullah had represented, and what future reformers would represent. They wanted to replace the Islamic code as the basis of the state by secular law. They were Pashtun nationalists, demanding Pashtun-occupied territory from then British-occupied India. Later, after 1947, their co-thinkers would demand it from Pakistan, with momentous consequences.

Attempts by Afghanistan in 1919 and again after 1945, as Britain prepared to leave India, to renegotiate the Durand Line border, which arbitrarily cut the Pashtun people in two, would meet with dismissal. Pashtun nationalism would, by pushing Afghanistan into the Soviet orbit, shape Afghanistan's history in the second half of the 20th century. Young Afghanistan had links with the USSR. But after 1933 they ceased to be a force.

In the 1930s, Afghanistan took some German credit and German goods; and in 1937, Afghanistan joined Turkey, Iran and Iraq in the Saadob Pact, to resist Russian expansion. But in the 1939-45 war Afghanistan remained neutral, and on the USSR-British side. In 1941 it expelled German and Italian diplomats.

A national bank which regulated trade had been founded in the 1930s, but Afghanistan remained underdeveloped and stagnant.

Another modernising movement, in its ideas the heir of its predecessors such as Young Afghanistan, came into existence in reaction to Afghanistan's stagnation in the years after the Second World War. This movement was called Awakened Youth ["Wikh-e-Zalmayan"]. It too was made up of educated middle and small bourgeois, members of the intelligentsia and offspring of the elite, even of the large royal clan. These were the sort of people who made up the early Russian revolutionary movements of the 19th century, the Decembrists of the 1820s, and the populists of the 1870s and after, who "went to the people". And, like their Russian analogues, they would prove incapable of transforming the social situation they were trapped in.

The programme of this movement was broadly the same as those of its predecessors: modernisation, developing the economy, and strengthening the state, which also meant strengthening the towns — islands of half-modern life in a prehistoric sea — against the countryside. It was Amanullah's programme, or a variant of it. Some of the people in Awakened Youth would turn into Stalinists. Out of Awakened Youth or from its periphery came "Democratic Reform", which had a radical left wing led by Noor Mohammed Taraki, who would organise the Saur Revolution of 1978 and become President of Afghanistan. They talked of "democratisation" and of rising living standards; they won a number of deputies to the "People's Council".

Another such movement (1950) was Watan ("Homeland"). It had a broader political and economic programme: democratisation of political institutions; removal of political restrictions; a free press; free parliamentary elections; the right to form political parties; and economic development, which meant state economic activity.

One faction of Watan, calling itself Voice of the People ["Nida-I Khalq"] organised a political party in Summer 1951; it was quickly declared illegal. The insuperable problem of all these movements, with their similar programmes (though these post-war movements, lacking proposals for equal treatment for women, lagged a little behind Amanullah) was that the class that might elsewhere have pursued and fought for their ideas was very weak. Their weakness was illustrated by the cardinal fact about Nida-I Khalq: it had a cadre of ten men, just ten, and was mainly active amongst medical and law students at Kabul University.

The oppositionist "movements" of disgruntled elite youth naturally enmeshed and overlapped with the ruling elite. As Amanullah had been involved in Young Afghanistan, so now Sardar Mohammed Daud, the king's first cousin and later brother-in-law, was in and of the elite modernising movements of the 1940s. When he became prime minister in 1953 — he had already been a minister for some years — Daud, the most important elite reformer/revolutionist-from-above in 20th century Afghanistan, would play a decisive role in developing Afghanistan and putting it into qualitatively closer relations with the USSR.

When, in the elections to the 8th National Assembly, in April 1952, none of the oppositionists managed to gain election as a deputy, the protests by students at Kabul University against election-rigging were led by Babrak Karmal. The son of a general, he was the future head of the government that the Russians would install in 1980.

The government began to crack down on the opposition, doing so with the customary Afghan mix of benign and savage repression. The youth organisations were banned, some leaders were arrested and jailed, others were exiled on government service. Noor Mohammed Taraki, who would become Afghanistan's head of state after the "Saur Revolution", was exiled to Washington as press attaché at the Afghan Embassy there. But progress did not depend on victory for the opposition – something unthinkable – nor did their being banned and persecuted rule it out.

Into the USSR's orbit (after 1953)

I N 1953, when Mohammed Daud became Prime Minister, he vigorously took up the old cause of modernisation and development. He proclaimed "guided elections", instituted a five-year economic development plan and took Afghanistan closer into the orbit of the USSR. It is important to understand how and why this happened. Without it the 1978 Stalinist coup would not have been possible.

Pashtun nationalism was central to the upper-class modernising "opposition" movement that emerged after the Second World War. They demanded that the Pashtun districts of Afghanistan and of Pakistan be unified as part of the Afghan state. They insisted that the Durand Line dividing Afghanistan and British India (since 1947, Pakistan) was arbitrary and wrong, artificially dividing the Pashtuns. In the mid-1940s, as Britain prepared to leave India, and before India and Pakistan divided, the Afghan Pashtun elite tried unsuccessfully to negotiate with Britain for their "Pashtunistan". By 1950 Afghan-loyal guerrillas were active in the Pashtun areas against the Pakistan state; and by the early 50s, there was considerable tension between Afghanistan and Pakistan over the question.

The USA needed Pakistan as an ally in the region against both Russia and China, where the Stalinists had consolidated their control in 1949. When Daud tried to get US arms in 1953, the USA said no and told Daud to settle Afghanistan's quarrel with Pakistan. Essentially, the USA took sides with Pakistan. In the bipolar world of the Cold War, that left the USSR as ally and model for Afghanistan.

Russia was coming out of the inflexible foreign policy of the first years of the Cold War. It was seeking influence in Third World countries. The USA and Russia would soon compete in offering aid in a bid for clients and friends. Later in the

Left: Mohammed Daud, reformer-from-above. Right: Hafizullah Amin, revolutionist-from-above

decade, Egypt, refused western aid to build the Aswan High Dam, would turn to the USSR and for over a decade move into the USSR's orbit. The USSR established friendly links with other "progressive" rulers such as Sukarno in Indonesia and, after 1958, Kassem in Iraq.

So, after 1953, insulted, Afghanistan turned for aid to the USSR, already a very important trading partner. One account of it is that Mohammed Daud, knowing that the USA would favour Pakistan, wanted to be insulted by the USA so that he could whip up support for the turn to the USSR he wanted to make anyway, and wrongfoot conservative opponents of such a turn. Daud was engaged in a new drive to modernise Afghanistan and in an attempt to strengthen the state and the army, on which everything would depend. Like other Third World rulers, he was willing to learn from the USSR experience of using state power to organise economic development.

In 1955 the USSR granted Afghanistan a long-term loan of $100 million. Afghanistan already got most of its manufactured goods from the USSR — for example, 50% of imported machinery, and 85% of petroleum goods. Now the USSR would undertake to equip the Afghan armed forces with planes and tanks and artillery, and train Afghans to run and maintain those modern machines of war. It would organise Afghan telecommunications and air communications; build trunk roads and bridges; install hydro-electric power; and construct elite housing enclaves in Kabul. In all these things, but most significantly, in connection with operating and maintaining modern ground and air war machinery, Russian advisers and technicians came to Afghanistan to train Afghans. Steadily growing numbers of Afghan officers went to the USSR for education. The USSR thereby gained a shaping influence on the key layers of the officer corps of the air force and the army and tank regiments which it now undertook to equip and train.

To the feeble merchant bourgeoisie was added a more modern-minded element, and a more dynamic one — yet one rooted not in the development of

Afghan industry and technology, but in the importation into one of the most backward societies on earth of advanced military technology.

If the cities were islands in a prehistoric sea, a thousand years ahead of the countryside, the armed forces, flying and maintaining modern planes and running tanks and modern artillery, were the representatives and embodiment of a technology 100 years ahead of the average level of the towns. Tsarist Russia had imported capital and Western industrial technology, and created giant concentrations of workers who shaped the future of Russian society; but the workers, though a small minority of Russia's population, were themselves numerous, and had contact with the peasantry from which they had emerged. Afghanistan imported military technology and gained a comparatively narrow layer of educated military technicians. They too would shape the future of their society, though in a very different direction. The officer corps was numerically small, and it tended to be detribalised, and thus to have even less contact with the people than the bourgeoisie and the royal modernisers had. Its relationship with the numerically large rank and file of the armed forces was one of a hierarchy of command, not of political leadership.

By the end of the 1950s, Russia, which in November 1957 had put the first man-made craft into orbit around the Earth, had great economic prestige. For the educated layers of a country like Afghanistan, even those who would not become "Communists", Russia's statised economy offered, in whole or in part, a model of quick development and modernisation. The lure of the Russian model was powerful. And so Daud initiated the closer links with Russia that led ultimately to the Saur Revolution. He was concerned to strengthen the Afghan state against internal and external opponents: of course, he hoped to keep control, but he found that at the end he did not control the state. People working closely with the Russian state were able to use parts of "Daud's" state to make a strange coup-revolution.

Stalinism in Afghanistan (from the 1950s)

S TALINISM in Afghanistan cannot be understood outside of Afghanistan's interaction with the USSR. But it also cannot be understood except as the heir of all the movements — from "below", or at least from not quite the top layers, by the youth of the elite, and from above, by those who controlled the state itself — for modernisation and development. In its aspirations, it was a mutant variant of what the non-Stalinist reformers sought, taking the USSR as model of what was "modern" and "developed"; in its origins, driving forces, and brutal bulldozing methods once in power, it was a direct outcome of their repeated failures.

In Afghanistan, movements for reform "from below" — in the sense that they sought to build a political opposition — tended to come from among the upper reaches of society, amongst the young and sections of the intelligentsia. The reformers-from-below had virtually one recurring programme, and that was identical with the programme of the reformers-from-above — development, and one degree or other of "democratisation". Young elite reform movements from "below" tended to divide into those whose origins, family and connections already overlapped with the establishment and the personnel of the state, and who evolved into reformists-from-above, the only possible sort of practising reformer — from Amanullah to Daud — and those who remained outside and really "below". Many of those became Stalinists.

There were Stalinists and Stalinist sympathisers in Afghanistan in the 1930s and 1940s. In the 1950s, one immediate consequence of the agreements with Russia was a loosening of repression against pro-Russian Stalinists. That was when the nuclei of the future Stalinist parties took shape in the form of "discussion groups", though a Stalinist party, the People's Democratic Party of Afghanistan, was not founded until 1 January 1965. Within two years of the founding of the PDPA, the organisation would split into two groups, both claiming to be *the* PDPA and distinguished by the names of newspapers their organisations briefly published in the 1960s, *Parcham* (Flag) and *Khalq* (People, Masses). After a decade at war with each other — during some of which, after 1973, Parcham was part of Mohammed Daud's republican government which persecuted Khalq — they united again in 1977 to prepare for the April 1978 coup. Within weeks of the coup they had split again, bloodily.

Probably the distinction between Parcham and Khalq existed in the "discussion" groups of the 1950s. In any case the PDPA was never more than two brief and unstable conjunctions between two distinct parties.

Because of Russia's direct influence on layers of the Afghan elite, both PDPAs, Khalq and Parcham, were unique among Stalinist organisations. These were not to any degree working-class or peasant organisations. They were both rooted in sections of the Afghan state elite and bits of the bourgeoisie and intelligentsia. They were organisations of segments of the urban elite, of the ruling class — segments distinguished from the rest of their class by belief in a "Russian" way forward for Afghanistan and commitment not to a bourgeois model of Afghanistan's development but to a bureaucratic Stalinist model. They aspired to switch Afghan history on to the Stalinist track of development; already part of the Afghan ruling class, they wanted to transform themselves into a bureaucratic elite after the model of what existed in Russia. They had many things in common with, for example, the bureaucratic elites selected as their satraps by the Russians when they transformed the East European societies into replicas of the USSR, but they were selected in a unique way because of the close relationship that had developed between the USSR's ruling class and the rulers of Afghanistan.

They never developed anything remotely like a mass following. They could make the Saur Revolution only by winning over the key segments of the military elite.

In the passage quoted at the head of this article, Leon Trotsky truly wrote of the leadership of the Stalinist parties that:

"The predominating type among the present 'communist' bureaucrats is the political careerist... Their ideal is to attain in their own countries the same position that the Kremlin oligarchy gained in the USSR. They are not the revolutionary leaders of the proletariat but aspirants to totalitarian rule. They dream of gaining success with the aid of this same Soviet bureaucracy and its GPU..."

The degree to which that "type" would "predominate" would vary from party to party, and within the parties from layer to layer of the party leadership. There never was a Stalinist party – and not only the leadership of the party, but the whole organisation – that corresponded more closely to what Trotsky wrote in 1940 than did the Stalinists of Afghanistan.

The leading figures of Afghan Stalinism had a considerable political history by the mid-1950s. Noor Mohammed Taraki, future leader of Khalq and President of the People's Democratic Republic of Afghanistan proclaimed after the Saur coup, was a Ghilzai Pashtun, born about 1917 into a semi-nomadic family of livestock dealers. The Ghilzai were hostile to the ruling Durrani Pashtuns. Taraki worked in India in 1935-7. Possibly he was even then sympathetic to the Communist Party of India, and he may have joined it.

What "communism" meant even in comparatively underdeveloped India, where there was a proletariat and a bourgeoisie, bore some relationship to what it meant in Europe. But what did "communism" mean in tribal-feudal Afghanistan, where both proletariat and bourgeoisie were feeble segments of urban islands in one of the most backward countries on earth? Did it mean that "communists" would support bourgeois progress? Aspire to make a working-class revolution?

In fact, by now the Stalinists everywhere in backward countries – and not only in backward countries – stood for bourgeois-democratic revolution. In China already, and soon in Yugoslavia, Albania, and other countries, armed Stalinists would aspire to power, using "bourgeois-democratic revolution" as a flag of convenience. But for Afghanistan even the aspiration to a bourgeois-democratic revolution seemed insanely ambitious.

Taraki studied law and political science at the Kabul college for government employees, from which he graduated in 1941. Employed by the Ministry of Economic Development, he was a protégé of Abdul Majid Zabuli, Afghanistan's leading merchant and founder in 1934 of Afghanistan's first investment bank. He worked for Zabuli as a private secretary around 1937. Zabuli dealt much with the USSR and naturally had connections with Stalinist state officials. Even at the top of Afghanistan's merchant capitalist class there was already a considerable interpenetration with the USSR, Afghanistan's major trading partner.

Taraki fell out with Zabuli. He was, it seems, accused, but not charged, with stealing Zabuli's property. No longer Zabuli's protégé, he was fired from the Economic Development Ministry. He then worked his way up the bureaucratic ladder of the government Press Department, becoming Deputy Chief of the official Afghan News Agency in the 1940s. In 1951 he became involved with Awakening Youth and worked on its paper, *Angar* (Burning Ember), which was banned after four issues. The paper advocated the right to form legal political parties, free elections and a democratic constitution.

By now Taraki had some reputation as a poet and story writer. In the repression that, after the recurrent Afghan pattern, soon followed the period of "liberalisation", Taraki suffered only banishment – to Washington, as press and cultural attaché. When prime minister Daud recalled him in 1953, he asked for political asylum in the USA. This was refused. He called a press conference to denounce Daud. Then he disappeared for three years; he may have been in the USSR. Back in Kabul he worked as a translator. By 1962 Taraki was working as a translator for the US Embassy! He was a full-time organiser for the incipient PDPA by 1963.

Taraki was the leading writer and theorist of Khalq, and also a representative figure of the social composition of its leading layer. A first-generation-literate intellectual from a poor background, who had had to struggle for an education, he never lost the attitudes of rural Afghanistan to women, and had the "outsider" attitudes of a Ghilzai Pashtun towards the Durrani Pashtun elite and the Durrani

Mohammedzai royal clan who held, dispensed, and manipulated power. Taraki lived as an intellectual in a too-slowly moving society − a writer in one of the two dominant languages, in a society with only five per cent of town dwellers and two per cent of rural Afghans literate − connected, of necessity and for his living, with the civil service and the commercial bourgeoisie.

Babrak Karmal became the central leader of Parcham when his predecessor, Mir Akhbar Kyber, was assassinated − possibly by Khalq − on the eve of the April coup of 1978. His background and political history is as emblematic of Parcham as Taraki's was of Khalq.

He was born in January 1929, the son of an army officer, who retired with the rank of General in 1965. He was a Dari-speaking Pashtun from an urban pro-Mohammedzai royal family. He was suspected of being of Tajik origin, "passing" for Pashtun. The family was wealthy, and Karmal had the best education possible in Afghanistan. He helped form a student union at Kabul University in 1950, which was banned after a few months. He was jailed for three years in 1953, but he spent his time not where he would probably have died, in the killer medieval common jail, but, as befitted one of his class, in a well-furnished private room.

After two years as a conscript in the army, he returned to the university and completed his degree in 1960. Like Taraki, he studied law and political science. Karmal was an orator, not a writer. He too worked as a translator − from German, for the Minister of Education. He also worked for the Ministry of Economic Planning (Afghanistan had its own five year plans). He became a full-time political organiser in 1964, on the eve of the proclamation of the PDPA. Karmal lived in the large USSR-built housing enclave (Mikrorayon) near Kabul, which housed state bureaucrats and army officers.

From the mid-1950s, when the proto-PDPA came into existence, as discussion groups in Kabul, people like Taraki and Karmal had connections with students and armed-forces officers. But these "communist" discussion groups were not opponents of the Daud Government, which had turned its face decisively towards "friendship and cooperation" with the USSR. Communist Parties in countries friendly with the USSR were everywhere working with the "progressive" local rulers − with Sukarno in Indonesia, Kassem in Iraq (1958-63), and Nasser in Egypt. That phase of Russian policy for Third World states would shape Afghan Stalinism before 1965, when the declaration of the PDPA signalled a change of tack.

Though he acted in the name of the King, Daud had effectively been dictator. In terms of achievement, he is the most important of all Afghan reformers. Daud got rid of the compulsory veil for women. It was a milestone in Afghan social history when Daud, one day in 1956, appeared in public alongside the women of his family demonstratively unveiled. He built up the conscript army − that is the independent power of the state, raised autonomously above society, and potentially a force by way of which the towns could hope to subdue the countryside. He built up the economy using state resources, state planning and foreign help. He drew systematically closer to the USSR, thereby, to be sure, seeking to pursue his own goals.

For those in the proto-PDPA, Daud was doing pretty much what they wanted done − though not enough of it, and not fast enough. He was perhaps more satisfactory from the future Parcham's point of view than the future Khalq's. Daud was surely to Russia's satisfaction, and Daud's overthrow in 1963 was, for the Russians, decidedly unsatisfactory.

Daud was dismissed in 1963 by the King, who now took over the actual power for the first time. Though thirty years on the throne, Zahir had never ruled. His uncles, a repressive and then a more liberal one, and then his first cousin Daud, had ruled in his name. But Zahir too was now a reformer. In October 1964 he produced a new "democratic constitution". There would be an elected parliament, under universal suffrage. Women could vote and be candidates. The right to organise legal political parties was promised. Members of the royal family other than the king were legally banned from holding political office. Thus was achieved one of the goals of the old reform movements from below, the breaking of the Mohammedzai extended royal family's monopoly of power.

Elections were held in 1965. Four women were elected to parliament. However, only a tiny fraction of those eligible to vote, voted. The people were still enmeshed in the pre-state structures and limited "democracy" of the ethnic groups and their councils. The voting figures were a measure of the relationship of the towns to the countryside and of the central state to the Afghan people: the central government did not loom large in their concerns, and it had little impact on their lives. In fact, Zahir's new constitution was still only a half-and-half system; the king, not parliament, would in fact rule.

The dismissal of Daud in 1963 was seen as a blow to Russian interests in Afghanistan; one consequence of that was the drive to form the PDPA from the "discussion groups". Yet nothing fundamentally changed in Afghan-USSR relations. Major changes would come only after Daud's return in the mid-1970s. The response then, by the organisation created in response to Daud's fall in 1963, would be the Saur coup that buried Daud.

With the formation of the PDPA the old question of creating a strong state able to lever or dictate to society became fused with the Stalinist drive to create a totalitarian state. The "Great Saur Revolution" of April 1978 marked its seeming triumph. Its manifest failure then led to the Russian invasion, after which the drive to create a state strong enough to reshape Afghanistan against the will of its people then fused with Russia's attempt to replace the Afghan state by a state of the invaders and their collaborators. "Modernisation" moved from an Afghan attempt at strengthening the state to an attempt to replace it by foreign totalitarian rule, driving to revolutionise Afghan society not only from "above" but from outside. The outcome would be the utter destruction of the Afghan state, and the collapse of Afghanistan into warlord fiefdoms. But that is to anticipate.

The formation and splintering of the PDPA (1965-7)

THE PDPA was founded at a conference of 27 men, held on New Year's Day 1965 at the home of Noor Mohammed Taraki in a upper-class district of Kabul. None of those present were military men. Taraki was elected General Secretary, with Babrak Karmal as his deputy. The programme they adopted was one of national reform and development, a programme that was identifiably in continuity with traditional Afghan drives for reform and modernisation.

The congress called for "democratic change", for "democratic government serving the people", and for a non-capitalist way of development. The party's brief-lived publication *Khalq* put it like this: the PDPA "aimed to unite the people in their struggle against despotism and reaction, to show the working people the way to a free and democratic society." (April 1966)

"Democratic" was the "brand name" for what was done by Stalinist rulers who held that they themselves embodied "the people" and could substitute for them: when they ruled, the people ruled. "Non-capitalist" meant more than one thing here. It meant taking the USSR as a model of "socialism" and of a "free and democratic society". It also meant state enterprise such as Daud had organised, but more of it. Different parts of the PDPA would perhaps understand the term "non-capitalist" with, at least, different emphases. Some of them differed from

Daud in degree not kind, or, anyway, saw what Daud had done as a weaker variant of their own statist policy. That there was an overlapping and blurring of lines between Daud's programme and one section of the PDPA (Parcham) would, as we shall see, be important for the future.

Afghanistan was then experiencing something of a public debate on models of "national development". It was a time of almost universal faith in the state as the only possible force for modernisation and development in the Third World. The PDPA's programme was one — extreme — variant among others of a statist model of development for Afghanistan. There was no difference between the PDPA and non-Stalinist Afghan devotees of statism on the necessity for a privileged elite in the future. The only argument was about its character. The leaders of the PDPA saw themselves as an elite like that of the USSR, the rest had a more bourgeois — or maybe "Egyptian", that is, bourgeois-bureaucratic hybrid — notion of the elite.

It should be noted that the PDPA was not explicitly secular and it was not avowedly Marxist. It talked of a "National Democratic Front" to work for "progressive reform". The sprawling extended royal family of Mohammedzai, despite the limitations imposed on its members in politics by the reforming king Zahir, still monopolised lucrative posts, blocking advancement for those outside the big and ever-increasing ruling clan. Here the upper class, bureaucrats and bourgeoisie, still had reason for discontent: it fed into the PDPA as it had fed into the earlier reform movements of which the PDPA was a mutant, Stalinising, continuation and descendant.

Though the Khalq/Parcham identities did not emerge until 1967, the distinction probably existed in a more or less defined form from the beginning. The National Committee elected at the founding congress had more or less parity of future Parcham and Khalq, and it would be strange if this was an anticipatory accident and not a deliberate attempt to accommodate known distinctions. The open Parcham/Khalq distinction within the PDPA emerged around the question of how "oppositional" the PDPA should be. The Parchamis accused the Khalq of ultra-leftism.

It came about in this way. When in late 1965, a new press law legalised opposition papers, it was only one more round in an already familiar cycle of liberalisation followed by repression. As in 1951, repression would come close on the heels of licence. State control of the press was not in fact lifted. Harrying censorship continued. When the PDPA published the newspaper *Khalq* (People, Masses), it was suppressed after only six issues (May 1966). It was thereafter succeeded by occasional illegal publications. The response of the future Parchamis to the ban broke the PDPA in two.

Inside the PDPA, Babrak Karmal criticised *Khalq* for having been too openly "communist". The future Parchamis advocated more caution, more circumspection, more skilful camouflage. Daud and his faction were now in opposition too, and Karmal saw the PDPA as simultaneously competing with the Daudites for the more "advanced" layers of the reform wing of the establishment and collaborating with them. Caution, moderation, close links with the Daudites, that was how the PDPA should work: it was the old policy, applied now with Daud out of office. "Leftism" was the main danger here. "Leftism" had lost the party its newspaper. It was only a year after the military-Islamist backlash that followed a botched Stalinist half-coup had killed hundreds of thousands of Communist Party members in Indonesia. Caution was in order.

A small majority of the PDPA Central Committee rejected Karmal's criticism. Taraki then tried to secure his majority by co-opting some of his supporters to the Central Committee. In spring 1967 the PDPA became two bitterly hostile PDPAs. The split would last ten years.

Though the Central Committee divided almost 50-50, the majority in the PDPA were probably Parchamis. Neither of the two PDPAs was repudiated by the USSR. Each group made bitter public denunciations of the other and, what must have caused confusion and embitterment, both claimed to be *the* PDPA. The differences expressed in the dispute around the banned newspaper *Khalq* reflected radical social and political differences and a difference in orientation — between working with the Daudite section of the establishment or working on it from outside; between a reformist orientation, in essence a continuation of the old reform movements, despite the Stalinist dimension of Parcham, and a revolutionary, or more revolutionary, approach to getting done what they all agreed needed to be done. It is not at all likely that even the Khalqis at this point thought it even a remote possibility to go for the full Russian model that they would go for in April 1978.

The Parchamis were more cautious not only because they were more "establishment" in background and connections, more "traditional" in orientation, overlapping heavily with the Daud opposition forces, but also, it seems, because they were closer to Russia. In accordance with its conception of its "tasks", Parcham was more loosely structured than Khalq. Khalq were more "outsider" in composition and attitude.

Before they became groups whose most important segment was airforce and army officers, both PDPAs, Khalq and Parcham, were a movement of the Afghan intelligentsia, of students and teachers in a country where the literate were only five per cent of the urban and two per cent of the rural population. Within that layer, Khalq tended to attract the unemployed and less well-connected, though even here there was no absolute distinction: Parcham had a militant phase in the late 1960s. In 1978 Taraki said a majority of the members of the PDPA were teachers. In this lay the continuity with the earlier reform movements and the importance of the perennial activity among students — privileged student scions of the elite. In the 1960s and 1970s these were the main forces taking part in the PDPA-organised demonstrations.

After teachers, journalists on the official press and radio were the second most important group for the PDPA.

Increased state economic and other activity would create jobs for the educated unemployed or underemployed with no other prospects: such people would therefore have a natural bias towards a statist, or even the full USSR, model of economic development, even when they themselves were not directly trained or educated in Russia or by Russians. That is shown most clearly in the career of

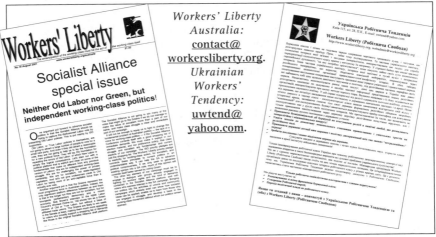

the PDPA-Khalq leader Hafizullah Amin – the organiser of the April 1978 coup, Prime Minister from June 1978, and President after September 1979. Amin was an educationalist by profession, principal of schools and colleges. Like a number of other leading PDPAers (for example Taraki and Dr Anahita Ratebzad) he spent time in the USA, where he worked for a doctorate. Before he focused in the 1970s on organising military officers for the PDPA, Amin organised in Pashtun boarding schools and among teachers.

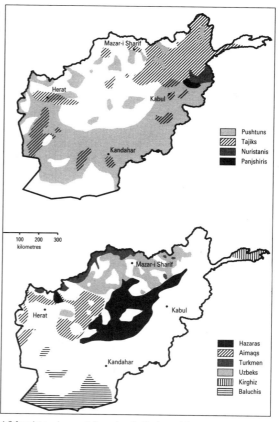

Afghanistan is a patchwork of ethnic and language groups

Let us finally try to sum up what distinguished the two Stalinist parties from each other. It was by no means clear-cut and stark on all points, but in general the two parties differed in the layers, upper or lower, of the old elite in which they originated, and in their connections with specific segments of the existing establishment.

The leading Parchamis were people whose origins tied them to the upper layers of the state bureaucracy, the bourgeoisie, the intelligentsia, and the armed forces. They were urban in origin and, like the state bureaucracy, included non-Pashtuns. They intermeshed with the layers engaged in "reform from above" to such an extent that they became part of the government set up after Mohammed Daud's republican coup in 1973. Conversely, in the Saur coup of 1978, they could pull some of those same upper-crust reform forces, disappointed with Daud, into the experiment of a different, Stalinist, attempt at reform from above.

Parcham was of the two parties the closer to the Russians; it was very much a Russian puppet. Parcham was the hybrid linking the "progressive" Afghan elite and the Russian bureaucracy. It was essentially a group of insiders, dealing in power, within and outside Afghanistan – always more reformers-from-above than revolutionaries. The "revolution" they made together with Khalq, though the prelude to an energetic attempt at reform from above, was only a "revolution" in the state apparatus. Within that attempt Parcham represented a cautious, long-term approach that, in fact, differed not all that much from Daud's approach.

Parcham was also more generally "modern-minded" than Khalq. It had a civilised attitude to women. It had women members and one nationally prominent woman leader, Dr Anahita Ratebzad. Here too they were flesh of the flesh of the non-Stalinist reformers from above, who in terms of women's rights, made the most important reforms in Afghanistan's history, in the 1960s – reforms that,

39

unlike what the post-Saur-Revolution Stalinists would decree, came into effect, and had more than a paper meaning.

Though Khalq was composed of people of the same social groups as Parcham, they were from their lower layers — teachers for example — and people of rural, and entirely Pashtun, origin. Though in power they would show a startling lack of astuteness in dealing with rural Afghanistan, they had more connections than Parcham with the countryside. More "outsider", less enmeshed with the upper class reformers-from-above, more distant from power than Parcham, their ambitions were correspondingly more radical, more "left", and more "revolutionary". Perhaps because they were more rural in their roots, they were also, notably, less "modern-minded in relation to women. There were no prominent Khalq women, if there were Khalq women at all.

But these were very small organisations. Split or united, the PDPA would never be other than a small organisation. In 1973 professional US observers and analysts of "communist" phenomena put both Parcham and Khalq at only a few hundred members each.

After the PDPA split (1967)

IN the late 1960s, foreign aid declined, there was an economic downturn, and job prospects worsened, especially for the educated aspirant state employees. It undermined the king's experiment in hybrid constitutionalism. The PDPAs grew. It was the time of spectacular student militancy all over the world, from the USA to Rome, London and Warsaw. It found echoes in Afghanistan.

The students wanted to modernise Afghanistan and secure their own futures. They demonstrated for changes in the law and also for the pass mark at the university to be cut to 50%. Both PDPAs were involved*.

The student segment of the Afghan elite were at this time what the military officers would be in the late 1970s, the striking force of the PDPA. For example, in October 1965, Karmal organised mass student demonstrations and a student occupation of Parliament. The issue was opposition to the king's candidate for Prime Minister, Dr Mohammed Yussef. The king was forced to retreat and appoint someone else.

There was also unrest in the small Afghan working class in this period. For example, there were 19 labour strikes and demonstrations in May-June 1968. Trotsky once observed of the student unrest in Russia at the turn of the 20th century that the students were to the workers as the leaves at the top of the tree to the rest of the tree. The leaves at the top move first in a gathering wind, but eventually the tree moves; the student "leaves" at the top of the tree were but harbingers of the deeper working-class movement. The working class moved in Kabul, but it was a tiny force, puny in relation to cities which were puny in relation to the country. It did not develop independent working-class politics. Working-class aspirations to transform society were not sustainable in 1960s Afghanistan. That fact was one of the preconditions for what happened in the 1970s.

Even in its most militant phase, Parcham was tied closely to the forces around

---

* They competed with a pro-Chinese and anti-Russian Maoist "revolutionary" movement, Sholay-e-Jaweid (Eternal Flame). The Maoists had an ethnic bias (Hazara) and were popular enough to seem to be serious rivals to the two small pro-Russian PDPAs in the late 60s. Unlike the two PDPAs they talked about "seizing power"; and unlike the PDPAs they advocated work with peasants. Their paper *Sholay-e-Jaweid* — founded in March 1968 — was suppressed in June 1969. But the Maoists went into quick decline. Some of their people would be involved in the anti-Russian resistance (after 1979) which China supported with material aid.

ex-prime-minister Daud. During the student demonstrations of 1969, the most militant in the long history of Afghan student unrest and dissatisfaction, Parcham acted as a link between Daud and the more militant students. For example, Parcham arranged for Daud to come in his Rolls Royce behind student demonstrations. This was thought likely to deter police violence – and it could not but help to build support for Daud. It is an example of how Parcham overlapped with Daud.

Parcham's paper was suppressed in June 1969 after a massive student strike and government lock out the previous month. Parcham collaboration and interlacing with the Daudites were now comprehensive and would lead to Parcham joining Daud's government after the 1973 coup. It would also lead to Parcham losing out in the competition with Khalq, which, remaining far more independent, would grow decisively while Parcham was tied to Daud.

Towards Mohammed Daud's coup (1973)

THE post-1963 regime had run into difficulties by the late 1960s. The king had raised hopes he could not fulfil and thereby had bred only disillusion and disappointment. As we have seen, there was economic decline, less foreign aid, and jobs and job prospects for students and graduates were correspondingly cut back. By the end of the 1960s, political stability had been shattered. Afghanistan's rate of growth and development gave no one grounds for satisfaction. In 1971-2 the country experienced drought and, in some areas, famine. The forces that created the PDPAs had been quiet while the "pro-Russian" Daud ruled, but now they were in active opposition, allied to Daud, helping whip up and organise the latest of the recurrent student and intellectual opposition movements into a strong movement of mass demonstration and strikes. That was part of the ferment that led to Daud's 1973 coup.

Daud had for ten years been out of power. The legislation banning members of the royal family other than the king from political high office forbade his return to power. Yet around Daud dissident layers of the Establishment grouped themselves, most importantly a group of airforce and army officers, many of them educated by the USSR. The conflict between Zahir and Daud divided the ruling class elite more seriously than at any time since 1929. The opposition was broad and powerful. About 50 key officers took part in discussions between Daud, the Parcham leaders and the USSR-trained airforce and army officers on what had gone wrong in 1953-63. Many did not yet feel obliged to choose between Parcham and Daud, whose forces overlapped.

Daud, though he was about to lead a sort of "bourgeois revolution" from above in the 1973 coup, operated still as a feudal chief: this modernising current was a primitive, pre-modernist, personalist movement around the Sardar, the chief. Daud relied on personal loyalty, not on ideas or programme, to hold his forces together and in step. He would be disabused. By the 1970s other factors, other modes and determinants, were loose in Afghanistan.

After experiencing Daud in power again, an important section of the Daudite military would go over to the PDPA, propelled by views about what had "gone wrong" before 1963 and in 1973-8 and seeking a firmer and more comprehensive drive towards "socialism". That would be a big factor in making the Stalinists' April 1978 Saur Revolution possible. Of the non-communist Third-World "pro-Russian" leaders of the 1950s, 60s and 70s, Daud would be the only one eaten up by his one-time partners.

There was another sort of opposition too – Islamic political fundamentalism. There had been ferment amongst urban Muslim intellectuals since the turn to

Noor Mohammed Taraki, the "Great Leader" of the Saur coup

Russia in the mid 1950s. Like the Stalinists of the proto-PDPA in the first Daud period (1953-63), they too had had their "discussion groups", and an important base at Kabul University. In May 1970, the Muslim Brotherhood organised rallies and demonstrations in Kabul, calling for a jihad against socialism and democracy.

There was also a feeble strand of "progressive" political Islam organised around certain mullahs.

In 1971-2 the PDPA led a wave of strikes. But the working class dimension was an utterly subordinate element in the build up to Daud's and Parcham's 1973 coup. Neither the 1973 nor the April 1978 "revolution" was shaped, led, made, or influenced by the tiny working class.

Economic downturn, disappointment with the 1963 reforms, a ruling class more seriously divided than at any time since 1929: in some respects, Afghanistan in 1973 approximated to Lenin's definition of the three prerequisites for revolution. The rulers could not go on in their old way; key sections, at least, of the people did not want to go on in the old way; and there was a viable alternative, driving for revolution. The future would be shaped by the ways in which Afghan reality differed from Lenin's formula.

Lenin's conditions for revolution were there in urban Afghanistan − in Kabul and the bigger towns. But the towns were not representative of Afghanistan. They were centuries ahead of most of the country. If during the French Revolution of the 18th century, important sections of backward rural France embodied counter-revolution − the Vendée − and suffered massacre and repression in their war with the revolution, in this case the whole of rural Afghanistan was an enormous Vendée waiting to be ignited. Afghanistan also diverged from Lenin's formula in that those driving for revolution were part of the old elite. They had more in common with enlightened despots and modernising rulers such as Frederick, Peter and Catherine (all called "The Great") then with any popular revolutionary movement. The urban forces of revolution were not a mass movement, or a movement able to evoke, rouse, or lead, a mass popular revolution. This fact expressed and defined the essential nature of Afghanistan's 1973 republican "bourgeois revolution", as of its April 1978 bureaucratic Stalinist continuation and successor.

Sardar Daud's republic (1973-8)

ON the night of 16-17 July 1973, officers led by Mohammed Daud and backed by the PDPA organised a more or less bloodless military coup. King Zahir Shah abdicated and Daud − the king's first cousin and brother in law − declared Afghanistan a Republic. He became its President.

A Republican Central Committee would rule. The symbiotic interpenetration of all layers of the elite in Afghanistan is made clear by two facts. The Minister of the Interior before the 1973 coup, the person whose job it was to prevent such a coup, Nehm Atullah Pazhwole, was a − secret − member of the Parcham PDPA! And the key organisers of the 1973 Daud coup would also, in 1978, be the organisers of the Stalinist coup, the "Great Saur Revolution".

1973 was a species of national bourgeois revolution, the best the progressive section of the Afghan elite could do. Parcham helped organise it, and some of Daud's officers were also Parchamis; indeed Parcham's leaders were central to it. Perhaps as many as 50 people in Daud's entourage were, loosely, Parchamis.

Daud abolished the Constitution, suspended parliament, banned political activity. The ban on political activity was partial, however. Parcham could open a public headquarters. Parcham was in government; half of Daud's ministers in 1973 were Parchamis. President Daud's first Deputy Prime Minister, Hassan Sharq, was Parchami.

Khalq, though it offered its support to the government (and in 1974 combined this with urging the exclusion of Parcham), was excluded from power. The relation between the Daudites and Parcham at this point was, though the details differ, reminiscent of the symbiosis between the Chinese Communist Party and Chiang Kai Shek's Guomindang in the Chinese Revolution of 1926-27 — but with a radically different outcome. Chiang Kai Shek slaughtered the Communists in 1927; in Afghanistan, as we shall see, ultimately the PDPA would slaughter Daud.

Daud, back in power in crisis-ridden Afghanistan, was at first the old pro-USSR Daud. For the Parchamis it was back to the pre-1963 days, except that now they had a substantial though subordinate share of power. Links with Russia had never been weakened, but now, at first, they were intensified. By 1977 115 enterprises were being built with Russian help and 70 were already in operation. In 1974, Daud signed a mutual "most favoured nation" trade deal with the USSR; in 1976 a long-term trade agreement was signed. Cars, cotton processing machinery, etc. came to Afghanistan from the USSR. and of course Afghans continued to be trained in civil and military technological skills in the USSR. Sections of the educated Afghan elite were already symbiotic with the bureaucratic elite in the USSR. That would increase. Between 1971 and 1974 500 Afghan students went for higher education to the USSR; 22% of Afghan specialists educated abroad went to the USSR. By now most Afghan medical doctors had been trained in the USSR. By 1977 3,700 officers had been trained in the USSR.

As we have seen, conflicts with Pakistan over "Pashtunistan" had been much more important than geographical proximity to the USSR in determining the closeness of Afghanistan's relations with the USSR. After 1973, Daud's foreign policy, too, was at first what it had been: he pursued not only "Pashtunistan" — the cause which had pushed Afghanistan into Russia's Cold War orbit — but also "Baluchistan". (Baluchis, too, live on both sides of the Afghan-Pakistani border).

Militant commitment to Pashtunistan, which had been central to the modernising oppositions such as "Awakening Youth", had defined Afghan nationalism — and defined it as Pashtun nationalism. It was also central to Afghan Stalinism. Both Parcham and Khalq were Pashtun and very much partisans of "Pashtunistan".

But in the mid-1970s Daud began to shift away from a central concern with Pashtunistan. After a quarter-century of animosity, he attempted to establish friendlier relations with Pakistan. This implied a loosening of relations with the USSR, or even a sharp turn away. Daud, of course, was neither Stalinist, nor a willing USSR puppet: he had his own goals and intentions. Deliberately he began to distance Afghanistan from the USSR. He began to weaken the power of Parcham.

The evidence suggests that Daud, as he strove to lessen Afghanistan's dependence on the USSR, seriously misunderstood how things stood, and failed to anticipate that a decisive segment of the airforce and army could be taken over by the PDPAs.

Daud sought and was promised an Iranian subsidy to the tune of $2 billion (in fact it was never delivered). Iran, which shares a border with Afghanistan, was then a regional "sub-imperialist" great power, and the USA's ally. Daud asserted Afghanistan's independence from the Russian bloc by condemning Cuba's "intervention" in Angola where, financed by the USSR, it acted as Russian proxy. In September 1975 Daud dismissed 40 USSR-trained officers. He sought facilities for training Afghan military offices in England and Egypt. The head of the airforce and a key organiser of Daud's coup, Colonel Abdul Kader, was disgraced and dismissed for saying that Daud's progress towards socialism was too slow. His demotion to the position of head of the Kabul military slaughterhouse was one of the decisive acts on the road that would lead to Afghanistan itself being turned into an enormous slaughterhouse. By late 1974, Parcham leader Babrak Karmal was under de facto house arrest, though the full break was still two years away.

After the Afghan pattern of hard and soft repression, alternating and combined, Parcham people were demoted and dismissed, some exiled overseas in Afghanistan's diplomatic service. But it was a selective purge to weaken Parcham's power and increase Daud's freedom of action: until 1976 there would still be Parchamis both in the government and in Daud's personal entourage. Daud would finally kick Parcham away early in 1977. (There is a curious symmetry between Parcham's experience of being kicked away by Daud after they had helped install him in power, and what Khalq did to them after the 1978 coup).

But this was no longer the same USSR as the one with which Daud had safely allied in the 1950s and 1960s. Nor were its devotees in Afghanistan, the PDPA, what they had been. As a result of the USSR's long-time influence, they now had, and were rapidly augmenting, special assets — de facto control of important sections of the Afghan state machine.

In the 1950s and 1960s, the Russian influenced Third World Communist Parties had docilely seconded "progressive" rulers and, in Egypt, they even dissolved its own organisation in deference to the Nasserite party. The policy of the Afghan Stalinists in their pre-PDPA phase had been a variant of that pattern. But by the mid-1970s Russia was in an aggressive, expansionary phase.

Stalinist victory over the USA in Indochina, and the setting up of Stalinist states there, seemed to have changed the balance of power against the USA and its allies. Quasi-Stalinist "anti-capitalist" revolutions and quasi-Stalinist USSR-client regimes had emerged in Africa. Just as the US military effort was collapsing ignominiously in Indochina, a Russian-financed Cuban Stalinist army crossed the seas to Africa to intervene in Angola. In Ethiopia, Angola and South Yemen — in fact, everywhere it thought it safely could — Russia pursued, with seeming success, an active expansionary foreign policy, linking up with client regimes that appeared to be following the Cuban pattern of radical-dictatorial regimes not initially Stalinist moving towards the USSR model and alliance with the USSR. The full-scale invasion of Afghanistan would be the culmination of this phase of Russian foreign policy. The PDPA coup of April 1978 was also part of it.

Preparing the "Great Saur Revolution"

PARCHAM had shared power. Khalq had not. In fact, when Khalq had been harried by the government, the Parchamis had actively participated in the persecution. In power, Parcham had forfeited the advantages of opposition. Trading acceptance of responsibility for only a share of power, and not the decisive share, Parcham inevitably suffered from disillusionment and impatience which undermined the Daud regime. Khalq had no such problem. Though it would have joined Daud's government if it could, in fact it had not.

While Parcham was enmeshed with Daud and part of his government, Khalq, with Taraki as theorist and politician and Amin as organiser and main practical man of business, built the decisive forces that would make the "Great Saur Revolution". They recruited the decisive leaders of the most important sections of the armed forces, those who could control Afghan state power. The proto-PDPA before 1965, and then the PDPA, had military connections, and probably some military cells; Parcham had the initial successes in organising officers. But from the 1973 Daud coup, Khalq, concentrating almost exclusively on the military, reaped the harvest that the Russian connection had sown.

The goals of modernisation and development, and acceptance of a central role for the state in the economy, were common ground in Afghanistan's elite: differences concerned the extent of statification. That common ground, together with disappointment at the failures of Daud after 1973, helped convince many of the military elite that Khalq, and then the reunited PDPA, offered a solution. The USSR wanted a coup; for them, the situation was by the mid-1970s not only ripe but overripe. Khalq's ability to recruit Daudite officers shows how ripe conditions were.

Khalq's concentration on military recruitment was part of a project, a plan for a special sort of revolution. A party as small as the PDPA, in a non-revolutionary situation, could realistically steer in a straight line for "revolution" only if the projected revolution did not depended on its own forces. As we saw in the passage from his official biography quoted at the head of this article, after April 1978 Taraki would boast that he had conceived of and carried out a new form of revolution. In fact it was a very old form — military coup — but with the tiny PDPA in control of the military.

The reunified PDPA (1977–8)

ONCE Parcham was out with Daud, once the whole orientation towards Daud had ended as it had, the reunification of Parcham and Khalq became a possibility. The Russians wanted it, and insisted on it. By now, Parcham was by far the lesser force both among PDPA members and, most importantly, in its implantation in the officer corps. It was not Parcham but Khalq that that reaped what the Russians and modern Afghan history had sown.

All the moves in this period strongly suggest systematic preparation of the "instrument" that would carry out the Saur coup. The coup was probably the USSR's project, or a project of a section of the USSR state — maybe the KGB. It was, in that respect, and at the other end of the Stalinist Empire, a variation on what had happened a decade earlier, in 1968, when Czechoslovakia had looked set to loosen its ties to the Stalinist bloc. Only the mechanics, the techniques, were, at first, different. In Czechoslovakia the invasion came first.

When the Russians had invaded Czechoslovakia in August 1968 the Russian ruling class had proclaimed the "Brezhnev Doctrine". Where "socialism" had been established, the USSR and its "Warsaw Pact" would not peacefully let it be overthrown. Afghanistan had effectively been a client state of the USSR. With the active participation of Afghan Stalinist forces, Daud, the pro-USSR dictator of the 1950s and early 1960s, had made a "pro-USSR" coup in 1973. Having got that far, the USSR would not just let Afghanistan move out of its orbit. The countdown to the Stalinist coup began once Daud's new international direction became clear.

In July 1977, exactly four years after Mohammed Daud's coup and just nine months before the "Great Saur Revolution", the two PDPAs held a unification conference. Though Khalq was three times bigger than Parcham, a Central Committee with equal numbers of Khalq and Parcham was created. This was a

Russian-enforced shotgun marriage.

Secretly, they set their goal as the deposition of the royal Republican Daud. They decided to create "mass organisations" of women, peasants and youth. There are no reliable figures for the numbers involved in the joint Parcham-Khalq PDPA Mark 2, but nine months later, after the coup, the PDPA claimed to have 8,000 members. The CIA and other professional Stalinist-watchers put the figure at not more than half of that.

The PDPA was not only a creature of the towns, but disproportionately Kabul-centred, though very small even in Kabul. Ninety per cent of the population of Afghanistan lived in villages. More than that: politically the party was politically underdeveloped and primitive. The PDPA's leaders, writers and speakers and their deeds in power testify to that. Its ignorance of the countryside – and specifically Khalq's ignorance, though Khalq had stronger rural connections – would be a factor in what happened when they seized state power.

The "Great Saur Revolution" (April 1978)

ON 27 April 1978, Afghan Stalinism launched its bid for power in the form of another military coup. Indeed, organised by the same leading military men, it looked remarkably like the same military coup as that of July 1973, but this time against Daud. There was about it something of military leaders taking back what they had given Daud, to bestow it elsewhere.

With the PDPA also there was an element of seizing now for itself what it had in the past bestowed on Daud. Five years experience had politically reshaped some of the formerly Daudite officers, and not only those who were already PDPA or close to it in 1973. Daud had moved too slowly towards "socialism". He was not fully committed to the USSR model, and of course he had begun to veer away from the USSR itself. The inadequacy of what Daud had achieved, coming to power amidst economic collapse, measured against what the urban elite urgently felt Afghanistan needed – that was the spur. That widespread feeling among not-quite-PDPA officers is what gave the tiny PDPA and its officers the initiative.

The founder of Parcham and its political-theoretical leader, Mir Akhbar Kyber, was assassinated on 17 April 1978 in Kabul. Two men came to his home and shot him dead. It is likely that Khalq, or the Amin segment of Khalq, killed him. Bitter hostilities and rivalries between Khalq and Parcham were still rampant in the "united" PDPA. Those denounced for the killing by Daud's police, the brothers Mir Siddiq Alemyar and Mir Aref Alemyar, would be given high office under Amin, and would later be shot by Parcham, in June 1980.

Variously blaming the CIA and the Muslim Brotherhood, the PDPA organised Kyber's funeral as a large protest demonstration in Kabul. Ten to fifteen thousand people took part. In response Daud attempted a large-scale crackdown on the PDPA.

Daud's police arrested seven leaders of the PDPA – Taraki, Karmal, Amin and four others. Symptomatically, a Khalq agent in Daud's intelligence system, Lieutenant Colonel Pacha Sarbaz, gave Amin, the organiser of Khalq's military men, advance warning. The other leaders were held incommunicado in jail. Amin, the lynchpin organiser, was held only under house arrest and thus left in a position to trigger what must have been a prepared coup. The initiative lay with the PDPA's military men, who now acted under Khalq's and Amin's control.

It has been suggested that, though the PDPA had been preparing for a military rising – probably set for August 1979 – the Parcham leaders were, in April, pulled along behind Khalq and Amin. But only some details of what happened were happenstance and accident. The main lines of development – a military coup at the moment the PDPA chose – would have been the same. Everything points to that.

Unlike 1973, which was a bloodless coup, 1978 was a very bloody, fierce and merciless battle for control of the state between sections of the armed forces. As many as 10,000 people died. Daud and 18 members of his family were killed. Of 1,800 members of Daud's bodyguard, the Republican Guard, there were few survivors, and those were later killed in jail. Perhaps 30,000 people were wounded.

The ferocity showed that something very serious was happening: it also pointed to the high-Stalinist ferocity that would soon find outlet in the PDPA factions slaughtering each other. But this, nonetheless, was a coup, a struggle for power among the samurai, not a revolution. The people were not involved – not at all, not even as a token gesture by the PDPA towards "Marxism". The people of Afghanistan were objects, not subjects, in the "Great Saur Revolution".

The PDPA in power (1978-9)

FOR a few days after the putschists had won control in Kabul, power was said to reside in a Military Revolutionary Council, with Lieutenant Colonel Abdul Kader, returned from the Kabul slaughterhouse, as Head of State. On 1 May 1978 the "military" designation was dropped. The Military Revolutionary Council became the Revolutionary Council. Taraki was named Head of State, President and Prime Minister. Babrak Karmal was named First Deputy Prime Minister. Amin was another Deputy Prime Minister. The state was renamed the "Democratic Republic of Afghanistan".

The new rulers denied that they were "communist" or "Marxists", or that the Afghan state had ceased to be "non-aligned". They addressed Pakistan and Iran as brother Islamic states. They solicited aid from sources other than Russia. Their Russian ties, the new leaders said, would be no greater than Daud's. Their country was "free and neutral".

At first this won widespread international belief. The Saur Revolution was not at first widely seen as "communist". This was a revolution by the old state machine and a segment of the existing elite, not their overthrow.

They insisted they were Afghan nationalists, concerned to modernise and develop the country. They denounced Daud's backsliding after the 1973 coup. The government declared itself devoutly Muslim. One article of the credo of State – a continuation of an article in the 1977 Daud constitution – said: "Internal policy is based on the foundations of the sacred Islamic religion".

"We are free and move ahead according to the circumstances prevailing in our society," a press conference was told in Kabul in June 1978. Guarantees were offered to private property; bank deposits were declared inviolable by the government. But from the beginning the government committed itself to land reform.

Taraki said the "present stage" was one of national democratic revolution. This was disingenuous. As Taraki would soon begin to boast, this was a "communist" revolution such as had not been seen before.

The "Great Saur Revolution" was a political revolution, something on top of and not in society. Even as such, it was peculiar because the Afghan state had only a loose and distant relationship with rural Afghanistan – with 90% of its people. The Stalinists in fact now had "the power"; and yet they had a great deal less power than they seem to have believed they had.. There was always an element of blundering and misunderstanding, of people who had gone to the wrong place, the weak state of Afghanistan, for power.

Their internal programme – even in its drive to strengthen the state – was essentially an accelerated and intensified version of what Daud had been doing; their self-belief that they could do it was essentially a belief in the unbridled use of state power, of force, to shape society as they should choose to reshape it. This was their "communism": the goal of a forced-march social and economic development like that of Stalin's USSR, and a belief that state force was the sufficient and essential precondition for that. There were differences in degree here between Parcham and Khalq, but only in degree.

The way they had made their revolution – through the armed forces – could not but greatly reinforce the typical Stalinist belief in the self-sufficiency of force and of the state. It would disorient them and confuse them about who they were, where in social history they were, and what they could hope to do. It would help undo the native Afghan Stalinist regime.

In terms of achievements Daud was, as has already been said, by a wide margin the most effective reformer and moderniser of 20th century Afghanistan. From about 1950 (when he was a minister, before becoming Prime Minister in 53) he had created an Afghan army by deliberately elevating officers from minor nationalities in an effort to knit together an Afghan state above the big ethnic groups. With USSR help – like Chiang Kai Shek in the 1920s – he had strengthened the state. After 1973 Daud nationalised the banks, fixed working hours, instituted paid leave, improved education and made a beginning with medical care. The land reform the PDPA announced in 1978 was more impressive – on paper, not in life. In fact, everything that socialists and consistent democrats can approve of in the PDPA regime's reform decrees existed largely on paper, not in reality. Those that had any effect on Afghan society produced opposite results to the goals proclaimed.

Criticising Michael Bakunin in 1870, Karl Marx had said what needs to be said about the post-Saur regime. The "charlatan and ignoramus" Bakunin proclaimed "the abolition of inheritance" as the "first requirement" of the social revolution. But:

"If you have had the power to make the social Revolution in one day... you would abolish at once landed property and capital, and would therefore have no occasion at all to occupy yourself with *le droit d'heritage*. On the other hand, if you have not that power (and it is of course foolish to suppose such a power) the proclamation of the abolition of inheritance would be not a serious act, but a foolish menace, rallying the whole peasantry and the whole small middle class round the reaction. Suppose, for instance, that the Yankees had not had the power to abolish slavery by the sword. What an imbecility it would have been to proclaim the abolition of inheritance in slaves. The whole thing rests on a superannuated idealism, which considers the actual jurisprudence as the basis of our economical state, instead of seeing that our economical state is the basis and source of our jurisprudence. As to Bakunin, all he wanted was to improvise a programme of this own making..."

(Karl Marx, letter to Paul Lafargue, 19 April 1870).

Taraki would have answered that he had the power meaning concentrated, state-organised, force. But the central truth here was put succinctly by Marx: "Force is the midwife of every old society pregnant with a new one". Afghanistan was pregnant with no new society, and Taraki looked to force to work miracles.

Frederick Engels, discussing the role of force in history, wrote in *Anti-Dühring*: "It is not by any means true that 'the primary must be sought in direct political force and not in any indirect economic power'. On the contrary. For what in fact does 'the primary' in force prove to be? Economic power..."

The experience of Stalinism everywhere, in which political force seemed all-powerful for so long, would ultimately prove Engels right — even in the most advanced Stalinist societies. Afghanistan, the most backward, would produce only a bloody caricature of Stalinism elsewhere. The gap between Kabul and most of Afghanistan meant that the first task of those aspiring to do what the PDPA aspired to do would have to be the military conquest of the country.

The PDPA government's public programme was not their "full" one. Amin would proclaim the goal of the revolution to be a "full socialist" society "with collectivised agriculture and the elimination of the private retail sector". Obfuscation and conflicting statements dominated. Unguarded comments, alternating with subterfuge, camouflage and pledges to Islam, would continue even after the Russian invasion.

What the PDPA regime *did* was clear enough however. Within a month, over 20 new agreements were concluded with the USSR and USSR "advisers" had tripled their number.

The comment by Amin about "full socialism" indicated a cauterising ultra-Stalinist programme to be implemented as soon as the PDPA was strong enough to carry it through. Collectivisation of agriculture makes sense or not depending on whether or not agricultural machinery is available; whether it is voluntary or compulsory is largely decided by the advantages the farmers would see in it. Even with imported Russian machinery, it would be a long way ahead in terms of general economic development in Afghanistan, and a considerable time, before collectivisation would be other than a fantasy or an attempt by a totalitarian state to slave-drive the people — or both.

In power, the tiny group of PDPA people ensconced in a bureaucratic state machine faced the peoples of Afghanistan as an antagonistic force. They would discover that though power grows out of the barrel of a gun, they had not sufficient power to make a revolution — and that there were a lot of other gun-empowered forces in Afghanistan ready to contest the power with them.

What social forces had made this revolution? Not the Afghan peoples or any of the subordinate classes of Afghanistan. Even passive support was limited to a section of the urban population. The PDPA was very small: we saw that the highest PDPA claim for its membership was 8,000, and that the real figure in April 1978 may have been half that. The party was essentially an organisation of the pro-Russian elite. Its strength and power lay in the officers of the armed forces, especially of the technologically most advanced parts of it, the air force and tank regiments, and among intellectuals and others within and on the fringes of the state machine.

How many officers were PDPA? Again, suggested figures vary. The PDPA claimed 2,000, 20-25% of the officer corps. Western (CIA, etc.) analysts put the number of PDPA (Khalq and Parcham) officers, in April 1978, at 200.

The conscript army was 80,000 strong. History knows examples of hybrids, of armies that were also parties and parties that were also armies, from Cromwell's Ironsides to Mao's "Red Army". The new Afghan military elite which had been formed under Russian influence, or the key segment of it which became the spearhead of Afghan Stalinism, was not one of those. The Stalinist officers' relationship with the rank and file was military and hierarchical, never a political leadership capable of rousing large numbers to action.

A very small group of PDPA, mainly Khalq, was attempting to drive a military machine, constructed for another purpose, as an engine of revolution in a country in which they had virtually no support outside of Kabul. It was a variant of the East European Stalinist revolutions carried out in the late 1940s from within the state machine. There, Stalinists had been installed in the key positions, specifically in control of the police and army, not by a military coup, but by the Russian Army. They stealthily and slowly, piece by piece, using what Matyas Rakosi in Hungary called "salami tactics", remoulded the East European societies. Here the PDPA was trying to apply the same method to a primitive society in which the writ of the state machine they now controlled scarcely existed outside the cities.

The meaning of the Great Saur Revolution

IN the Communist Manifesto Marx and Engels observe that in serious class struggle there is either the victory of the progressive class or the mutual ruination of the contending classes. The war between town and country is a form of class struggle. In Afghanistan that war — it became open war soon after the April 1978 coup — intertwined with a Russian war of colonial conquest and resistance to it, to bring ruin and destruction to Afghanistan comparable to the destruction inflicted on Germany during the Second World War.

Let us try to sum up what the Stalinist revolution in Afghanistan was. The "Saur Revolution" was a very bloody though brief civil war between sections of the armed forces — fought, lost and won, above the heads of the people, even the people of Kabul. There was not even the mimicry, or the pretence of working-class action such as the PDPA could perhaps have arranged — strikes in Kabul, for example — had it wanted to pretend, had it felt any need to square what it was doing with the hypocritical formulas and the pious dogmas of even the Stalinists elsewhere. That was not what the PDPA was about. The PDPA believed itself to have found a new road to revolution.

As we saw in the quotation at the head of this article, the new head of state, Taraki, claimed that the PDPA had found a way to "wrest political power through a shortcut" via the armed forces. Learning from Daud in 1973, the PDPA decided that it could go into the coup business for itself; and could in that way arrive at the same relationship to society that the USSR-imposed regimes in Eastern Europe had by the mid-1940s.

By infiltration of the air force and army officer corps, the PDPA used sections of the state apparatus to suppress and destroy the rest of it, and took over the state. Many details were different, but in its own peculiar way, adroitly using the strength and influence of Russia in Afghanistan, the PDPA had put itself in the position of the East European Stalinist parties after 1945 — or so it looked from the top, anyway. Russia was both prerequisite and prime mover, in Afghanistan as in Eastern Europe, though in Afghanistan it worked its effects through decades of influence and primary selection of the elements of a Stalinist bureaucracy out of the Afghan elite and not through invasion. Invasion would come not at the beginning of the process, as in Eastern Europe, but when it failed.

After the "Great Saur Revolution" the PDPA had the state power, and they had immediate Russian help on every level. The efforts of the previous "developers" of Afghanistan, and in the first place of Daud, provided them with a state stronger than anything Amanullah 50 years before could dream of — a conscript army of 80,000 men. Yet the issue was still between one sort of reform from above, one programme of development, and another. "Revolution" here could only be a political revolution, on the level of the state. In the Afghanistan of 1978 there was no ripe or developed society or economy, ready to burst out of constraints and restrictions. There was no social revolution — not even a bourgeois revolution — there for the making, waiting to break out of the restraining shell of the old society.

The state could be taken by force. But society? Every Stalinist state, beginning with Stalin's "Second Revolution" in the USSR after 1928, was unripe for rational or democratic collectivism, and its rulers had to adapt their programme to that fact, combining precocious collectivism with the work of development done in the advanced countries by capitalism. It was not the working-class "expropriation of the expropriators", as will be socialism when it emerges from advanced capitalism, but a matter of the exploitative totalitarian state bureaucracy statifying everything it could in order to eliminate small-bourgeois competition for a share of the wealth, acting to develop the forces of production, telescoping stages of development that took decades and centuries in Western Europe. Not socialism, but developmentalism under totalitarian rule — that was Stalinism. Trotsky once described the bureaucracy, in its relations with one of the oppressed nationalities of the USSR, the Ukraine, as "the rapists of the Kremlin". There is that aspect at the heart of every Stalinist revolution. The Stalinists raped History, who eventually took her revenge. But in Afghanistan, History proved more, and more immediately, resistant.

While the PDPA and the pro-PDPA officers firmly controlled the state, they did not, as events would very soon show, control Afghanistan. The PDPA and the officers had only made a coup, not a revolution. They did not understand the difference between a coup and a revolution, or between what the bureaucracy in the USSR and its all-powerful state routinely did to the pinned-down people, and what the PDPA proposed to do to the peoples of rural Afghanistan. They would soon learn the difference.

They had power only in the cities. Rural Afghanistan was still, after decades of "reform from above", suspicious of the central state power; many men bore arms, and many lived in a vast expanse of mountains and hills from which in the past both central government and foreign invaders — most recently, the British in 1919 — had been successfully resisted.

The PDPA in power mimicked the Russian bureaucratic elite. Immediately all the obscene paraphernalia of Stalinist style and language, worship of the "Great Leader" (Taraki), and so on, blossomed forth. They seem to have thought that within certain limitations — like making a few would-be bamboozling noises about their respect for Islam — they could behave as an all-powerful bureaucracy like the Chinese and Russian bureaucracies. They acted as if the state could command the social and economic forces and tides by its decrees, as if their "Revolution" were already made, as if their state could relate to society as an irresistible totalitarian force — the sort of force that had turned the USSR upside down in the 1930s, and done the same in China more recently. They acted as if they thought that they, like the rulers of the USSR, China, North Korea, etc, could do anything they liked with an atomised and defenceless population. But the population was not defenceless. The PDPA did not have totalitarian power in Afghanistan.

The Saur Revolution was the reductio ad absurdum of "revolution from above" because of its strange military-bureaucratic "instrument" at one pole and its lack of popular support at the other — and, in general, because of the economic and social level of Afghanistan. Afghanistan had further to develop than any other Stalinist state. Power could be taken in Kabul for a proto-Stalinist bureaucracy; but then what? Amin might talk of collectivising agriculture and eliminating private retail. At Afghanistan's existing level of development such measures could only be bureaucratic formalities, and perhaps only on paper. That would be true even if Afghanistan were effectively annexed to the USSR.

Judicious state enterprise and economic activity could surely have helped develop Afghanistan. But if the Stalinist state, inheriting the traditional relationship of the Afghan state to society, that is its traditional weakness, encountered powerful resistance and provoked civil war, then not progress and development but regression and disintegration might follow. That is what did follow "Great Saur".

The coup produced spreading circles of resistance almost from the beginning. "Taking power" in Kabul, though bloody, proved comparatively easy for the PDPA; it had yet to "take power" in Afghanistan. Here the underlying identity with the Communist Parties in Eastern Europe, ensconced in their state machines, ceased, because it was a different sort of state.

Because of their militarist-elitist notion of the "revolution", the Khalq-PDPA leaders went through the months between April 1978 and December 1979 as deluded, inept and increasingly desperate people, suffering from a hopelessly confused perspective on history, misunderstanding both their own place and that of the Russian bureaucracy – which they aped – in it.

The regime knew it lacked popular support. It never overcame that problem, not with the youth movement was initiated, not with its drive to build "trade unions" (controlled by a policeman and forbidden to strike), and not with its "Democratic Organisation of Afghan Women".

The regime never had and never managed to call forth sufficient active or even passive support in the population to carry through the reforms it promulgated. The relationship of even the PDPA's upfront reform programme to Afghan society – that is the relationship of the new rulers to Afghan society – is summed up in the fact that many peasants refused to take land under the land reform on the ground that for Muslims it is a sin to take other people's property. They had not been convinced even that they had reason for resentment about land ownership. The PDPA simply had no links with them.

When it decreed the peasants' debts to usurers – a major yoke on their necks – abolished, the result was an immediate drying-up of credit for the peasants and then a steep decline in agricultural production. The government was not in a position to organise an alternative system of credit. It is difficult to imagine quite what they thought they were doing: did they believe in magic? No, but they believed in the primitive magic of the Stalinist state.

Afghanistan responds to the Stalinist coup

D ESPITE its public proclamations and readings from the Koran, the government immediately fell foul of the Muslim religious leaders. Already by late June 1978, eight religious groups had declared war on the government. Its first offence seems to have been insufficient consultation with the religious leaders. But the unavoidable conflict had secular roots too, in the fact that many of the religious leaders were landholders likely to be affected by land reform.

Ninety-nine per cent of Afghanistan's people were Muslims, 85% Sunni and the rest Shiite. By contrast with Iran, where the Shiite hierarchy formed a powerful cadre of what was a virtual mass party, the clergy in Afghanistan were not organised hierarchically, and therefore were less of a coherent national force.

Nevertheless they were a very powerful force, and from the start the regime was opposed by a clergy commanding huge influence and wielding it in alliance with the landlord class and the royalists and the outsiders who increasingly took a hand in Afghan affairs to thwart the Russians.

When the government decreed its land reforms without having mobilised rural support, the clergy was able to rally mass opposition and the government had only the army to back it up.

Within six weeks of the April 1978 coup, armed Muslim tribal bands were reported to be in rebellion against the new regime. But at first the rebellions were small-scale and localised. Opposition to central government, normally, even when dormant, a stable part of the outlook of the Sardars (chiefs), now became active opposition to the "pagan" and "infidel" regime.

The paradox is that what fuelled and spread the mass revolt, and fatally undercut the government, was its reform decrees — decrees that should have benefited many millions of Afghans, but in fact clumsily antagonised even their putative beneficiaries. In the 19th century, Russian populists who "went to the people" were beaten up by the peasants they sought to rouse and handed over by them to the Tsar's police. In Afghanistan after April 1978, the "reforming" government stood in something like the same relationship to those whom their reforms would ostensibly benefit.

The Taraki government decreed the abolition of peasant debt to the village usurers; drastic land reform; abolition of the practice of charging a bridal price for women; and, building on the reforms of the last 15 years, compulsory education, including education of girls. The PDPA's declared programme also included a seven hour day; an anti-illiteracy campaign; and some price controls.

Land holdings were declared limited to a maximum of about seven hectares — a drastic levelling which alienated all the leaders of rural society. With the help of the priests, the rural ruling classes were able to mobilise most of those due to gain from the land reform against the government. Most of the upper layers, the "lords temporal and spiritual", of Afghanistan's semi-feudal and rigidly hierarchical society moved into opposition to the central government; and the revolt slowly spread until it threatened to overthrow the PDPA regime.

The PDPA found that they had little but increasingly naked force to back up their decrees. Had the ruling classes been able to overcome their endemic tribal and other divisions, and unite in opposition to the government, then the weight of the potentially overwhelming forces opposed to the PDPA and prepared to take up arms against it would probably have brought the PDPA regime down by mid-1979.

It would be a mistake in judging such a society from outside (or from "above", from the heights of state power, which is probably the point here) to assume a seething rebelliousness (as distinct from grievances) at the base of society. Far from it. Living as they did in rural isolation and medieval backwardness, the rural Afghans would have had to make an immense mental leap to reach the possibility of even conceiving of a different arrangement of society, let alone of committing themselves to a struggle to attain it by breaking up the existing social structures — pulling down their huts before any replacement was assured, to use Isaac Deutscher's image. That would be true even for the most oppressed of them, and even for those who felt themselves to be oppressed. And of course the fabric of such a society is woven from many ties of mutual responsibility and personal and family loyalties between the members of the different hierarchical layers, ties that remained intact after April 1978.

To revolutionise such a society, to wean the lower layers from the existing structures, more than decrees were needed. But — apart from brute force — only decrees were available. The revolutionary regime had not been installed by the people or a hegemonising section of the people. Not even the example and the prodding of substantial bourgeois areas in Afghan society, of areas that had developed beyond the semi-feudal level, was available. No part of Afghan society had achieved sufficient bourgeois/capitalist development to give the government an adequate base-area from which to begin to transform rural

53

society, to suggest or provide alternatives to the semi-feudal relations around which the lives of the masses of rural Afghans were organised.

As we have seen, the central government did not even have the resources to organise an adequate alternative credit system when it decreed peasants' debts abolished — an act which should have benefited, and thus affected the attitudes of, millions of peasants.

Thus the decrees of the "infidel" central government and its disorganising "interference" appeared mainly as a disruptive intrusion and a threat to the rural poor. Because the government failed to ignite them against the upper social layers whom the nascent Stalinist bureaucracy aspired to replace, it had no alternative but to continue to rest, fundamentally, on the army, and on methods characteristic of armies, which are not the best tools of delicate social reform.

Even the land reform, designed to benefit the 700,000 landless peasants and millions of others, did not polarise rural Afghanistan to the benefit of the new rulers against the old, or rally a strong layer of the rural poor to the government which made the revolutionary decrees. It did not even generate enough passive support or tolerance to make a difference. Poor rural Afghans refusing to accept redistributed land became it was immoral to take another person's property: that was the level of the gap between the bureaucratically decreed social reform and rural Afghanistan.

Using slogans about the defence of Islam against the infidel government, the Sunni Muslim priests, and the landlords and royalists, rallied the people against the government before the government's decrees could even begin to achieve the beginnings of a class polarisation in the rural areas and allow the new elite to mobilise the poor against the old. The government's lack of a serious base in the population was decisive here. Which is only to say in a different way that the "Great Saur Revolution" was not a revolution, but a coup d'état.

And of course the popular distrust of the PDPA regime was not just a misunderstanding that separated the peasants from those who only wanted their good — like the Russian peasants rejecting the revolutionaries from the cities who were honestly trying to liberate them. The PDPA's land reforms at best would have rallied the peasants to the aspirant bureaucratic ruling class forming itself around the new state power and helped it eliminate its opponents in the old ruling class. Time and again in Stalinist revolutions, such overtures had been followed by forced collectivisation. So here Allah did protect the Afghan peasants — by way of their responsiveness to such cries as defence of Islam — from being duped by the aspirant Stalinist ruling class.

To try to deflect the revolt, the Stalinist government stepped up its attempts to compete with the priests for the Islamic banner, mimicking their petrified obscurantism. On important occasions the "Marxist" revolutionary Taraki publicly prayed for the revolution in Kabul mosques. The 1,410th anniversary of the Koran was celebrated officially throughout the country.

The regime felt sufficiently sure of its standing here to denounce its Muslim opponents for "un-Islamic activities". They declared a jihad (holy war) against them in September 1978. Soon, after the empty decrees on land and women in the autumn of 1978, the forces against the government had gained sufficient strength to be able to declare their own "jihad" on the government, in March 1979.

The striking way in which the material interests of the ruling class were mixed together with the prejudices of the Muslim faith and with the enormous ignorance of the rural population was captured by an anonymous writer in the *Economist*.

"In fact no restrictions had been imposed on religious practice: the mosques were always open, and were particularly thronged with worshippers during the

Id festival last weekend. The Shari'a courts continued functioning.

The acts that were interpreted as anti-Islamic measures included the fact that the new regime ignored the religious leaders, the introduction of the red flag (removing the green of Islam), the enforced education of women (a first step, the mullahs claimed, towards their being sent to Russia to live lives of shame), the land reforms (many of the mullahs are landowners), and the use of the words 'comrade' and 'hurrah' (this cheer word, the mullahs said, was really the name of Lenin's mother)" (1 September 1979).

But maybe they'd heard about the "Lenin" mausoleum and the obscene quasi-religious cult centred around the remains of the great iconoclastic revolutionary. They surely knew about the PDPA (Khalq) leader cult of Noor Mohammed Taraki.

The priests were encouraged by events in Iran, where the Khomeini movement took power early in 1979. A Muslim priest told a *Daily Telegraph* reporter that they would fight with the Koran in one hand and a gun in the other. For they were "fighting a pagan regime which has no place in Afghanistan... This jihad will surely mean the end of the Communists, and the triumph of Islam, just as it has triumphed in Iran and Pakistan". (An Islamicising military dictatorship, under Zia ul-Haq, had held power in Pakistan since July 1977).

Beginning as a series of limited local revolts in summer 1978, the rebellion spread until by the end of 1979 the Muslim insurgents could plausibly claim to dominate 22 out of Afghanistan's 28 provinces. A big factor in this process and in the speed with which the Muslim masses were polarised against the reforming government must have been the brutality with which the government reacted.

From the summer of 1978, that is from the first and extremely limited localised revolts, the government bombed and strafed tribal villages. Eventually, by mid-1979, it was using napalm on the rebels and engaging in military sweeps which pushed many thousands across the border as refugees.

It is not clear how much of the land reform was carried out before the government called it off in mid 1979. But when the government did finally abandon land reform, with the patently untrue claim that it had been completed already (and six months ahead of schedule!), it was left with no possible means of appealing to the lower orders of traditional Afghan society against the landlords and the priests. It thereby acknowledged defeat in the competition with the old ruling class for the support of the people. Now it could rely only on the potent argument of the MIG, the helicopter gunship, and napalm against the vast majority of the Afghan population.

Long before the Russian invasion, the government of Afghanistan was behaving as if it were a hostile government of occupation, using the methods that the US used in Vietnam. The initial policy of reforming decrees plus repression soon became just a policy of more and more unrestrained repression, escalated simply to enable the government to survive. The very early resort to savage repression flowed, like so much else, from the lack of an adequate base of support for the government; but it inevitably increased and deepened the government's isolation. They were caught in a vicious circle of violence. It would become a cyclone that would ravage the country for more than two decades.

The Muslim revolt continued to grow and spread. In late March 1979 there was a mass uprising in the town of Herat, during the suppression of which perhaps 5,000 people were killed; it seems likely that some at least of the insurgents were Afghan workers who had recently been expelled from Iran. Army mutinies occurred and sometimes whole army groups deserted to the rebels.

In June there was fierce fighting around the strategically very important town of Jalalabad. In August a four-hour battle with mutineers took place in Kabul itself: they were routed by tanks and helicopter gunships.

In July 1979 the Muslim groups claimed to have set up an alternative government (though in fact they remained incapable of co-ordinating their combined forces).

More and more of the countryside was controlled by the rebels, and the government securely controlled only towns, garrisons, and wherever its army had asserted physical control at a given time.

As the war of attrition between the government and a large and steadily increasing part of the population became more vicious, the flow of refugees across the border into Pakistan grew into a mass exodus. The figures tell their own story. In December 1978 there were 10,000. In March 1979, there were, according to Pakistani government figures, 35,000 refugees in Pakistan. In June it was 100,000. By July there were 150,000; and some of them had napalm burns.

By the end of 1979 the Pakistani government was citing a figure of more than 400,000.

Outside intervention in Afghanistan

OTHER than the Russian involvement with the PDPA regime, and long before the full-scale Russian invasion and the reactions to it, the Afghan civil war had already developed international ramifications.

Pakistan, pursuing its old conflict with Afghanistan had helped the political Islamist movements that opposed Daud. In the mid-70s it gave those of them who fled Daud's repression a base and material help. The spreading chaos after April 1978 gave Pakistan — now ruled by the Islamicising military dictator, Zia — unprecedented opportunities and Pakistan's government seized it. Ultimately Pakistan's intervention would take the form of giving irreplaceable help to the Taliban, which in some key respects might be described as a creation of the Pakistani state, to take over Afghanistan.

The anti-PDPA forces were allowed to base themselves in Pakistani territory. They were given material support to train and arm there. Money flowed to them from the Gulf states. Emissaries toured Muslim countries — Egypt and Saudi Arabia, for example — to get support and money for their holy "anti-communist" war. By February 1979 the leaders of one of the Pakistan-based Islamist parties, Hisb-i-Islami, claimed they had so far raised and spent £400,000 on weapons. The Muslim insurgents had Chinese rifles, and the Chinese government sent soldiers to Pakistan to train them.

"... When (Pakistani) drug enforcement agents spotted some Chinese in the tribal border areas, an urgent message was sent to the Pakistani government demanding immediate action. The official reply was that the Chinese had nothing to do with drugs and were to be left alone.

"Members of Pakistan's narcotics control board later learned that the mysterious visitors had been sent by Peking to train Afghan guerrillas"

(*Economist*, 23 April 1979).

The same issue of the *Economist* gave details of just how accommodating to the needs of the anti-PDPA forces the Pakistani government was being. The drug trade was already very important.

"... The war inside Afghanistan does seem to be financed increasingly with the proceeds of the illegal opium trade. Feudal Afghan landlords, whose holdings are threatened by the Taraki government, are bringing their poppy crops into Pakistan and using the proceeds to buy arms in the town of Darra, where rifles, machine guns, explosives, even cannons, are available to anyone with cash in his pocket. The arms merchants of Darra report that business is booming". (*Economist* 21 April 1979).

Guns also came from Iran:

"... a burgeoning opium-for-guns trade with dissident groups and Baluchi tribesmen in Iran has built up... Narcotics experts believe that an increasing amount of the 300 tons of opium produced annually along Afghanistan's southern fringes is being funnelled into meeting the growing demand from Iranian addicts, and for refining in Iran to supply Western markets for heroin. In return many of the guns seized from Iranian armouries during that country's revolution are finding their way into Afghanistan, probably with the knowledge of some Shi'a Muslim clergymen who want to help the overthrow of the 'kaffir' or infidel regime in Kabul" (*Economist,* 19 May 1979).

The CIA? A recent statement from Zbigniew Brzezinski, who was National Security Adviser to US president Jimmy Carter, suggests that there was a lot more US aid to the rebels before December 1979 than had previously been reported:

"According to the official version of history, CIA aid to the Mujahedeen began during 1980, that is to say, after the Soviet army invaded Afghanistan, 24 December 1979. But the reality, secretly guarded until now, is completely otherwise. Indeed, it was July 3, 1979 that President Carter signed the first directive for secret aid to the opponents of the pro-Soviet regime in Kabul. And that very day, I wrote a note to the president in which I explained to him that in my opinion this aid was going to induce a Soviet military intervention".

(*Le Nouvel Observateur,* 15 January 1998).

Already, Afghanistan was becoming an international cockpit.

The PDPA splits again

P URGING those in the army and airforce officer corps who were not fully PDPA – and very soon, bloodily purging the PDPA itself – would be a major element in the 20 months during which the PDPA was in power. Like a man smashing with a sledge at the fragile edifice on which he stands, from the very beginning the PDPA acted to weaken the forces and the instruments on which it depended, not only the armed forces taken over from the old state (like the bloodshed during the Saur coup, this might have been thought inevitable) but the PDPA itself.

As the Muslim revolt became serious, and right through to the Russian intervention, purge followed bloody purge, like an amalgam of Robespierre's reign of terror during the French Revolution and Stalin's destruction of the officer corps of the Russian Army in 1937. To the armed forces' other inadequacies as an instrument for changing society was soon added an inevitable collapse of morale.

The division between caution and "revolutionary" bulldozing, which had been there in the Parcham-Khalq split in the mid-1960s, would now re-emerge – between Khalq and Parcham, between Khalq and the Russians, and then finally, as we shall see, between sections of Khalq itself. That same choice between caution and "adventurism" had separated the non-Stalinist reformers, too, If the Parchamis had much in common with Daud's approach, King Amanullah was, so to speak, an early Khalqi.

Comparative numbers in the PDPA heavily favoured Khalq, especially the number of the PDPA airforce and army officers it brought to the "united" party. Symbolically, on 27 April, Amin, the organiser of Khalq's work among the officers, was in a position to introduce the leading PDPA officers – those who had made the revolution – to the PDPA's Central Committee. Khalq was the dominant segment of the PDPA in the coup and in the regime it produced.

The 1977 unification seems to have been not real but merely formal. Cooperation even in the coup had been less than smooth. Within weeks of the coup, Khalq had pushed aside, jailed, or, in the Afghan fashion, exiled to embassies overseas, all the Parcham leaders. Babrak Karmal was banished to Prague; Dr Anahita Ratebzad, head of the "Democratic Organisation of Afghan Women", to Belgrade. Soon all six of the leading Parchami ambassadors were recalled on charges of high treason. But they did not come back, nor did their hosts send them back.

The Parchamis were accused of planning their own coup. Those accused included the Minister of Defence, Abdul Kader, military leader of the April coup (as of Daud's coup in 1973!), and the Chief of Staff, General Shahpur Khan Ahmadzai (who was shot). Taraki took over from Kader as Minister of Defence. After a month in custody Kader confessed to anti-revolutionary activities and treason: his confession was published by the Ministry of Defence, now headed by the other hero of the April coup, Khalq member Abdul Watanjar. The Minister of Planning, Sultan Ali Kishtamard, the Minister of Public Works and four Central Committee members were accused of plotting to create a broad national front that would bring in non-PDPA people, including Daudites, to run the country. Whatever about the "plot", this is likely to have been the Parchamis' political programme – and that of the Russians too. It is what Babrak Karmal would try to do once the Russians in 1980 had reinstalled Parcham in power.

On 24 July, less than three months after the coup, Taraki could announce that now all army commanders were supporters of Khalq. Khalq in power divested itself of the cautions and restraints of Parcham, and there was in this an element of making a final break with the Daudites too. Parcham, as we have seen, had been entwined with the Daudites, not only politically – as regards programme and tempo of change – but also socially and psychologically. Some of the Daudites' typical attitudes and approaches were dominant in Parcham. The differences lay in relations with the Russians and in the Parchamis' ultimate ideal of an all-out USSR model for the future of Afghanistan. With Parcham as with the Russians, Daud's turn from Russia was probably decisive motivation for the coup. Khalq might reasonably have asked: what did we make the Great Saur Revolution for if we do little more than Daud, except that now Afghanistan is organically tied to the USSR?

Probably there were two distinct reasons for making the Saur coup and two conceptions of what the revolution was about – that of the Russians and Parcham, and that of the more "outsiderist" and more subjectively revolutionary Khalq. Yet the methods they had used – a "coup", a "political" revolution inside the state, with little popular support – were more appropriate to the slow and cautious manipulation favoured by Parcham and the Russians, than to the revolutionary drive Khalq wanted – immediately, the radical reforms that roused Afghanistan against the new regime. From the Russians' point of view, the ascendance of Khalq was the ascendancy of the wrong Afghan Stalinist Party.

There may also have been differences between

Khalq and Parcham on the extent of USSR's control in Afghanistan: Khalq was more rooted in Afghan/Pashtun nationalism, less "cosmopolitan" and less inclined to "take orders" from the Russian co-thinkers of Parcham.

If in Afghanistan the whole history of 20th century Stalinist revolutions from above and from outside is reprised as caricature, and all the elements scrambled, Taraki and Amin had elements in them of the "national Stalinism" represented in Eastern Europe by those purged as "nationalists" and "Titoites" in the late 40s and early 50s — Gomulka, Nagy, Rajk, etc. — and then by Dubcek's Czechoslovakia in 1968, and Ceaucescu's Rumania.

The Russians invade (December 1979)

JUST as the 1978 coup is not to be understood outside the long perspective of the struggle of sections of the Afghan elite for modernisation and development — not as a sudden radical break, but as a break within a long process of evolution — so too with the Russian take over of Christmas 1979. It was no sudden break but the logical culmination of a long evolution.

Afghanistan had been connected to the USSR for a very long time and had, though formally still "neutral", experienced a qualitative shift into Russia's Cold War sphere in the mid-1950s. That relationship was reinforced in the early period of Daud's second rule, after 1973. Russia's "advisers" had long had great influence in the armed forces.

By mid-1979, because of the devastation in the air force caused by purges and Khalq-Parcham faction-fighting, a majority of the pilots running Afghan government planes were Russians. By autumn 1979 there were three or four thousand Russian advisers in Afghanistan. Like the USA in the 1960s in Vietnam, Russia was drawn inexorably towards occupation. When the PDPA regime's difficulties threated to lead to its collapse and the expulsion of Russian influence from Afghanistan, the USSR would finally invade. But first it tried another way to reshape events in Afghanistan. It tried to organise a new coup.

Khalq's "adventurist", "revolutionary bulldozing" approach had been tried and had failed to the extent that the survival of the regime was in question, very much as with King Amanullah 50 years earlier, at the beginning of 1929. In mid 1979 the government had retreated from land reform, with the lie that it had been completed ahead of schedule. That did not improve things. Further retreat, including perhaps the creation of a broader government, was indicated: that is what Babrak Karmal would do when the Russians put him in power at the end of the year. But Hafizullah Amin was, it seems, reluctant to retreat. The Russians were "Parchamis", exercising pressure for "moderation" and caution. Parcham itself was still weak; but under Russian pressure the old Parcham-Khalq division emerged within Khalq itself. The Russians tried their last gambit before full-scale invasion.

In September 1979 they attempted to organise a coup against Amin, utilising the "Father of the Revolution" and President of Afghanistan, Noor Mohammed Taraki. But Amin won the ensuing gun battle at the Russian embassy, and captured Taraki, who would be strangled in jail some weeks later. The Russians decided to invade.

Though Russia had long been sidling towards full control in Afghanistan, it was nevertheless a qualitative jump into a new situation when Russia's army and airforce occupied Afghanistan on 24-27 December 1979.

We have seen that Russia had been "expanding" for the last half of the 1970s. People linked or soon to link with Russia, or considered "communists", had seized control of Ethiopia, Mozambique, Angola... In mid-1979 a Castroite movement, the Sandinistas, had won the Nicaraguan civil war and set up a government in Managua. Iran had, with Russia's support, been taken out of the US imperialist orbit.

But the invasion of Afghanistan was something else. This was expansion by way of direct seizure of territory by the Russian Army, for the first time since the end of the Second World War (or since North Korea as Russia's proxy invaded South Korea in June 1950: the Korean war that followed had ended in mid-1953 with an armistice on the 1950 borders). Both Hungary and Czechoslovakia, where the Russian Army had "intervened" in 1956 and 1968, were internationally recognised as part of Russia's Eastern Europe satellite empire: Britain and the USA behaved accordingly during the very bloody reconquest of Hungary in November 1956, and the invasion of Czechoslovakia in August 1968.

The USSR had much expertise in the techniques of "intervening" in foreign countries to draw upon. General Yepishev, who had masterminded the invasion of Czechoslovakia in August 1968, was sent to Afghanistan to report on the situation...

When full scale invasion came in December 1979, there was no resistance to it. 5,000 Russian troops were airlifted to Kabul, where they seized the airport and public buildings. Over the next few days, more soldiers poured in. An additional 40,000 Russian troops occupied the provincial towns. By the end of 1979 Russia had control of all key towns, airfields and highways. (In December 1979 there were only 2,500 kilometres of asphalt roads in Afghanistan).

The number of USSR advisers was more than doubled: they may have outnumbered the purged and ravaged PDPA, which according to some estimates had at that point perhaps as few as 3,000 members, including, maybe, 700 Parchamis. By late February there were 75,000 Russian troops in Afghanistan.

What did Russia say it was doing? It had been invited in by President Amin to help defend Afghanistan; a "limited contingent" of its forces had been sent to defend the country from foreign attack. Crude and stupid lies like that were still typical of the "internal" propaganda of the Russian bureaucracy but had been rare in international affairs since Stalin's death. In fact, one of the first things the invaders did was to attack the Presidential Palace, seize Amin and, possibly after a "trial", shoot him. They accused Amin of collaborating with the CIA and of planning to form a non-communist government. A few days behind the Russian army, Babrak Karmal, like the East European leaders who came home in 1945 in Russian planes, with the proverbial Stalin-like pipes in their mouths, was flown in to be head of the government. Parcham had finally taken power.

But in fact the invasion marked the end of what there ever was of an independent regime: Parcham would only be the Afghan glove on the USSR fist.

At least seven Central Committee members died in the Russian take-over (Amin, Jauzzani, Hashemi, Katawazi, Misaq, Wali and Waziri), and 17 vanished. The Central Committee suffered a 75% casualty list. Babrak Karmal appointed 19 new Central Committee members and 34 new Revolutionary Council members. But this was now only an apparatus, not a party.

The "moderate" policy that Parcham and the Russians had wanted was now pursued — incongruously combined with the "extreme force" of a Russian invasion. Babrak Karmal tried — with little success — to create a broad-based government. Soon the PDPA Afghan flag was changed back from red and gold — which had caused great offence — and replaced with black, Islamic green, and a small red star. In April 1980, Karmal promulgated an interim constitution. The first sentence defined the Peoples' Democratic Republic of Afghanistan as "an independent democratic state belonging to all Muslim working people of Afghanistan." Article 5: the People's Democratic Republic of Afghanistan will ensure "respect, observance and preservation of Islam as a Sacred Duty". They preached a "new evolutionary phase of the Great Saur Revolution". There was retrospective ideological rectification. Saur was emphatically redefined as a "National Democratic Revolution". Several ex-Daudites were co-opted, as were fragments of the shattered Khalq.

But all political measures were now out of date. Essentially the Russians sought to group and regroup elements from various parties into a ruling apparatus. It was what they had done in Eastern Europe after 1945. From a position of immense and seemingly irresistible power they set out to impose themselves and their social system on Afghanistan, in a process whose first step was the shaping of a political instrument out of the remnants of Parcham, bits of Khalq, and other elements.

Eighty per cent of the officer corps that had survived to January 1980 were Khalq or Khalq-loyal. Thus, the efforts to create a broad, "moderate" government in the first months of 1980 had to go side by side with the continued purging of the PDPA, which also meant purging the officer corps. Now it was again the turn of the Parchamis, who had helped persecute Khalq under Daud in the mid 1970s. Khalqis were still being shot in the middle of 1980. An author connected to the US intelligence authority, Anthony Arnold, accurately summed up the situation as the USSR put Parcham back in power: "Parcham was a beleaguered faction of an unpopular Communist minority of a discredited intelligentsia in an over-whelmingly conservative non-literate and increasingly hostile population."

The Russians tried to use the blueprint used to shape instruments for "communist" rule in Eastern Europe after 1945: to organise a pliant instrument around a USSR-loyal Stalinist core, bribing, co-opting, intimidating elements of other parties and none into accepting the new situation and the new dispensation. The difference was that, unlike in Eastern Europe after 1945, Russia did not control Afghanistan. Like the PDPA after the 1978 coup, it was faced with first conquering the country, or, more precisely, with finishing the conquest the PDPA had been attempting.

At first, the Russians, where possible, acted only as back up to the Afghan army, providing helicopter gunship support, etc. But the Afghan army had begun to crumble in 1978-9, and the Russian occupation accelerated the process. Two thirds of the 80 to 100,000 strong Afghan army deserted, many soldiers going over to the Muslim forces. Whole units deserted, taking their equipment. The Russian invaders inherited the situation the PDPA (Khalq) regime had faced in December 1979, when it had at best controlled only the main towns (and uprisings in Herat and Kandahar had demonstrated how unsure and insecure that control was). Essentially, the Afghan state had been shattered. The Kabul regime was not too far from being just one sort of warlords – urban warlords – among warlords: controllers of segments of Afghanistan, not a government of Afghanistan. Russia could with security take over only the PDPA areas.

The invasion intensified and broadened the opposition – even within the towns. Even segments of the PDPA (Khalq), their power shattered, and their Pashtun-Afghan nationalism outraged, would join the anti-Russian resistance. (Remnants of the old Maoist organisation had already been involved in resistance to the PDPA regime.)

The Russian invasion quickly turned the very extensive but, in December 1979, still disparate and distinct regional rebellions into something like an Afghan-wide resistance, though in no sense a united movement. In February 1980 there were strikes – primarily of shopkeepers and such people – against the Russian occupation forces. There would be other such strikes throughout the Russian occupation. A month after the invasion a number of organisations would form an Islamic Alliance.

Islam had after April 1978 been the central rallying cry of the gathering opposition to the PDPA regime — as indeed it was against Amanullah 50 years before. In 1979 political Islam was becoming an important force in the world. Political Islam, Sh'ia not Afghan Sunni, had already installed an "Islamic Republic" in Iran. Political Islam would remain a great force in Afghanistan long after the Russians had been driven out.

Why did Russia invade?

WE have seen that invasion was the logical development of all that had gone before in Afghanistan. Like the USA in Vietnam, Russia in Afghanistan had been drawn into a progressively more active and direct role. By December 1979, such was the extent of opposition to the pro-USSR regime that it must have seemed to Moscow that they must either invade or accept the likely victory of those in Afghanistan who would take the country further outside of Russia's orbit than at any time for 25 (or even 60) years. To let its clients in Kabul be overthrown could not but damage Moscow's standing in the world, and the standing and security of its client states.

Invasion would be a dramatic throwing over of the international modus vivendi with the West and maybe of détente, which had been formalised in 1969 and had held, despite the USA's bloody work in Indochina, for a decade. But because Russia had made great gains in the world in the 1970s, and seen the USA suffer humiliating defeat and setback, Moscow — or some key people in Moscow — must have felt themselves on the crest of a rolling wave of history. Their power was at its greatest ever, and their place in the world vis-a-vis the USA greatly strengthened. Moscow thought of Afghanistan as its own. It would not let go. Russia invaded:

● Because it lacked confidence in the "leftist" and intransigent Amin regime to stabilise Afghanistan.

● Because for the USSR to allow the defeat of its client would have undermined its relations with other client states like Ethiopia.

● Because the USSR feared the destabilising effect in its central Asian republics of Islamist victory in Afghanistan. In the 1920s there had been Muslim uprisings in the central Asian republics, similar to what the PDPA had faced, repressed with difficulty and much bloodshed.

● Because — and this is probably the fundamental thing — the disarray and weakness of US imperialism following its defeat in Indochina and the then recent collapse of Iran as a military power seemed to allow the possibility of the Russian bureaucracy expanding its area of control with military (though not political) impunity, in a strategically very important area.

Throughout its history the Stalinist bureaucracy took opportunities as they arose to gain and plunder new territories, seizing what it could. As Trotsky indicated nearly half a century earlier:

"The driving force behind the Moscow bureaucracy is indubitably the tendency to expand its power, its prestige, its revenues. This is the element of 'imperialism' in the widest sense of the word which was a property in the past of all monarchies, oligarchies, ruling castes, medieval estates and classes".

Since World War Two the USSR had increasingly been the co-equal of the west in terms of military power, in a world where the H-Bomb had ruled out full-scale war as a means for the two great world blocs to try each other's strength.

The occupation of Afghanistan brought Russian within sight of the old Tsarist Russian goal of a warm water port (it is less than 500km from Afghanistan's south-west corner, through the Pakistani province of Baluchistan, to the sea). In the heady late 1970s, further Russian expansion through areas of Pakistan in which ethnic conflicts with the Pashtuns and the Baluchis might be exploited, may not have seemed over-ambitious to the rulers of the Kremlin — if they could consolidate "communist" rule in Afghanistan.

The Russian invasion of Afghanistan triggered a freezing new cold war in the early 1980s. On 28 December 1979 US President Jimmy Carter denounced the Russian "intervention" and called it "a grave threat to peace". In January 1980, the United Nations, by 108 votes to 18, called for the withdrawal of "foreign troops" from Afghanistan. Every year for a decade, with slightly varying but always massive majorities, the UN would pass a resolution to the same effect. Carter declared that the USA would resist further Russian expansion and called for international support for the USA in doing this. The USA embargoed the export of its grain to the USSR. Sixty countries, including the USA, would boycott the July 1980 Olympic Games in Moscow. In 1981 the European Parliament resolved to recognise the anti-Russian resistance as a national liberation movement.

Russia's Vietnam War (1979–89)

T HE Russian invasion ended for a decade the autonomous development of Afghan society. It fragmented and fractured what had been built of a national state-wide identity over 100 years — or, rather, what was still intact of it after the April 1978 coup and what followed. That the USSR garnered and deployed shreds and shards of the PDPA and other things Afghan does not qualify this judgement. The simmering conflict between town and country that the April 1978 Stalinist coup had exacerbated to unprecedentedly intense open war was now subsumed in war between Russia and most of Afghanistan's people, intermittently including most of the inhabitants of the towns. It became a war of colonial conquest identical in essentials with all such wars, and even with the most barbarous of such wars in the 20th century — with what the US did in Indochina, the French in Algeria, the Italians in Ethiopia, and the Nazis in Poland, the Ukraine and other places in Europe's East inhabited by "Untermenschen".

We will not need to follow the story of this war in great detail. The story of Afghanistan's Stalinist "revolution", though it reprised so much, was unique. Russia's colonial war was, unfortunately not unique and it does not have the same interest for us.

Three things shaped the Russian war and determined its duration and final outcome: the indomitable resistance of the Afghan peoples, the faltering power of the USSR, and outside intervention on the side of the Afghans. The Afghan resistance was weakened by ethnic and other internal disunities and conflicts. Russia never deployed the full military might necessary for full conquest. Russian troops in Afghanistan never numbered more than 120,000. Western experts calculated that perhaps four times as many — together with internment camps for a large part of the Afghan population — would have been required to "pacify" Afghanistan on Russian terms.

Outside help for the anti-Russian forces by the USA, China, Iran, Saudi Arabia and Pakistan, fighting a proxy war, eventually, by the mid-1980s, reached the extent of supplying the Afghan resistance with Stinger missiles which gave them the power to bring down Russian MIG fighters and helicopter gunships.

For the anti-Russian mujahedeen the war with the Russians was from the beginning the continuation of the war with the Khalq-PDPA regime — intensified. Before the invasion the Kabul regime had lost even notional control of most of rural Afghanistan. The Russians too never, except episodically, held more than the towns, and even in the towns it never had more than an occupiers' presence.

The invaders moved around the country in convoys, subject to frequent ambush and attack, and sometimes suffering heavy casualties. An army of occupation in a hostile land, the Russian army related to the hostile people as all such armies relate to those who refuse to submit: with repression, massacre and reprisal for resistance. Attacks on the Russians and their allies, routinely led to the shelling and napalming of nearby villages. Crops were burned from the air in reprisal and as policy in the fight to destroy the capacity of the people to resist.

A third of the people — up to six million at the highest point — would be driven over the border as fugitives and refugees. Perhaps one and a half million Afghans would die.

As early as March 1980 there were reports of heavy Russian casualties; there were also reports of the use of poison gas by the Russians. The basic pattern of the ten year war existed already and it would not change. The ferocity of the warfare and the effectiveness of the Afghan resistance grew.

Central to the course of the war was this fact, which needs to be explained: once in Afghanistan and meeting with such resistance, the extent and duration of which they seem not to have expected, the Russians never committed the forces necessary to bludgeon Afghanistan into submission. Why? It was no longer the same Russia. From the early 80s, the USSR, so confident in the 1970s, suffered an accelerating collapse of energy, drive and will in the ruling class.

Brezhnev, the neo-Stalinist dictator died in early 1982, and the Stalinist political system slowly spun into the crisis from which it would never emerge. Yuri Andropov succeeded Brezhnev. In February 1984 Konstantin Chernenko succeeded Andropov, and then in March 1985 Mikhail Gorbachev opened the last chapter in the history of the USSR. The crisis would culminate in Gorbachev's "glasnost", the loss of the political monopoly of the Communist Party, and the disintegration and collapse of the whole decayed totalitarian edifice.

How much did the Afghan resistance contribute to the changes in the USSR? It was, at the least, one of the things that convinced Andropov, a former head of the KGB, the only organisation in this opaque totalitarian Stalinist system able to assemble comprehensive information about the real state of USSR society, that despite the USSR's international victories of the 1970s, the system was internally decrepit and rotting. Already in 1983, Andropov told Zia ul-Haq, the military dictator of Pakistan, that he wanted to get out of Afghanistan and would go if Pakistan stopped backing the resistance. What would prove to be years of international negotiations would soon commence in Geneva. But the slaughter would go on — in such ways as the saturation bombing of hostile villages and the surrounding territory, which was a regular feature of the war. So would torture. In 1985, the UN Human Rights Commission reported "gross violation of human rights" by the USSR and the Karmal regime. In November 1986 the Commission declared that conditions were "serious" especially among women and children. Amnesty International concluded that torture of political prisoners, sometimes under Russian supervision, was routine in government prisons. The mujahedeen routinely tortured and butchered their opponents.

The International Institute of Strategic Studies would estimate total USSR casualties in Afghanistan as 20 to 25,000. From 1985, as the regime in the USSR "liberalised", USSR's ex-soldiers who had been part of the bloody colonial war in Afghanistan would begin to demonstrate in Moscow against the war. Though the protests were never on the same scale and made nothing like the same impact as the 1960s and 70s anti-Vietnam war movement in the USA, they belonged to the same order of things.

By the mid-1980s, even the old PDPA strongholds – in so far as it ever had strongholds – such as Kabul, were not safe from mujahedeen attack. Even the Russian "Embassy" was not safe from rocket attacks. Kabul was surrounded by no less than three defensive rings, but bombs and rocket attacks were a nightly occurrence there. For example, on 25 October 1984, there were heavy rocket attacks on government buildings in the centre of Kabul: a rocket exploded in the building housing the Prime Minister's office. The KGB office in the centre of Kabul was hit by a rocket. The offices of the Afghan secret police, the Khad, were attacked in the same way.

In October-November 1984 the USSR lost control of the southern Afghan town of Kandahar, which had a population of 100,000. The Russian Army recaptured it after extensive bombing: like the alien military power at war with a whole population that it was, the Russian army burned the crops in the area surrounding Kandahar.

In November 1984, after the anti-USSR resistance forces captured 100 USSR soldiers and killed another 30 near Kandahar, a week-long wave of air attacks on the people of the area followed. As the Afghan government army melted away, the war was more and more exclusively a matter of the invaders' army pitted directly against most of the people of Afghanistan. A trickle of Russian soldiers deserted to the Afghans. From September 1986, when the US began supplying radio-guided Stinger missiles that reduced the effectiveness of the Russian planes by forcing them to fly high above their putative targets, the military balance tipped against the Russians. They begin to incur heavier losses. In 1984 the US Congress had voted $280 million a year to the Afghan resistance. In fact, the USA, with Pakistan as conduit, had already been helping finance the resistance.

The economy was wrecked: agriculture was being ruined. The area under crops was down by maybe as much as two thirds. And, something of immense importance for the future – though there was an Afghan resistance there was no longer an Afghan state. The country had broken up into local rulerships, warlords, and fiefdoms, sometimes tenuously united against the Russians. What had already been true of the PDPA government before the Russian invasion was also true now of the invaders also: the Kabul regime and the Russians were no more than the biggest, but also one of the lesser, of the warlords – big in power and resources because Russia was big then; small, smaller than most of the rural warlords, in popular support.

Despite the Geneva negotiations and Russia's sometime declarations that it wanted an orderly withdrawal – hoping to leave a Russian-friendly regime ruling Kabul – the deliberate and systematic integration of Afghanistan with the Russian economy continued. Concern for possession of Afghanistan's minerals was an important motive for what the Russians had done in Afghanistan. Here too it was an old-fashioned imperialist-colonialist enterprise. But by now, Afghanistan was less an asset to the USSR than a bleeding wound which Russia repeatedly said it wanted to heal by way of a negotiated withdrawal.

In March 1986, Mikhail Gorbachev – who had taken over in the USSR in March 1985 – told the 27th Congress of the CPSU that Russia would withdraw in the "near future". In June, visiting the USA, Gorbachev pledged his support for a negotiated settlement and Russian withdrawal. In fact, it would take another three years of negotiation and slaughter. For example, in April 1986 there was fierce fighting in the "rebel" stronghold of Zhawar in Paktia Province near the

Pakistan border, with hundreds of casualties on both sides. Using American ground to air rockets the Afghans downed a dozen Russian fighter planes. Three hundred Afghan government soldiers were captured. The Russians were strong enough to win the immediate victory. And then? They withdrew and their opponents "inherited" the area. It was an insecure army of occupation.

In the period after Stalin's death in 1953, liberalisation in Russia had led to the removal of discredited Stalinist "hardline" leaders in the Eastern European satellites. So now, in Afghanistan, with Gorbachev's liberalisation in the USSR. On 4 May 1986 Najibullah replaced Babrak Karmal as Prime Minister. If it was a Gorbachevite face lift, those controlling it had a curious idea of it. Najibullah had been the head of the political police.

Russian control of even key institutions grew increasingly insecure. In December 1986 helicopter gunships were destroyed on the ground when the guerrillas attacked Jalalabad and there was fighting in Herat.

At the end of 1986, Najibullah proclaimed a ceasefire and an "amnesty" and promised that a new constitution would proclaim Islam as the religion of Afghanistan. Nobody cared. The Mujahedeen refused to talk to Kabul about a ceasefire: they would talk about it only directly with the Russians. The seven main resistance groups had formed an alliance in May 1985. On 12 January 1987 they met in Peshawar, Pakistan, and set up a Mujahedeen High Command. It was very late in the war, which showed how things stood with the Afghan resistance.

Renewed warfare broke out in the PDPA, now between supporters of Karmal and of Najibullah, requiring Russian troops and tanks to keep the peace. In October 1987 15 prominent PDPA leaders — that is, leaders of the ruling state apparatus — were removed from office, and perhaps 2,000 PDPA members purged and expelled, that is, repressed by the Stalinist police state. Najibullah was preparing for Russian withdrawal. As the life of a drowning man is said to run through his mind as he drowns, while the USSR died Afghan Stalinism continued to be a grim reprise of Russian and East European Stalinist history.

In April 1988, exactly 10 years after the "Great Saur Revolution", accords were agreed in Geneva for the gradual withdrawal of the USSR from Afghanistan. The United Nations would oversee a five year period in which a political settlement would be worked out. Russia promised that it would withdraw in 1988. Yet still the war and the slaughter and the Russian bombing continued.

Russian withdrawal began in May 1988. This development was inseparable from the accelerating collapse of Stalinism in the USSR. The USSR would complete its withdrawal in February 1989. The question of a transitional regime in Kabul was now central. The return of the king was mooted, but the more fundamentalist mujahedeen opposed the return of King Zahir Shah.

The nature of the Islamic opposition

THE green flag of Islam was the banner under which rural Afghanistan mobilised against the infidel PDPA regime after April 1978, and against the infidel Russian invaders after December 1979. Ulema, mullahs, sardars, landlords, peasants, teachers, nomads, layers of the bourgeoisie, rose, so they said, in "defence of Islam". It was the old mediaevalist cry of conservative rural Afghanistan against change, against progress, against the unknown. King Amanullah had heard it in the 1920s and gone down before its force. Yet, in the war of resistance to the Russians, the most powerful of the resistance groups were not the village-based, deep-rooted, "conservative" and "traditional" forces of Islamic Afghanistan, but those promulgating militant Islam as a modern revolutionary political philosophy, a set of social recipes derived from their own interpretation of the teachings of Islam, to be imposed on Afghan society.

They were in fact the mirror image of the Stalinists – procrustean Islamism and procrustean Stalinism alike were eager to shape and reshape, chop and stretch, the existing society.

"Procrustean Islam", unlike procrustean Stalinism, could hope to cut along the grain of existing society. The radicalism of its different organisations, the degree to which they were willing to try force as a tool of social engineering, varied from mere propagandists for their own version of social Islam, in the 1950s and '60s, to the Taliban of the 1990s, which mutated out of its predecessors into a Jacobin-Islamist movement intent on using the state and state terror to reshape society.

Like Stalinism, "procrustean Islam" originated in the towns, and primarily in the universities. It emerged to engage in a parallel enterprise to that of the Stalinists. On a certain level, therefore, it is misleading to see the Islamic resistance to the PDPA and the Russians as just the rural Islamic past in revolt against modernising trends and the modern world. It also embodied those "Jacobin-Islamist" elements of the modern world, dressed up in the garb of the past, but advocating a set of doctrinaire political proposals and recipes for reorganising society. It might be called Afghanistan's "reactionary Third Camp", a force seeking an alternative to capitalism and to Stalinism in a projection of a half-imaginary past – its own modern construction of the past – onto the present and the future.

Karl Marx once wrote that the past weighs like a nightmare on the minds of the living. The present feeds on the past, and on the ideological forms provided by the past – yet the living force is not the past, but the present, consuming, reshaping and putting its stamp on the malleable memory-traces of the past. People try to recreate the past; in fact they bring mystification and confusion to the present. Their enterprise is in the present; their mimicry of the past can only be a way of confronting the present, and inevitably only a historical charade.

It is always the present that is depicted in the garb of the past; the "past", in such enterprises, is always the present in disguise – as, for example, in the productions from age to age of classical drama. It is the present that we project on to what we see and hear on the stage, and it is largely within present-day terms and concerns that we understand what we see and hear: how could it be otherwise?

That is true also of modern political Islam, and it is fundamental to it. It is mummery, mimicking, and pantomiming of the forms of the past in response to the 20th and 21st centuries.

The Islamic reaction in Afghanistan, of which modern political Islam was only a part, developed into a powerful force in reaction against a foreign-inspired coup, then against a foreign invasion and Russia's colonial war – not, as for example in Iran in the 1970s, against the disintegrationist social consequences of native capitalist development. Yet one of the striking thing about political Islam in Afghanistan, one of whose mutations would be the Taliban, is how far back its roots go.

It did not begin as primarily a reaction against Afghan Stalinism, but rather against Daud's closer ties with the USSR. Both Afghan Stalinism and political Islam in Afghanistan "took off" in the 1950s as responses to Daud. They were parallel formations, though it would be a quarter of a century before the PDPA coup and the Russian invasion, together with Pakistani and US largesse, gave the Islamists the possibility to grow into a major force.

Pakistan was the patron of Islamic reaction in Afghanistan from early on, as it would later be the patron, and in part the organiser, of the early Taliban. The conflict between Afghanistan and Pakistan over "Pashtunistan" had led Afghanistan to alignment with Russia, and the USA's patronage of Pakistan had led Afghanistan to closer partnership with the USSR. Afghanistan had intervened in Pakistan, sponsoring small guerrilla armies in Pakistan's Pashtun territory. From the mid 1970s, when Afghanistan's political-Islamist leaders fled from Daud, Pakistan would return the compliment. The antagonism remained powerful, even after Daud in the mid 1970s began to back-pedal on "Pashtunistan".

Starting under the populist Prime Minister Zulfikar Ali Bhutto, Pakistan retaliated by backing the Islamist opposition to Daud, giving them money and bases in Pakistan. This continued after the Russian invasion of Afghanistan and the overthrow of Bhutto by the Islamicising military dictator Zia ul-Haq. It would continue under other military dictators and under Zulfikar Ali Bhutto's daughter Benazir Bhutto. Pakistan would help to create and sustain the Taliban and the Taliban regime, and back it until after 11 September 2001.

The Islamist leaders who fled from Daud to Pakistan in the mid-1970s had started out in politics at Kabul University in the 50s and 60s. Surprisingly, but symptomatically of what political Islam is, a number of them had been students there not of theology but of science-based subjects such as engineering. (For example, Ahmed Shah Masud, a leader of Jamiat-i-Islami.) The first organisations of political Islam in the 1950s were "discussion groups" at Kabul University, paralleling the proto-PDPA "discussion groups". By 1978, there were a number of organisations of political Islam. The shortest way to survey them is to look at the organisations recognised by Pakistan after the Russian invasion. Of the seven organisations recognised by Pakistan's military dictator Zia to be recipients of Pakistani and US aid, four were political Islamist and three "traditionalist".

Jamiat-i-Islami had begun informally in discussion groups in the 1950s and 60s. Formally it dates from 1972, in the era of post-liberalisation instability, on the eve of Daud's coup. Its leader was no rural religious tub-thumper, but a professor of Islamic theology at Kabul University, Burhannudin Rabbani. It had links with the Muslim Brotherhood in Egypt, where Rabbani had studied. He was a Tajik, and the would-be organiser of the detribalised national minorities, especially the Tajiks. He opposed Daud, and opposed Afghanistan's links with the USSR, but he too wanted a revolution that would reshape Afghanistan — only according to "Islam".

But "Islam" could not speak for itself, and thus it fell to Rabbani and his friends to decide what the Islamic social programme was. They felt that the age-old tradition was being overthrown by the modern world, and they wanted to restore it — but their politics were in the present, not the past; not in the words of the holy books, but in the words and deeds of their interpreters, their modern political "messengers".

In 1974 Rabbani fled from Daud's attempts by repression to control the Islamic recoil. However, Rabbani was an advocate of reform, not of radical, procrustean political Islam. He wanted not "Jacobin-Islamic" dictatorship to impose change from above but the transformation of Afghanistan to correspond more closely with his views of how things should be by way of a more long-term, evolutionary, educational, cautious pushing and nudging. Perhaps, here, Rabbani had a more realistic conception of the confines which the limited power of the Afghan state still imposed on all projects of transformation of Afghanistan from above, whether Stalinist or Taliban.

He believed in working through the traditional organs of Afghanistan, such as the Jirgas and the Loya Jirga. His not being Pashtun — and his organisation never having a Pashtun base — may also have imposed on Rabbani a sober assessment of what could and could not be imposed.

There were two groups called *Hisb-e-Islami*, distinguished from each other by the names of their leaders – *Hisb-e-Islami (Hekmatyar)* and *Hisb-e-Islami (Khalis)*. They emerged in 1979 from splits in Jamiat-i-Islami. Both were more Islamist-radical than Jamiat-i-Islami. The founder and leader of the Taliban, Mullah Omar, was with Hisb-e-Islami (Khalis) in the years of the anti-colonial war.

Hisb-e-Islami (Hekmatyar) was led by Gulbuddin Hekmatyar, a Pashtun who studied engineering at Kabul University in the 1960s and who fled to Pakistan from Daud's repression in the mid-70s. Hekmatyar thought that the Islamists should learn from the Stalinist "party" structure. His Hisb-e-Islami was organised on Stalinist lines, as an Islamist "revolutionary party". Built with carefully selected and educated members, it was organised in a hierarchy of cells, under a rigidly centralised command structure.

Together with adopting an "Islamic Stalinist" model of organisation, Hekmatyar also adopted a Jacobin-Stalinist model of revolution – Islamic revolution – from above. Hekmatyar's Hisb-e-Islami believed in changing social conditions and practices which it found uncongenial by the imposition of those it thought more desirable. The Taliban would be the only political-Islamists to arrive in a position to do that; the way the Taliban regime, caught between the blows of the US Air Force and popular Afghan resentment, crumbled, would show that the political-Islamists misjudged what could be done in Afghanistan scarcely less than the Stalinists did.

Hisb-e-Islami appealed to the better-educated, and, within that middle-class catchment area, to those with a technical education: man does not live by bread and technology alone... It was the protégé of the Pakistani intelligence agency, which was generous in providing it with resources. As a tightly selected and educated party, Hisb-e-Islami (Hekmatyar) stood somewhere between the Stalinists and the future Taliban, having features of both.

Khalis, founder of the other Hisb-e-Islami, had studied Islamic theology. He publicly opposed Daud's reforms and fled from Daud's retribution. His organisation based itself much more on traditional Islam.

Ittihad-i-Islami was led by a former lecturer in Islamic theology at Kabul University, Abdul Rasoul Sayyaf. He had been Rabbani's deputy in the early days of the political Islamist ferment at Kabul university. Ittihad-i-Islami was a narrow Sunni sectarian movement, the spawn and stooge of Saudi Arabia.

Jamiat-i-Islami and its splinters were, from the 1950s, the Islamic counterparts to the Stalinists, developing in parallel to them and largely in response to them. For the first 25 years, Afghanistan's Russian connection gave the situation its dynamic, and the pro-Russians the initiative. The Islamists were on the "other side" of Daud and Zahir Shah after 1963 – on the "right" of Daud where the Stalinists were to his "left", if you like. But left and right are meaningless words here. The Stalinists were "left" only if totalitarianism is "left", and it isn't.

Alongside Jamiat-i-Islami and its more militant splinters, there were three other organisations.

Those were Islamic, but not radical, political, Islamist. Based on the power structures and on the ruling class of pre-1978 Afghanistan, they were conservers of what was under attack in Afghanistan rather than people pursuing an "Islamic revolution" and a remade Afghanistan of one sort or another.

Unlike the four radical Islamist organisations listed above, whose roots go back to the 1950s and 60s, and for whom the Russian invasion was a great opportunity to fight, amidst disruption and an Afghan war of liberation, for their own "revolutionary" transformation of Afghanistan, the three "traditionalist" groups arose as a specific response to the Stalinist coup and Russian invasion.

Harakat-i-Inquilab-i-Islami was led by Nabi Muhammad and involved the ulema and mullahs of the villages who organised and led the revolt against the PDPA after the April coup. Large, loose and amorphous, Harakat-I-Inquilab-i-Islami represented traditional Afghanistan and traditional Islamic rejection of modernisation, expressed in such things as the desire to have only Islamic law, the Shari'a, and not secular law in any form. Here it overlapped with and shared general Islamist objectives with the narrower and more specific organisations of political Islam.

Mohaz-i-Milli-i-Islami was the party of the Afghan Durrani establishment overthrown in 1978. It was led by Pir Gailani, connected by marriage to the royal family, an Afghan "liberal", and a representative of the ruins and remnants of the educated professional classes. Geographically they were centred around Kandahar.

The Afghan *National Liberation Front* was formed in 1980 by Sibghajullah Mujadidi, a Pashtun who had been jailed under Daud (in 1959, for publicly opposing a visit by the Russian leader, Nikita Khrushchev). It advocated the return of king Zahir Shah.

All seven groups were recipients of Pakistani and US largesse. They had shifting relations with ancillary, allied, and subsidiary groups. They either ran their own refugee camps or — with Pakistani government encouragement — had organising centres in the camps run by the Pakistani government. They controlled the distribution of relief, including food. Refugees had to affiliate to the organisation dominant in a particular camp or go under.

Thus, as well as producing material resources and political encouragement and help for the seven selected organisations, Pakistan, with the USA standing behind it, ensured that they would have a supply of people. The ruling Stalinists in Afghanistan, and then Russia, ensured that it would be an abundant supply, continuously replenished.

All seven organisations were Sunni, and six were Pashtun. In addition, there were two organisations of the Afghan Shi'a minority, linked to Iran — Hisb-e-Wahdat, who took over Hazarajat in central Afghanistan in 1987, and Harakat-i-Islami, consisting of educated urban Shi'ites.

In the course of fourteen years of war before February 1992, against the PDPA regime, the Russian invaders, and the post-Russian Najibullah regime, these organisations and their local military commanders fought and manoeuvred with each other, openly and covertly, sometimes bloodily. Afghanistan, as we have seen, was a conglomerate of peoples, never a nation, and it had never had much of a modern state. What there had been of integration and of a modern state broke down after April 1978, and decisively after December 1979, into a shifting patchwork of warlordships overlapping with political and religious sectarian fiefdoms.

The opponents of the PDPA and the Russians were by every measure other than their opposition to Russian conquest utterly reactionary. Hisb-i-Islami (Hekmatyar) was an Afghan equivalent of fascism in the West.

The Najibullah regime

IT was widely expected that the Najibullah regime could not long survive the departure of the Russians. In fact it lasted until April 1992, when the Tajik and Uzbek mujahedeen took Kabul from the Pashtun control embodied even in Najibullah. Najibullah fled to refuge in a UN compound in the city. Four years later the Taliban would hang his body alongside that of his brother on public show in a Kabul street. It was 14 years almost to the day since the Saur

Revolution.

During the years of Russian power, in the towns, there had been a sifting and selection of political allegiance. The Stalinists had a base in the towns, much of it people who thought them the lesser of evils. The urban population had been swelled by migration of less tribalised people such as Tajiks from the north to "their own" in cities like Kabul. The prospects of being conquered by the illiterate and envious rural armies of Muslim bigots will not have appealed to the dominant layers in the cities and big towns, where the standard of living remained vastly better than that in rural Afghanistan, and still less to the newly arrived refugees and half-refugees. In any case the Khad, the Stalinist political police in the cities were a formidable force against dissent and for keeping the regime going: one estimate has it that in this regime-sustaining Stalinist police terror, the victims of Najibullah's political police over those years numbered perhaps 80,000. The Afghan Stalinists were brave fighters. They did not slink into their graves, but went down fighting.

How did the Najibullah regime compare to that which the Russians had come to save from defeat by the peoples of Afghanistan? Was the Kabul regime the Russians left behind the same regime that they had come to prop up? It was its descendant after almost a decade of Russian rule, during which it had been a quisling administration. If, like the PDPA regime established in April 1978, it was aligned far more with the modern world – on women's equality, notably – than with rural Afghanistan, it was also aligned with foreign conquest.

In the eleven years between the "Great Saur Revolution" and Russian withdrawal it had been demonstrated that though both the Russians and their Afghan allies and stooges stood in theory for the equality of women, in practice that mainly took the form, especially for rural Afghans, of killing women and children on an equal basis with killing men.

By February 1989, when Russia withdrew, the Kabul regime was a Stalinist state apparatus in urban enclaves disconnected from most of the country – an apparatus that, beginning with what could be put together from the shattered PDPA, had been selected, reselected and repeatedly purged in the 11 years since the Great Saur Revolution and the nine since the Russian invasion. Politically it represented – a bloody decade on – what the Parchamis had represented, which, to a considerable degree, was what Daud had represented, but now with no hope of imposing itself throughout Afghanistan.

The cities were, even more than in April 1978, urban islands in a hostile rural sea. When, in 1986, Babrak Karmal had been replaced by Mohammed Najibullah, former head of the political police, in an attempt to strengthen the regime in preparation for a Russian withdrawal, that move had led to new open civil war among the Afghan Stalinists. But until its final collapse in 1992 the Najibullah regime would continue to control the main cities and towns – Kabul, Mazar-i-Sharif, Kandahar, Herat, Jalalabad and smaller towns.

Why and how did the Kabul Stalinist regime survive the departure of the Russians? Indeed, by a few months, survive the collapse of the USSR itself which the colonial war in Afghanistan had helped bring about?

After February 1989, the Russians continued to supply the Kabul government with weapons and money. The Russian withdrawal removed from the many-headed opposition armies the only thing that had given a collection of warlords and warring political factions even a semblance of unity, the resistance to the invaders. Some of them were now bought off by Kabul, which still had pipelines to the Russian treasury – the Uzbek warlord Rashid Dostum in northern Afghanistan, for example.

On that level, the departure of the infidel invaders increased the power of the government it left behind. Najibullah proved better now at finding, buying and using allies for the regime than Karmal ever was.

Mohammed Najibullah's urban Afghanistan was for a while rendered more viable than its enemies had though possible. Stripped of the Russian superimposition, it was urban Afghanistan against rural Afghanistan. The Russian invasion had put an end to the Afghan state, finally and for more than two decades. Local rulerships defined by shifting relationships of ethnicity, religion and dominant political formations had replaced it. Russian military power could sustain for the Kabul government the pretence to be a national government. But in most of Afghanistan it was the power only to raid and destroy before its forces retreated to towns and fortified bases. To conquer and "pacify" the countryside was beyond its power, and by the mid 1980s probably beyond its aspirations.

Even the power to strike out murderously had been diminished from 1986 by the effectiveness of the mujahedeen's newly US-supplied rockets in knocking USSR planes and helicopter gunships out of the Afghan skies. With the Russian army and airforce gone and Russia reduced to the role of Kabul's quartermaster and financier, the Najibullah regime shrank to a series of precariously linked urban centres in a hostile rural world. Kabul's power to buy and bribe warlords could last only so long as Russia was there to provide the means for it, so long as the Kabul regime was still propped up by the USSR financially and with armaments. Afghan Stalinism might have survived for much longer had the USSR itself survived.

When, after the collapse of the USSR, resources for bribing and paying tribute to some of the lords of rural Afghanistan dried up, the Najibullah regime fell. The desertion of the regime by Rashid Dostum would precipitate the fall of Kabul in April 1992, a surprising three years after the Russian withdrawal.

The origins of the Taliban (1994)

THE downfall of the Taliban regime in December 2001 ended Afghanistan's twenty-three-and-a-half year cycle that began with the PDPA coup of April 1978. The regime brought down at the end of the cycle had a great deal in common with the regime born of the coup at its beginning and with all the Stalinist regimes that had ruled in Kabul for 14 years.

Like the PDPA, the Taliban put themselves in control of the state not by way of a campaign that won sufficient support for their goals, but by conquest. Like the PDPA, the Taliban then tried to engineer a revolution from above. The revolutions were, to be sure, very different, but both were inimical to much of the population. Procrustean Islam ended the cycle that procrustean Stalinism began.

Though some who would be Taliban, including its founder and leader, Mullah Omar, had fought the Russian invaders, the Taliban movement did not emerge until more than five years after the Russians had withdrawn and more than two years after the fall of the Najibullah regime.

The Taliban was a movement of religious zealots convinced that they were called by god at that exact moment to wage a jihad to put down the festering disorder into which Afghanistan, shattered into warlordships and bandit fiefdoms, had collapsed, and to restore a unified Afghan state dominated by Durrani Pashtuns. They combined fanatical commitment to a supposedly universal god with narrow tribalism. In that the Taliban continued a drive to create an Afghan state, strong and controlling, that goes back to the 1880s. They aimed by way of the state to make themselves absolute masters and to impose a radical Islamic social regime on the peoples of Afghanistan − what they believed would be the first truly Islamic state anywhere since the 7th century.

Their conception of the proper Islamic state was unique to themselves — involving among other things the imposition in Afghanistan of a system of rigid gender apartheid, sustained by an all-pervasive state persecution of women and girls without precedent even in the sorry history of Islam.

When God called the Taliban to do his work in Afghanistan he didn't take any chances. He made sure they had adequate help. Without that help the story might have gone differently. The Pakistani state, specifically its military intelligence agency, helped originate, organise, finance and arm the Taliban. It deployed adroit political, logistical and diplomatic support when the Taliban needed it. That support was probably irreplaceable at the Taliban's beginnings. The Taliban, from the start, also had the active support, material, political, diplomatic, of Saudi Arabia.

The early relationship between the Taliban and Pakistan has more than a little in common with the relationship between the PDPA and the USSR, especially the Khalq PDPA, which was never a puppet and later threw off the USSR leading strings.

The Taliban originated in Pakistan among refugees created by the Russian invasion, most of them boys educated in primitive religious schools where the curriculum consisted of rote learning of the Koran and Islamic law. Teachers were by all accounts at best no more than semi-literate themselves. They learned nothing of science, secular literature, history, maths or the modern world in this medievalist education.

Those living in the refugee camps and growing up in them did not in their own lives have many points of contact with the modern world, either.

By late 1978 refugees had begun building up in Pakistan and Iran. By the end of the Russian occupation, six million, a third of Afghanistan's population, had fled the country. Afghanistan was a place of interminable political and ethnic civil wars that continued after the fall of the Stalinist Najibullah regime in 1992. Most of them did not return to the Afghanistan after the Russian withdrawal or after the end of urban Stalinism. The refugees had a tenuous, constricted place in the world. Many were orphans.

Children and young men living in narrow poverty and narrower ignorance, dependent for food and safety on compliance with whichever of the political-religious groups was dominant in their refugee camp, were easy victims for systematic indoctrination in an all-embracing religious-totalitarian view of the world. Young men for whom circumstances offered little in life to compete with God and the other-worldly paradise promised to those who would be warriors of god, and guaranteed to martyrs for the faith — they were the catchment area of the Taliban.

Marx wrote of the "heavenly" other-worldly fantasies of religion that they are "the heart of a heartless world" — compensatory fantasies about this world. The religious fanaticism of the Taliban, too, reflected the grim and heartless world in which these boys grew up back on to them, fantasised — still nightmarish, but now a world which they, as soldiers of god, could hope to find a better place in, dominate and revenge themselves on.

The history of Islam has many examples of religious zealots bred in the poverty, the asceticism, the narrowness, the ignorant bigotry and the mysticism of the arid desert sweeping down in warlike waves on richer settled communities, as god's own god-like tyrants to purge and scourge the apostates back to true religion. The Taliban too swept out of the desert, but out of the man-made deserts of the refugee camps in Pakistan, to impose themselves and their starved and delirious ideas on Afghanistan.

Outsiders first became aware of the Taliban when they took the Pashtun city of Kandahar in October 1994. The organisation appeared fully-formed, without a history or visibility to outsiders while it was growing. It could do so because it was not alone. At that stage it was heavily a creation of the Pakistani state — Pakistan's PDPA.

On 12 October 1994 200 Taliban attacked the garrison at the Afghan border post of Spin Boldak, an important desert fuelling post for Pakistan-Afghan transport held by Hekmatyar's soldiers. Almost without a fight, the Taliban won control of Spin Boldak, thereby capturing 18,000 Kalashnikov rifles, large quantities of ammunition, and artillery and trucks in the nearby arms dump. The material had been moved just over the border from Pakistan to comply with an international accord of 1990, and was nominally held by Hekmatyar.

This well-chosen target, which brought so much to the Taliban at the beginning of its campaign, showed a level of military intelligence that points straight to a central feature of the early Taliban: they were being helped, shepherded, organised and directed by the Pakistan intelligence agency. The vast haul of arms at the very beginning was a birthday gift from the Pakistani state parent of the Taliban. The new force was Pakistan's protégé — Pakistan's attempt at a solution to the chaos in Afghanistan.

The Taliban next "appeared" at the beginning of November 1994, acting as an auxiliary force on the ground for the Pakistanis to free a large convoy of Pakistani trucks being held to ransom by a group of warlords. The Taliban attacked, defeated the warlords, and publicly hung the body of the warlord Mansur from the barrel of a tank.

The Taliban immediately moved on the large city of Kandahar and in a mere two days of very desultory fighting subdued the city's defenders. What would be a surprising characteristic of many Taliban victories was present here from the beginning: Mullah Naquib, the leading militarist in the city, with 2,500 men under his command, did not fight. He had been handsomely bribed by the Taliban's Pakistani sponsor, the ISI intelligence agency. Russian money had helped keep Najibullah in power; Pakistani money helped the Taliban rise to power.

Naquib's men enlisted with the Taliban. Here too the Taliban acquired new large stocks of weapons and additional tanks, armoured cars, and MIG-21 fighter planes. It would be a year before the Taliban would be able to deploy airpower, but Pakistan would fix that for them too.

In just a couple of weeks, the unknown force had captured the second largest city in Afghanistan, with the loss of just a dozen men. Ahmed Rashid, author of the best history of the Taliban, sums it up: "In Islamabad, no foreign diplomat or analyst doubted that they had received considerable support from Pakistan."

Yet they would quickly demonstrate that they were not quite Pakistan's puppet, whatever the Pakistan government may have intended or expected. They showed it first by what they did in the cities they captured. We will first complete the story of the Taliban conquest of Afghanistan and then return to that.

Pakistan's immediate concern was to re-establish sufficient order in Afghanistan to make something like normal trade possible. In the longer term, Pakistan was concerned to make Afghanistan, which, after nearly two decades of internal war, was not a state, but a wilderness infested by big and small bandit warlords, exacting tribute and protection-money from anything that lived and moved, its satellite state. On a hundred miles of road there might be a dozen or 20 separate posts at which heavy tribute would be exacted from traffic for the right to proceed. Acting directly or immediately as the agent of Pakistan to clear the roads and allow economic life to revive, the Taliban cleared the highways of the warlords and their tolls, establishing only one toll, their own. It was the advantage of a single state as distinct from many petty "states". One of the historic tasks of bourgeois revolutions, like that of 18th century France, was precisely such work of clearing away the myriad restrictive tolls and exactions that inhibited and strangled trade. In 1990s Afghanistan that prerequisite for trade and economic life beyond local production had to be performed by those who thought they were taking Afghanistan back to the 7th century – and in the chaotic conditions created by the sequels of the Great Saur coup d'état, made by those who thought they were taking Afghanistan by a short cut into the 21st century.

The chronic distress in Afghanistan; the magnetic power that success in Kandahar gave the Taliban to attract recruits; the money, expertise, organisational scaffolding and safety-net provided by the Pakistani state and its agencies – all these guaranteed that the Taliban became, from 1994, a spectacularly growing force in Afghanistan. Recruits flocked to join the new movement. By December 1994, 20,000 students from Pakistan, as well as Afghans from the refugee camps, had rallied to Kandahar.*

A Pakistani Minister openly claimed the Taliban as "our boys". One of the central things "going for" the Taliban was that its links with Pakistan raised it above all the mere warlords of Afghanistan – and would eventually raise it above the Kabul government.

Three months after taking Kandahar, the Taliban controlled 12 of Afghanistan's 31 provinces. Like Chiang Kai Shek's Guomindang in the mid-1920s marching north across China to unify the country by eliminating its proliferating warlords, the Taliban began to march north across Afghanistan to unify and restore an Afghan state. Their many victories served to testify that the Taliban was indeed the hand of god, bringing order at last to Afghanistan.

Its reputation for invincibility, rooted in its early quick, Pakistan-managed successes in and around Kandahar, helped it cow some of the bigger and lesser warlords.

Pakistan's money helped it neutralise others. But so far this was a Pashtun movement in Pashtun territory. The prospect of peace without rampaging banditry in power disposed many in its favour. For such a movement to unify multi-ethnic Afghanistan under its control would present complications that would become clearer with its further success. But the first results of initial Taliban success was an immense rallying of support.

Who rallied? War-weary people enticed by the reputation the Taliban acquired for putting down banditry and warlordism and for disarming factions other than their own. Bourgeois forces with their minds focused on peace and order as the pre-conditions of trade.

The Taliban sprung from its success in Kandahar north to the outskirts of Kabul and west to Herat. It had now become a force for consideration in the combinations and recombinations of the political, ethnic, and religious (Sunni-Shi'a) factions. In fact, the Taliban was unrelenting and uncompromising in its opposition to all others. What it did and did not do was shaped by its drive for total power and by a vision of the unique goal which god had bestowed on Mullah Omar and the elect of the Taliban.

The Taliban soon revealed itself as not an Afghan but a Pashtun force – and not an Islamic, however puritanical, but a Sunni-sectarian movement. Early in 1995, the Hazara forces holding some suburbs of Kabul, faced with a dangerous offensive by the warlord Masud, did a deal with the Taliban, surrendering weapons and positions. But the Hazaras are not only not Pashtun, they are Shi'a. Their version of Islam was not recognised as any sort of Islam by the Taliban.

---

* This, by the way, was a very unexpected realisation of the slogan some leftists favoured in the late 1960s, "student power"!

When the Hazara leader, Abdul Ali Mazari, fell into the hands of the Taliban, they killed him out of hand. It showed the ethnic and religious-sectarian character of the Taliban early and unmistakably.

Simultaneously the Taliban's mystique of god-guaranteed invincibility was debunked when, in March 1995, Masud drove them out of the positions surrendered to them by the Hazaras in the suburbs of Kabul. This event proclaimed and emphasised something basic to the situation in Afghanistan: already the Taliban, having taken the Pashtun areas in the south, had reached the end of its natural Pashtun "constituency". From here on in it was faced with the ethnic/national conquest of the rest of Afghanistan – with acting as a conquering Pashtun-imperialist power. It would in the next 18 months conquer a great part of non-Pashtun Afghanistan, but never all of it.

Now, after the setbacks of March 1995, Taliban control shrank from 12 to eight provinces. The Taliban, which had an abundance of guns and vehicles from Pakistan and their other steady backer, Saudi Arabia, spent the summer rebuilding and preparing. With the help of Pakistani military intelligence officers, they created a new command structure. The religious levée en masse character of the Taliban would never entirely disappear, but from now on it would be far better organised.

Like an enabling, busy parent, Pakistan acted as a go-between to secure a secret agreement for the Uzbek forces of General Rashid Dostum to provide technicians to repair the Russian-built planes and helicopters which the Taliban had earlier taken when they took Kandahar. Thus the Taliban acquired airpower, courtesy of Pakistan and of Dostum. It would take the ethnic and other warlords time to learn that the Taliban was not one warlord group among others, prepared to play their eternal game of alliance, doublecross and recombination. The Taliban was out to exterminate the warlords, not to settle down in coexistence with them.

Early in September 1995 the Taliban took Herat, their second great city. Herat, unlike Kandahar, was not Pashtun and not Sunni. There, the Taliban were foreign conquerors, and a force for religious oppression of Muslims whom they did not recognise as Muslims.

Immediately after they overran Herat, the Taliban in October and November 1995, once more concentrated on taking Kabul, which they were already besieging. Here too, and yet again, they were not dependent on the success of their arms only. They were in a position to buy the surrender of some of the Kabul Government's front line commanders. Still shepherding and outriding for the Taliban, the Pakistani government summoned the anti-Rabbani warlords, Hekmatyar, Dostum and others, to try to get them to ally with the Taliban against the nominal government in Kabul, headed by Rabbani. But if Pakistan was not yet convinced that the Taliban could win outright victory, the Taliban were in no doubt of it. They knew which side god was on, as they would know it six years later when they defied the USA. They boycotted the meeting, denouncing the warlords as "communist infidels". Pakistani and Taliban goals and strategies were no longer identical, but Pakistan – and Saudi Arabia – would continue to back the Taliban. (With Iran, Russia and India the prime backers on the other side.) Pakistan would make new efforts to ensure that the Taliban had sufficient military supplies.

The USA, which had been seriously involved in financing the anti-Stalinist mujahedeen in the 1980s and early 90s, had lost interest after 1992, when Najibullah fell. Now, in 1996, it was mainly interested in peace and conciliation. It urged the Kabul government and the Taliban to come to an agreement. Its direct concern was to facilitate the laying of a gas pipeline from Turkmenistan through Afghanistan to Pakistan. Even though US enmity to Iran led it to give subtextual backing to the Taliban and Pakistan, it had low expectations of the Taliban. At the UN, in April 1996, the US proposed an arms embargo on Afghanistan.

In May 1996, Hekmatyar allied with the Rabbani government against the Taliban and entered Kabul, large parts of which his rocket-fire had reduced to rubble, for the first time in 15 years, to become Prime Minister. The Taliban launched a massive rocket attack on Kabul in response. The Taliban had now been camped outside Kabul for a year, raining rockets on the "infidels" and non-Pashtuns within. In April 1996, for example, the Taliban fired 866 rockets, killed 180 civilians, wounded 550, and destroyed large chunks of the city. That was on top of what Hekmatyar had done between 1993 and 1995.

Saudi Arabia and Pakistan, despite favouring and advocating a Taliban alliance with other warlords against Kabul, backed the Taliban in another attempt on its own to take Kabul. The intelligence services of both Saudi Arabia and Pakistan were involved in discussing the plan of attack; both the Taliban's patrons stepped up supplies. But first, before attempting to take Kabul, the Taliban moved east in August 1996 to take Jalalabad. There too they had help. Saudi Arabia and Pakistan helped arrange the flight of the head of the Jalalabad garrison, Haji Abdul Qadeer, by way of a bribe, reportedly US$10 million in cash. The Pakistani government sent hundreds of armed refugees from the camps in Pakistan to attack Jalalabad from the east. On 10 September, Qadeer fled to his substantially augmented bank account in Pakistan. On 11 September, Jalalabad fell with no more than 70 casualties. The extent to which things were "arranged" from afar for the Taliban could not be clearer.

The Taliban immediately moved on Kabul in an impetuous and, as it proved, unstoppable offensive. Facing attack from four directions, Masud decided not to fight in the nearly ruined city. The Taliban took Kabul on 26 September 1996.

Symbolically, they took the ex-Stalinist President (and former political police chief) Najibullah, together with his brother (his successor as chief of the Stalinist police) and, after torturing and mutilating them – Mohammed Najibullah was reportedly castrated – hanged them up for all to see in the centre of Kabul.

To the supporters of Rabbani's defeated Afghan government, the advance of the Taliban was an advance for Pakistani rule in Afghanistan. This would prove not to be true, but it brings into focus the degree of Pakistani support on every level which added greatly to the power of the war waged by the Taliban on the ground. The speedy collapse of the Taliban regime under the American attack that began early in October 2001 would show how insubstantial the base of that regime was, especially in the non-Pashtun north; in retrospect it suggests that without the outside help it had, the Taliban would not have conquered Afghanistan.

With the capture of Kabul, most of Afghanistan was under Taliban rule. But the war was not over. On 10 October 1996, the enemies the Taliban had routed – President Rabbani, Masud, Dostum, and the Hazara leaders – met on an Afghan roadside and formed a "Supreme Council for the Defence of the Motherland". In the five years they had before US bombs brought down their regime in December 2001 the Taliban would never complete the conquest of the country

Victory and heavy Taliban casualties once more brought hordes of students – Afghans and Pakistanis from the refugee camps and the religious schools of Pakistan, and Islamic enthusiasts from further afield – eager to participate in the triumph. Some religious schools shut down entirely and thousands of students went to fight in the holy war with the Taliban, bussed in by Pakistan's funda-mentalist political parties with the encouragement of the Pakistani government. The difficulties of Pashtun-imperialist conquest of the whole of the non-Pashtun north, where over 60% of Afghanistan's agricultural resources are, would defeat them.

The Taliban focused on taking the last stronghold of the anti-Taliban, the city of Mazar-i-Sharif, controlled by Dostum. Dostum's Uzbek forces were the nearest thing to a remnant of the Stalinist regime, in which Dostum had been a pillar until near the end, when his defection signalled the end of the line for the Najibullah government.

The Taliban took Mazar peacefully by buying General Malik Pahlauan, Dostum's second in command. Pahlauan had fallen out with Dostum and looked to the Taliban to help him defeat his former chief. Dostum fled. In May 1997 2,500 Taliban came in pick-up trucks to take over Mazar peacefully. But Pahlauan had misjudged the Taliban. They came not as he expected, as allies, but as Pashtun conquerors and masters. Even now, the "exclusive" centralising Pashtun nature of the Taliban could surprise those who for their own reasons thought they could ally with it.

The Taliban, strangers from the south, immediately started to disarm the Uzbek and Hazara soldiers and to impose their ideas about the place of women in society. The Taliban's "minders" from Pakistan sent diplomats and intelligence agents to try to moderate relations between the Taliban — who saw themselves as conquerors, with the rights of conquerors — and the Mazaris, who thought they had reached an agreement with the Taliban, not surrendered to them.

On 28 May 1997, some Hazara soldiers resisted disarmament, and sparked a general uprising. Hundreds of Taliban were killed and a thousand captured. The Taliban defeated, the Uzbek soldiers then set to looting the city. The Taliban had suffered heavy casualties. But the resources of religious barbarism were not exhausted. Once again, recruits — five thousand of them, Afghans and Pakistanis — were hurried from the religious schools in Pakistan to replenish the Taliban. In August 1998 the Taliban retook Mazar and, according to Ahmed Rashid, "went on a killing frenzy" for two days, slaughtering between five and six thousand people.

The Taliban in power (1996–2001)

I N their campaign to take over Afghanistan the Taliban had their activities co-ordinated and orchestrated by the Pakistani state. They were given material help and provided with diplomatic and other expertise that was not the Taliban's own and which can in retrospect be seen to have been irreplaceable.

In their capacity of people working for both their own and Pakistan's immediate objectives, the Taliban cleared much of the country of "wild" warlords and bandits, restored political and economic unity to as much of the country as they could conquer, opened the warlord-blocked and bandit infested roads, and lifted most of the tolls and taxes exacted by the local holders of power on trade and enterprise, including the trades associated with the production and export of heroin. Pakistan saw them as Pakistan's. It was true, but it was far from the whole truth. In the way the Taliban ruled, they were never just anybody's puppet.

In their ethnic/national policy within Afghanistan, they were Durrani Pashtun chauvinists. In their capacity of being a religious movement, they persecuted the Shi'a and imposed a social and religious programme unique to themselves. The more civilised, multi-ethnic, and secularised a given city, the more at odds it was with the Taliban and the more savage its treatment.

They imposed it first on the Pashtun city of Kandahar, in November 1994, immediately after they took control of the city. They banned women from working outside their homes and closed down girls' schools. By banning women teachers they in fact thereby closed down boys schools as well. Forty-five of forty-eight schools were closed. Women were forbidden to go out without being draped from head to toe in a moving personal tent with only a narrow latticed slit to peer through, which restricted their vision like blinkers on a horse. Women were beaten up if any part of them could be seen. Wherever the Taliban ruled, women and girls would be a conquered, persecuted species.

The Taliban banned virtually every form of entertainment, of amusement, and all spirituality other than those of its religious forms that they themselves prescribed and licensed. TV, video, films, music, kite-flying, card-playing, chess and other such games, and many sports were proclaimed non-Islamic. Bans and restrictions on some or all of these things has been common to all societies where clerics have influence. In Catholic Ireland, for example, from the 1920s to the 1950s, the clergy unrelentingly campaigned against dance halls as "occasions of sin" and armed with sticks, would patrol nearby fields and dark places to make sure no one seized on the occasion to sin. Religion-based restrictions on what could be done on a Sunday existed in Britain until recently. What was unique in Afghanistan under the Taliban was the comprehensiveness of the bans. It was a religious-totalitarian state, rigorously enforcing its prohibitions with unrestricted violence. The regime imposed minutely-detailed regulation on dress and appearance. They imposed their own primitive version of Islam's Shari'a law. It has been described as "the strictest interpretation of Shari'a law ever seen in the Muslim world." Men were compelled to grow long beards. In the non-Pashtun and more "westernised" cities which they would conquer, ethnic and other oppression would be added to enforced cultural monolithism.

Unrepentant heirs of the iconoclasts, they banned images of people and even of animals as idolatrous; and yet much of their cultural programme, what they banned and what they imposed, was itself a great debauch of superstitious negative and positive fetishism. That summed up what the Taliban were. There was about the Taliban a terrifying simple-mindedness – a murderous innocence. They identified virtue with trivial external things of dress and fashion, things which are very historically-specific and historically malleable. They defined themselves, and tried to define the good Afghanistan they worked for, in terms of such things as the length of beards! Mullah Omar issued a directive about the angle at which the requisite turban should be worn. Silly rules on a vast range of fashion-conscious trivia were enforced by the grim and all-too-serious state,.

It was "secondary narcissism", the feeling individuals and societies attach to such elements of their own identity as regional accents, "national dress" and so on, intensified to the level of clinical paranoia. The fetishism and perpetuation of historically specific secondary and tertiary things – food, ritual, dress, morality – is commonly the daily stuff of most religions. Hasidic Jews go around London and New York dressed as 17th century Poles. Catholic bishops wear ancient Roman mitres. All religions preach as "eternal" moralities codes of behaviour that in fact are rooted in specific societies and in certain levels of material production, or (for food rituals) in climate. The change in sexual morality over the last 40 years is the clearest example of this historic malleability.

Ruling elites sometimes make gods and universal patterns of themselves – thus the literature, music and art which were promoted, and those which were restricted and banned and persecuted in Stalin's Russia, were determined as much by the narrow personal taste and knowledge of the bureaucratic ruling class parvenu elite as by the need of the totalitarian state to control everything and its bias towards propagandist simplicities in the arts.

But even in this tradition, the Taliban's outlook — a uniquely narrow and singularly unenlightened backwoods Islam, wrapped up in naïve self-approbation — was a thing of its own. They tried to cut Afghan society down to a replica of the Taliban itself. Their fanatical fetishism of cultural trivia like the length of beards was intended to ward off the hostile worlds beyond the camps and the schools and protect an inner vision of ancient Islamic virtue and glory — for people using Toyota pickup trucks, helicopters, radios and telephones from the hostile modern world, people promoted, protected, financed and armed by a Pakistani state which has the nuclear bomb. The gallant incomprehension of the relationship of forces, and what that inevitably meant, with which the Taliban defied the Americans in 2001, was all of a piece with the naïve, fear-ridden, superstitious incomprehension that characterised their entire political career.

The capture of Persian-speaking, non-Pashtun Herat by the Taliban marked the point at which Pashtun oppression of the other Afghan peoples became an important aspect of Taliban conquest of Afghanistan. The rule they imposed on Herat was government by a Durrani Pashtun army of occupation and administration by Pashtun Taliban, many of whom did not even speak the local language — rule by an ignorant, rural, alien, new theocratic elite. Of 45,000 children in Herat's schools in the mid-1990s, half were girls. The conquering Taliban closed every school in Herat and forbade girls to study even at home.

Such oppression of women, and of everyone who did not share their beliefs and had to have them imposed on them, was a facet of Taliban rule everywhere. Kabul, though Pashtuns had ruled there continuously until 1992, was very mixed ethnically, and more Tajik than Pashtun. Even in September 1996, though it was as bombed and broken as Berlin was in 1945, Kabul was still greatly distant in terms of historical time from the rural, mono-cultural, narrow and bigoted Durrani Pashtun barbarians who conquered it.

For the cities like Kabul, it was as if a gigantic explosion in rural Afghanistan had blotted out the light, and ash and all-clogging dust were raining down on them, suffocating thought, movement, and life beyond those of its rudimentary forms recognised by the Taliban. Immediately they had Kabul in their grip the Taliban banned all women from working — in a city where one in four civil servants was a woman. The school and college education of 70,000 girls and young women was immediately cut off — as was the entire elementary education for boys. The Taliban knew its priorities: the women teachers on whom the boys' schools depended could not be allowed to go on working. Women, when not imprisoned at home, were compelled to become tented beings. The many thousands of families dependent on the earnings of war widows were reduced to destitution and threatened with starvation.

Barbarous medieval Islamic laws were promulgated: thieves would be mutilated by amputations, adulterers stoned to death. Men were arrested in the street for being clean shaven. A dictatorial committee of six Durrani outsider Pashtuns was set up to rule Kabul. None of the members of the committee ruling over the 1.2 million people of Kabul, most of them non-Pashtun, had ever lived in a large city or even visited Kabul.

We have already seen something of what happened in Mazar-i-Sharif the following year — in a sophisticated quasi-secular modern city vastly distant, in everything from its ethnic character to the treatment of women there, from the Pashtun countryside and the world of those who had known little but the refugee camps in Pakistan. As if the prime business of their war was the subjugation and degradation of girls and women, the Taliban's first act, even before they had disarmed the old garrison in Mazar-i-Sharif, was to shut down the university and the schools where girls were taught and women did a portion of the teaching, and to whip women off the streets.

Taliban rule was dictatorship over 90% of Afghanistan by an armed party consisting in the main of the most backward narrow, naïve, ignorant, and comprehensively inexperienced people in Afghanistan and in the Afghan refugee camps — young men in the grip of a mass paranoid self-righteousness that allowed them to project their conception of themselves onto urban Afghanistan as a moral imperative and, guns in hand, impose it by conquest. Could they have done it without outside help? It is not at all clear that they could have reached "take off" without the shepherding, orchestration, and various forms of practical, political and diplomatic help which Pakistan and Saudi Arabia gave them.

Their rule, which I have been describing above, shows that they were, however, an autonomous movement driven by religious politics that went far beyond the goals they had in common with even the Islamist elements in the Pakistani state which helped them. As they overran Afghanistan their independence from their backers was correspondingly enlarged.

The fall of the Taliban

T HERE was something akin to heroism in the way that, after 11 September, the Taliban, rulers of one of the most backward states on earth, stood up to the USA, the mightiest power on earth, with a military budget greater than those of the nine next-biggest powers all added together, roused to vengeful rage by the Al Qaeda attacks in the USA.

They would not bow down before the great Satanic power, nor would they betray the heroic Islamic fighters of Osama bin Laden. Let the USA first provide proof that bin Laden was responsible for the attacks in America, they insisted, pettifogging and procrastinating, but doing it with considerable dignity. It was as if they simply did not know what the USA could do to them. As if such things as relative power and strength did not matter in a world where the hand of god was everywhere.

After all, eschewing realistic calculation and the horsetradings and the combinations with the warlords it indicated, even against the advice of their Pakistani and Saudi patrons, they had conquered most of Afghanistan: God himself had guided them. In fact, as we have seen, it was the ministrations of the Pakistani intelligence agency, and Pakistani money, that had provided the "magical" element in the Taliban's conquest of Afghanistan. But who, if not God, had inspired Pakistan to do what it did for the Taliban? God would look after his own people, the Taliban, now too.

Thus, characteristically living in their own obsessions, worrying about the length of beards and the angle of turbans, heroically fending off the incalculable harm that a woman's naked face or uncovered arm might do, dreaming happy, foolish, simple-minded, barbarous, religious dreams, the bigoted rulers of Afghanistan sleep-walked to their destruction.

The events of the unpeeling of the Taliban regime are quickly told. In face of US threats, the Taliban's Pakistan and Saudi backers deserted them. God deserted them, too. Where they had conquered Afghanistan in an aura of miraculous competence, now they could do nothing right.

The USA started bombing on 7 October. After a month of bombing, the Northern Alliance enemies of the Taliban exploded from their narrow part of northern Afghanistan and, with even greater speed than that with which it had expanded out of Kandahar in 1995-6, Taliban rule contracted. The Taliban regime proved far more fragile, shallow-rooted and insubstantial than anyone had suspected.

First, the Northern Alliance took Mazar-i-Sharif (7 November) and then marched on to take Kabul (13 November) and Herat (12 November). The scenes in the cities that followed the rout of the Taliban were joyful scenes of national and social liberation. The Taliban lasted longer in the Pashtun lands and in the city of Kandahar, but even there they did not last long.

The base of the Taliban was narrowly Durrani Pashtun. The Ghilzai Pashtuns were easily turned against them. No doubt the weapon − gold − that had played such a large part in the expansion of the Taliban from Kandahar after 1995 played its part now too. Kandahar fell on 9 December 2001 and Mullah Omar became a hunted fugitive, pursued by the agents of Satan.

An uneasy coalition of warlords rules in Kabul, for now invigilated by the international powers that blasted a road to power for them. An Afghan state still does not exist, only warlordships. Foreign troops keep order in Kabul. Large-scale foreign aid is promised. Unquestionably Afghanistan, its economy blasted, the intricate irrigation system on which much of its best agriculture depended deliberately wrecked in the wars, its capital Kabul in ruins, is greatly worse off than it was on 27 April 1978.

Conclusion: Afghanistan and the shape of history

WHEN the USSR attempted to annex Afghanistan it was at the height of its power. Or so it appeared to the rulers in the Kremlin. The USSR was the second superpower, "an industrial giant". Yet, according to the basic ideas of Marxism and of those who made the Russian Revolution, the USSR should not have survived the 1920s. Indeed, the survival of the USSR had seemingly refuted all the old Marxist ideas about the shape of history and the provenance of socialism.

For Marxists, the democratic collectivism that is socialism grows out of capitalism, and cannot come about otherwise. Capitalism develops and socialises the forces of production. It develops the working class. It creates the preconditions for transition to a higher social system − that is, for the material abundance without which exploitative and privileged classes and castes emerge and re-emerge in history, and socialism, the end of exploitation, is impossible.

Those who made the Russian Revolution believed that too. The only correction that they thought history, through their action, was making to the Marxist scheme was that the working class could temporarily take power in a backward country, in itself far from being ripe for socialism and indeed in many ways pre-capitalist. The Russian workers could take state power, but unless the working class in the countries of advanced capitalism which were ripe for socialism soon also took power, the workers could not stay in power in what Lenin called "backward, semi-Asiatic Russia". They would be overthrown by the native and foreign bourgeoisie.

In fact the isolated Russian workers' revolution did not fall quickly. It survived and degenerated. The working class was not overthrown by the bourgeoisie but by a bureaucracy made up of remnants of the old Tsarist bureaucracy and upper classes and of bureaucrats extruded from the working class. They constructed a totalitarian state that gripped society in a vice for sixty years.

The first Stalinist state came into existence in the late 1920s, and set out on a forced march to catch up with and outstrip capitalism. When the emerging bureaucracy, still calling itself Marxist and socialist and Bolshevik, first proclaimed such a course, they called it socialism in one country. Trotsky and the working-class Bolsheviks objected to it as utopian absurdity, a reversion on a gigantic scale to the old mid-19th century "utopian socialist" project of building communist colonies in the wilderness that would compete with and surpass capitalism.

Capitalism could only be superseded, overtopped in history, from its own furthest point of development; otherwise, the preconditions for a socialist alternative to capitalism would not exist, as they did not exist in the USSR. Before there could be any question of capitalism being overtaken by such "utopian" competition from the periphery of world development, advanced capitalism would first have to lose its dynamic, decline and regress.

Every one of Trotsky's objections to "socialism in one country" applied equally to a USSR conceived of as a distinct form of class society (bureaucratic-collectivist or, for that matter, state-capitalist). It was still backward, starting from a very low level, compared to advanced capitalism.

Unless advanced capitalism ceased to advance, unless it regressed, unless it was to spiral down in a series of world wars "that would be the grave of civilisation", the bureaucratic collectivist system would not overtake and supplant it*.

The survival and expansion of Russian Stalinism to the position it had at the end of the 1970s seemed to have refuted all such considerations. The shape of history was not as pre-Stalinist Marxism had seen it. Stalinist bureaucratic collectivism, coming from its own line of development parallelling capitalism, refuted it. It refuted Trotsky's view that the Stalinist social system, however defined, could not survive; it refuted the position of those such as Max Shachtman in the 1940s who developed Trotsky's ideas and, while clearly designating the USSR as an exploitative class society, continued to see it as a historical aberration, something that could not survive, an unexpected temporary contradiction of the Marxist conception of the shape of history as an inverted pyramid with world capitalism spreading out at the top and socialism rising out of that. The survival of the USSR, but also the spread of Stalinism, refuted those ideas. There was not one world but two; not one line of historical development — feudalism, capitalism, socialism — but two equally important parallel lines. In the Stalinist line of historical development, capitalism played little part; the Stalinist social system was, so to speak, in itself simultaneously both historical "capitalism" and early socialism. (That was, for example, Isaac Deutscher's view).

In that view of history, Afghanistan too, one of the most backward societies on earth, could be switched onto the alternative, faster, line of progress. All that was necessary was that the right people had the state power and could muster sufficient strength of compulsion.

Isaac Deutscher, a reluctant but wholehearted and poisonous apologist for Stalinism and proponent of the idea that Stalinism had wrecked all the old Marxist ideas about the shape of history, put it with brutal simplicity when explaining why the governing idea of the Bolsheviks, of Lenin and Trotsky, that the bourgeoisie would overthrow the Russian Revolution if the workers did not soon take power in advanced Europe, had been proved false. Deutscher conflated

---

* These considerations are at the heart of Trotsky's seemingly incoherent way, at the end of his life, of discussing the question of what exactly the USSR was, both in class terms and in terms of the Marxist idea of the shape of history. Trotsky, whose writings established incontrovertibly that the rulers of the USSR had, as he put it, all the vices of all the ruling classes of history, refused to designate the USSR a new form of class society for exactly the same reason as he had rejected as absurd the idea that the USSR could build socialism in one country. When he changed his view on this question (in September-October 1939) he did so in the perspective of a decline of capitalism through economic regression and world wars. See *The Fate of the Russian Revolution: Lost Texts of Critical Marxism.*

the October Revolution with Stalinism, but his words contain an important truth: "Not for a moment did Trotsky imagine... that the Russian Revolution could survive in isolation for decades. It may therefore be said, as Stalin was to say... that he 'underrated' the internal resources and vitality of revolutionary Russia... This error, if an error it was, was intimately bound up with his conception of the revolution... It did not occur to him that a proletarian party would in the long run rule and govern an enormous country against the majority of the people. He did not foresee that the revolution would lead to the prolonged rule of a minority... [That] would have appeared to him, as to nearly all his contemporaries, incompatible with socialism. In fact, he did not imagine, in spite of all he had written about Lenin's 'Jacobinism', that the revolution would seek to escape from its isolation and weakness into totalitarianism". (*The Prophet Armed*, 1954).

When Mao Zedong wrote that "power grows out of the barrel of a gun", he meant the gigantically inflated power that he exercised deliriously — the power to remake China according to his will, and at a tempo he could force, by the unrestrained use of violence against the Chinese people. Taraki's idea of a shortcut to power, after which Afghanistan could be reshaped at will, fell down not as a calculation of what was possible to the PDPA, which could and did take state power, but as an understanding of Afghanistan and the Afghan state. Yet, if the USSR had not begun to spiral into collapse in the 1980s, soon after invading Afghanistan, it would have mobilised sufficient power to compensate for the incapacity of the Afghan state to subjugate the peoples of Afghanistan. Afghanistan would have appeared as one more example of the futility of the Marxist idea of the shape of history and of the revolutionary potency of totalitarianism — of magic-making force in history.

The collapse of the USSR clarified this situation and vindicated the Marxist idea of the shape of history. Capitalism will be superseded from its own furthest points of development by the proletariat it creates seizing control of the means of production it creates, or it will not be superseded at all.

Trotsky got many things wrong about the USSR, but in thinking that such a system was historically unviable he was proved right, though in a very different timescale from the one he used. Stalinism, whether conceived of as "socialism in one country" or as a form of exploitative class society, could not compete with advanced capitalism. Modern history does not have two lines of development; it has one, with some side-detours,

As if in a neat summary final chapter of a book, Afghan Stalinism sums up the experience of Stalinism in history. The Great Saur Revolution was made by a tiny elite — by members of the old Afghan ruling classes who desired to become a bureaucratic ruling class in a social system like that of the USSR — in one of the most backward societies on earth. They pitted themselves against the Afghan people. They thought they could use the state, and USSR help, to work social miracles. Instead, they brought catastrophe down on the peoples of Afghanistan, mass slaughter, mass displacements, apocalyptic ruin. Even in the scale of the bloodshed and the ruination at the end, the Afghan experience summed up, albeit as caricature, the whole experience of Stalinism in history.

Afghanistan, whose "Great Saur Revolution" was the bloody reductio ad absurdum of Stalinism in history, the absurdity too far, played an important role in the collapse of the USSR itself. Karl Marx, in his time, looked to Poland's struggle for independence to help bring down Tsarism. Poland was more developed than the Tsarist Russian Empire which kept it in subjection; Afghanistan, at the other extreme, was immensely less developed than the empire which tried to conquer it. Yet the resistance of the Afghan people to the Russians brought the USSR's rulers up against the state of their own system. They could not muster the will or the resources to complete what they began in December 1979 (or, perhaps better, in April 1978). They could not retreat without cost. They fought a bloody, inconclusive, colonial war for nine years that helped expose the decrepitude of Russian Stalinism.

The Afghan war caused none of it. The Stalinist system was rotten, and it began to totter under its own dead weight. But the heroic resistance of the Afghan rebels, who by every test of the 20th century except their resistance to subjugation were reactionary, helped trigger the final crisis that brought down the Stalinist empire. Having swallowed more than one camel in its history, Russian Stalinism choked on the Afghan gnat. By a strange dialectic, the resistance to Russian conquest of one of the most underdeveloped and "reactionary" collections of peoples on the planet played the immensely progressive role in history of helping bring down the great totalitarian empire.

Amongst other things, the wars of the Islamic tribesmen, who would not bow down before the enemies of their god, for their own freedom – in that, though in that alone, they acted in the spirit of real communism – helped win the freedom of the nations of Eastern Europe, Poles, Czechs, Ukrainians. Indirectly, they did what the USSR probably feared in 1979. They helped detach the central Asian republics from Russian rule. But the Afghans have paid a terrible price for the strange and unexpected role they played in the history of the 20th century. They are paying it still.

Bibliography

Anthony Arnold, *Afghanistan's two-party communism*. 1985.
Michael Griffin, *Reaping the whirlwind*.
William Maley (ed), *Fundamentalism reborn? Afghanistan and the Taliban*. 1998.
Peter Marsden, *The Taliban*. 1998.
Kamal Matinuddin, *The Taliban phenomenon in Afghanistan, 1994-7*. 1999.
Asta Olsen, *Islam and politics in Afghanistan*.
Ahmed Rashid, *Taliban*. 2000.
Tom Rodgers, *Soviet withdrawal from Afghanistan*. 1992.
Amin Saikal and William Maley (eds), *Soviet withdrawal from Afghanistan*. 1989.
Mohammed Nazif Shahrani, *Revolutions and rebellions in Afghanistan: an anthropological perspective*. 1984.
Sreedhar Mahendra Ved, *The Afghan turmoil*. 1998.
John O'Mahony [Sean Matgamna], *Afghanistan: Russian troops out!* 1985
John O'Mahony [Sean Matgamna], The invasion of Afghanistan (series of articles on Afghanistan in *Workers' Action*, January 1980.

Postscript:
The left and Afghanistan

THE Russian annexation of Afghanistan at Christmas 1979 led to a new USSR-Western Cold War of an intensity that had not been seen since the "thaw" that had begun with Stalin's death nearly three decades earlier, in 1953. The international left polarised for and against the Russians and the Americans. Independent working-class politics were greatly weakened. Most of those Trotskyists who had drawn sharply away from the USSR after the invasion of Czechoslovakia, but without breaking from the idea that the USSR remained some sort of a – degenerated – working-class state, were thrown backwards politically. In the newly re-polarised world of the Second Cold War they were flung to one side, the side of the Russian Empire which, despite everything, they believed to represent historic progress and progressive anti-capitalism.

After the invasion of Czechoslovakia on 20 August 1968 by the armies of the USSR and its Warsaw Pact satellite states, which was – revealingly enough – followed by formal East-West detente in 1969, even the "orthodox" Trotskyists who still adhered to the idea that the USSR remained "progressive" and in the last analysis should be supported against an "imperialist" attempt to destroy it, had drifted into a de facto acceptance that Russia was the second pillar of world counter-revolution and should be kept "ideologically" at a distance. The USSR was − as the invasion of Czechoslovakia to snuff out the reforming Dubcek regime's attempt to create "socialism with a human face" had shown − antagonistic to everything the left stood for, and especially antagonistic to labour movements and working-class freedom.

The invasion of Afghanistan forced all of us − the forerunners of *Workers' Liberty* were then still, by that stage very half-heartedly, in the "orthodox" Trotskyist spectrum − into sharp choices. We could assess what the USSR was doing on its merits. That meant recognising the invasion as a piece of Russian imperialist brigandage of the sort the old colonial and imperial powers of the West no longer practised on a large scale − even what the USA had done in Vietnam was not that sort of imperialism. Or we could follow the pattern of the new Cold War antagonisms, and side with the USSR because of its allegedly progressive place in historical evolution. That would mean supporting Russia's colonial war against the peoples of Afghanistan.

We could either think about the real world. Or we could enact a parody of what the (largely falsified) histories of the movement said Trotsky had done in 1939, when the USSR invaded Poland and Finland; we could refuse to see the annexation of Afghanistan as something that could be considered "in itself", apart from its place in the new world polarisation which it had brought about; we could see the invasion as a strange new upsurge of revolutionary anti-capitalism by Russia's bureaucratic rulers.

The "orthodox" Trotskyist forerunners of Workers' Liberty faced the choice of either supporting Russia's war of conquest or of looking afresh at the view that considered the USSR to represent the opposite pole in world politics to "imperialism" and so to deserve "unconditional defence".

We could not support USSR imperialism's colonial war. Lutte Ouvrière in France, never quite a fully "orthodox" Trotskyist group, but one that insisted that the USSR was still a degenerated workers' state, also argued straightforwardly that the USSR troops should get out. There was a big minority in the French Mandelite organisation, the LCR, which took the same view, and a small minority in the British Mandelite organisation − but all the other organisations of "orthodox" Trotskyism came out for the

Russians!

At first some of them proclaimed the wonder-arousing discovery that the Russian bureaucracy was "going to the aid of a revolution". That was the interpretation of the big section of the Mandelite Fourth International then grouped around the Socialist Workers' Party of the USA, which has since moved from kitsch-Trotskyism to kitsch-Stalinism.

The general fallback position, a few months later, after they had sobered up and realised that the USSR had embarked on its own Vietnam war, was that though they would not have advocated the Russian invasion, they could not now demand that the Russians withdraw, because that would help the counter-revolution in Afghanistan. This combined the joys of vicarious Stalinist realpolitik with revolutionary socialist virtue, by way of hypocrisy and incoherence.

Over the decade of the war, some of them abandoned that position; others − the Socialist Party is the most important example in Britain − supported Russia to the bitter end.

The SWP UK was at that time on a different trajectory. They did not adopt the bloc-politics approach until 1987, when they suddenly backed Iran against Iraq on the grounds that the US favoured Iraq. Whereas the "orthodox" Trotskyists rejected Third Camp politics because they thought of the Stalinist bloc as, in the last analysis, positively progressive, the SWP version of two-camp bloc politics today is entirely negative − against "imperialism", and for no matter who is fighting the USA, even if it is a more primitive and genocidal imperialism, like Serbia in the 1999 Balkans war.

By 2001, however, many of the orphaned "orthodox" Trotskyists, deprived by the collapse of Stalinism of what they had thought to be the actually-existing world revolution, embodied in the relatively-progressive USSR-centred pole of world politics, and having failed to learn from their experience, had collapsed into the same sort of "Yankophobia" as the SWP. There were some exceptions, at least partial ones. The LCR in France, and the Labour Party of Pakistan, said "No to [US] war, no to [Taliban/Al Qaeda] terrorism". But many of the same currents who in 1979-89 had sided with the USSR's attempted conquest of Afghanistan on the grounds that it was a lesser evil than the victory of the Islamist reactionaries, now sided with the Islamist ultras of the Taliban in a war with the USA which was not a war for Afghan rights against US conquest, but resistance to a bloody US "police action" in revenge and retaliation for Al Qaeda's massacre of civilians in the USA.

The rise of political Islam

By Clive Bradley

"T HE central axis of world politics in the future is likely to be... the conflict between 'the West and the Rest' and the responses of non-Western civilisations to Western power and values". So wrote prominent American intellectual Samuel P Huntington, in a much-hyped article in 1993, later a book, entitled *The Clash of Civilisations*. Influential though the theory was, as the United States and its allies have bombed Afghanistan they have been at pains to distance themselves from it, for fear of alienating allies in the region, mainly Saudi Arabia and Pakistan, which they fear to be vulnerable to Islamist revolt. Rather, Bush and Blair have defined the war as "civilisation" against terrorism. "Civilisation" (not just "western civilisation") now includes the rulers of Saudi Arabia, the military dictatorship in Pakistan, the Russian butchers of Chechnya, etc.; "terrorism" is a concept to be widened or narrowed as the need arises.

Indeed, the signs of the revolt they fear are there. Saudi Arabia's wealthy, corrupt and repressive ruling family has been scared of Islamists since the Iranian revolution of 1979. Egypt is feared to be extremely vulnerable. In Algeria, the Islamist FIS (Islamic Salvation Front) was set to sweep elections in 1992, prompting a military coup which plunged the country into civil war.

Western governments have been obsessed with "Islamic fundamentalism", especially since the end of the Cold War, scared the authoritarian regimes they support in the Middle East could fall to "Islam", and then terrified as on September 11 "fundamentalism" struck right in the heart of America. But the western left has tended to take the mirror image view, regarding Islamism as a legitimate expression of anti-imperialism, consequently to be supported. Because the Islamists cry "death to America", articulate regional and popular grievances against Israel, and generally decry "imperialism", many on the left have identified them as progressive, sometimes progressive, or "at heart", so to speak, progressive. Many of those now keen to find something progressive in Osama bin Laden were, when Russian troops were reducing Afghan villages to rubble, only too delighted to object to fundamentalism as reactionary; but then they saw fundamentalism as part of the imperialist camp.

Neither framework, "clash of civilisations" nor "anti-imperialism", grasps the complexity and nature of modern Islamism.

Terms like "Islamism" or "political Islam" can be misleading, encouraging the hasty reader to overlook the radical difference between Islamist politics and general Islamic religious sentiment. There are political tendencies which are broadly "Islamic" but not "fundamentalist". Yet the term "fundamentalism" can also be misleading. Christian fundamentalists believe in the literal truth of the Bible. The literal truth of the Qur'an is accepted by all religious Muslims. But modern "Islamic fundamentalism" is essentially a political, not a religious current. It denotes not especial devoutness, or devotion to the Qur'an, but political movements whose programme is to reshape societies into a template of an "Islamic state" which allegedly existed some 1,200 years ago. Revivalist movements, attempts to purge the life of Muslim communities of non-Islamic accretions and restore it to a more authentically Islamic form, have recurred many times over the centuries. But modern Islamism is distinctive in attempting to master the contradictions of already partly-secularised, partly-industrialised, partly-cosmopolitan societies by reverting to an imagined past and seeking to use the power of more-or-less modern military and state machines to do so.

Modern Islamism originates in the cities, not in the more tradition-bound countryside. Its core activists are drawn from the educated middle class (often young men, frustrated university graduates), not from the sections of the population most remote from scientific and "western" culture. But it is not an offshoot or outgrowth of national liberation struggle against imperialism. In the era when mainly-Muslim countries were struggling for freedom from colonial or semi-colonial domination, more secular politics dominated. They appealed to "the nation"; Islamists do not. Where national liberation struggle is still most sharp, among the Palestinians, Islamism was notably slower in gaining a grip.

Although some Islamist currents have been aided in their early stages by the USA or by pro-US governments which saw them as a safer channel for protest than the secular left, Islamism is not just a creation of such aid. It has its own roots. Although some Islamist currents have gained their strength in struggle against pro-US regimes, Islamism is not just a reflex, "spontaneous" expression of "despair and rage" against US imperialism, either. The Islamists may be violently opposed to the relative women's emancipation, the secularism, and the commercialism, which they see the USA as epitomising; they are not against capitalism, profit, inequality, or dealing with the IMF. The main target of their anger is not the remote USA, but the nominally Muslim governments and people of their own societies. They seek to replace the governments – and subjugate the people – by installing a more reactionary, more repressive, but more "Islamic", regime.

In the countries where Islamism has risen, capitalist development has ravaged old social relationships, but not created stable new ones. Pre-capitalist society has largely been eliminated. Huge fortunes have been made out of the oil industry, in particular. Universities, televisions, radios, cassette players, cars, bureaucracies, airports, skyscrapers have mushroomed; simultaneously, huge numbers of people have been thrown onto the margins of society, and a huge class of "new petty bourgeois" is tantalised, then frustrated, by the chaotic, lopsided development. Old exploiting classes – bazaar merchants, the religious establishment, sometimes landlords – remain, and are jostled and embittered by the process of change. While in advanced capitalist countries, most of the population is working class in the broad sense, in these societies the working class is still a minority, and there are huge numbers of marginalised sub- or semi-proletarian poor, and of distressed petty bourgeois. These are the social conditions in which Islamism emerges as a distinctive movement, combining some of the features of the "reactionary anti-capitalism" which Marx describes in the Communist Manifesto – a first reflex reaction by displaced elements of the relatively well-off to the disruptions of early industrial-capitalist development – with some of the features of fascism.

1. The historical background

MUHAMMAD, the author of the Qur'an and founder of Islam, died nearly 1,400 years ago. Within a very short time, his followers, from their base in what is now Saudi Arabia, had conquered large tracts of the Middle East. Islamic empires, controlling variable but large territories from India to the Atlantic, and from southern Europe to sub-Saharan Africa, were big powers from then right through into the 20th century.

For much of that time, the Muslim world was advanced and sophisticated in comparison with Christian Europe. When Europe was suffering the Dark Ages, Muslim Arab scientists invented algebra (which is an Arabic word) and brought the use of the zero and of decimal number systems from their Hindu inventors in India to the West. Islamic culture as a whole, in literature as well, for example, was far more developed. "The west" – Europe – was the source of barbarian hordes who periodically invaded Muslim lands, bringing slaughter and intolerance.

But European feudalism proved to be a more dynamic system than the state-centred tribute-paying system of the Islamic empires. Western Europe became capitalist. Britain seized India; the Netherlands seized Indonesia. By the middle of the 19th century, the remaining Islamic great power, the Ottoman Empire centred in Constantinople (Istanbul), was a decaying, stagnant hulk. From the 1830s, rulers in Cairo and Constantinople tried to modernise, to semi-secularise, to fend off the domination of Europe by emulating its achievements.

After World War One the whole structure came crashing down. Nearly 1,300 years of Islamic empire came to a shocking, sudden end. France and Britain divided most of the remaining Arab territories of the Ottoman Empire between them. In Constantinople, nationalists took power; established a new, aggressively secular, and Turkish state; and, without significant resistance, abolished the caliphate, the position which had been the peak of the religio-political hierarchy of the Islamic world.

More-or-less secular nationalism would dominate the politics of the Islamic world for the next 50 or 60 years. This secular nationalism was intertwined with "Islamic modernist" tendencies, schools of thought that wanted to revive Islam but also attune it to the modern world. Saad Zaghlul, the founder of the Egyptian Wafd Party after World War One, a modernising bourgeois nationalist movement which led a popular uprising in 1919 and dominated the inter-war period, had been a student of the most important early Islamic-revivalist thinkers, Jamal al-Din al-Afghani and Muhammed Abduh. Other intellectuals, notably the writer Taha Hussein, came from the Islamic-revivalist tradition but were forthrightly secular.

The Middle Eastern oil industry began in Iran and Iraq shortly before World War One, and expanded enormously after the 1930s. At first it was an enclave industry, run by foreign (mostly British or US) companies under the complacent eye of docile governments. Gradually, the local propertied classes became more assertive. The 'capitulations', arrangements which since the Middle Ages had given foreign business people immunity from local laws and local taxes, were abolished between 1923 and 1937.

After World War Two, a wave of popular movements across the Middle East which brought radical, secular nationalist governments to power. "Arab socialism" was declared in Egypt under Gamal Abdul Nasser, whose military government introduced land reform, nationalised the Anglo-French Suez Canal, resisted a disastrous Anglo-French-Israeli invasion, and then progressively introduced more and more widespread nationalisations, and aligned with the USSR. Nasser was a popular hero across the region, copied in various states (Syria, Libya, Sudan). In Algeria, a massive and bloody war of independence against France brought radical nationalists to power in 1962; in terms of real mass participation, this was the most thoroughgoing of the bourgeois revolutions of the period.

In Iraq, a popular nationalist movement took power in 1958 under Qassim, relying to a significant degree on working-class support; the strong labour movement was dominated by the Communist Party. That regime was overthrown, bloodily; after a few turbulent years, the right wing faction of the Ba'ath Party took power, and is still there. Saddam Hussein's regime veered between pro-Western and "anti-imperialist" policies, always savagely repressive of opposition movements and the national minorities such as the Kurds.

In Iran (a mainly non-Arab country; the majority nationality is Persian), a Nasser-type regime under Mossadeq, which nationalised the British-owned oil company, was overthrown, with CIA and British assistance, and replaced by the Shah. The Shah was extravagantly pro-Western, but carried through, for instance in land reform, many policies similar to the radical nationalists. He was overthrown in 1979 by an enormous revolutionary movement, in which Islamists under Khomeini ultimately dominated.

90

In the first part of the 20th century, foreign capital had dominated everywhere: but by 1960, the bulk of economic activity in the region, with the important exception of oil, had passed into the hands of the governments or the native bourgeoisies. The next two decades saw a powerful wave of statisation. Outside agriculture and housing, the national private sector was reduced to insignificance in Egypt, Syria, Iraq, Sudan, Algeria, Libya, South Yemen and Iran, and severely curtailed in other countries. The takeover of the oil industry since 1973 completed that process. Then, from the mid 1970s, the governments made a reverse move, towards privatisation and, often, encouraging foreign capital; local ownership, however, remains dominant, and local state ownership substantial.

Islam played a role in the ideologies of all these movements, to varying degrees: Qaddafi in Libya (whose "Green Book" evokes the symbolic colour of Islam) was considered by some to be an Islamic fundamentalist in the early years. The FLN in Algeria mobilised the cultural symbols of Islam as part of their nation-building project, as the common factor between Arabs and Berbers. Nasserist Egypt considered itself the centre of three worlds – the Arab, the African, and the Islamic; Nasser's successor, Anwar Sadat, made great play of his personal piety (he had the characteristic mark on his forehead which results from regular prayer) – though not enough to save him from assassination by Islamists. But the Islamic component in post-war nationalism played second fiddle to the secular. Even Pakistan, established specifically as a Muslim state after the partition of India in 1947, was not an "Islamic state" in any sense that modern Islamists would recognise. In Tunisia, the most secular of the secular-nationalist states, president Bourguiba banned the hijab and broke the Ramadan fast on television. Religion was declared a private matter.

Secular nationalism scored impressive victories, particularly in achieving independence, though it failed to bring about Arab unity. But by the 1970s it was reaching the end of its rope. It had achieved about all it could achieve, and brought little but frustration and dislocation to vast masses of the population. It was running up against the limits of the capitalist world market, limits that no amount of nationalist militancy could budge. Its success now seemed a wretched and pale thing compared to the glorious Islamic past.

The Arab states were humiliated by Israel in the June War of 1967. In the 1970s, Egypt moved towards the USA both diplomatically and economically, opening the country to foreign investment; it also negotiated a peace treaty with Israel (after another war, in 1973, in which the Arab states did considerably better). Other radical states followed suit in economic policy, though not on the question of Israel. The new economic policy – Sadat called it "infitah", opening – led to an attack on the system which had cemented popular support for the regimes. In 1977 there were strikes and riots when Sadat tried to remove subsidies from basic foods; on that occasion he was defeated, but over the next decade or so the subsidies were largely removed anyway. The state's promise of jobs to graduates began to prove costly. Soon unemployed students were a major pool of discontent. The government of Hosni Mubarak, which succeeded Sadat, became more and more repressive, especially towards Islamists, as resistance grew.

Elsewhere in the Arab world, a different process was taking place. In the oil-rich Arab states feudalistic/tribal monarchies, with colonial aid, transformed themselves into capitalist classes. In 1973, hiking the price of oil fourfold, the shaykhdoms became immensely wealthy. These ruling classes have enforced strict Islamic codes at the same time as gross inequalities have emerged as a result of oil wealth. In the biggest and most powerful state, Saudi Arabia, a tribal and puritanical Islamic sect, Wahhabism, has been the official religion of the government.

All the regimes, pro-western or more vocally nationalist and (until 1989-91) USSR-aligned, were authoritarian, often military in origin, sometimes brutally repressive. By the end of the 1970s they had generated vast sectors in their population for whom they represented nothing but broken promises, disappointment, disruption of traditional certainties, corruption, and shiftlessness. Partly because of the relative social weakness of the working class proper, but more decisively because the left, mostly Stalinist, had tailed the secular nationalists, the left had little appeal to those disillusioned masses. The Islamist movements were growing, entering the mainstream of politics as well as the radical fringes.

2. The Islamist movements

MODERN Islamist groups aim for an Islamic state, that is a government which bases itself on Islamic law, the shari'a, a system established about two centuries after the death of Muhammad and then maintained, with fluctuating degrees of erosion, into the 20th century. In the violence of its punishments (amputations, lashes, stonings, death) the shari'a naturally reflects the norms, values, and level of development of its time, 1,200 years ago. Parts of it draw on the social norms of the constantly-warring, clannish society of Arabia at the time of Muhammad; parts (notably the veiling, segregation, and subordination of women) on traditions of the extreme subordination of women in the territories the Muslim armies conquered; and parts on the need to rationalise the fact that as the Islamic empires consolidated, the Muslims came to constitute large class-divided societies, instead of being the cohesive military elite that they were at the time of the first conquest. For the Islamists, though, it has the sheen of a bygone age of harmony and order.

Islam, like Judaism and unlike Christianity, has generally been a religion expressed in public law rather than more abstract theology, private ethics or mysticism. Traditionally the interpretation of that law was the job of the ulema, the Muslim scholars, the rough equivalent in Islam of the Christian clergy. Khomeini in Iran, as we shall see, was an exception, but most modern Islamist theorists have not been clerics; they are Islamic "Protestants", asserting the original text (or their understanding of it) against the worldly-wise or pliant.

The Islamists appeal — ostensibly at least — to the Umma, the broad Islamic community, rather than to "the nation" (whether the Arab nation or a more narrowly defined one). For most modern, militant Islamists, their aim is both to revive, purge, and radicalise the Umma, and to extend it.

i. Egypt
It was in Egypt that the first Islamist organisation was founded — the Society of Muslim Brothers, by Hassan al-Banna in 1928. Arguably the early Muslim Brotherhood was closer to traditional Islamic revivalism than to modern Islamism, but in any case its history flows directly and continuously into that modern Islamism.

Egypt at the time was a British protectorate ruled by an unpopular king. The nationalist movement (principally the Wafd Party) was militant, but had proved unsuccessful, and was thoroughly bourgeois, making little effort to mobilise its popular support around social questions. The Muslim Brothers began as a conservative movement for social reform, aiming to encourage Egyptians — and later Muslims elsewhere — to rediscover their Islamic heritage and behave like proper believers. Its base, like that of later Islamist groups, was among the urban middle class, the "effendis".

Gradually al-Banna's organisation moved in a more overtly political direction. In the 1936-39 Arab revolt against Jewish settlers and British rulers in Palestine, they sent fighters. They played a part in making the question of Palestine, even at that early stage, an "Arab" or regional issue. At the same time, the Brothers moved further towards armed, terrorist-type action.

They had an uneasy relationship with the nationalist parties, but by the late 1940s, when al-Banna was assassinated, had developed a considerable base.

In 1952 the Free Officers overthrew the king and kicked out the British. Some of them had links with the Brothers. For a short while the Brothers supported, and even took part in, the new government. But they were hostile to the land reform which broke the power of the landlords, and quite soon the Brothers found themselves under arrest and facing persecution. As the regime became more radical, and began to introduce "Arab socialism" [state ownership], the Brothers opposed such atheistic heresy. They faced intense repression, along with other oppositional forces like the Communist Party. In the mid-60s, accused of an attempt on Nasser's life, thousands of them were rounded up.

One of those arrested, and executed along with other leaders of the movement in 1966, was Sayyid Qutb, who was probably the real intellectual founder of modern militant Islamism, at least in those lands where the Sunni (more Protestant-like) version of Islam dominates rather than the minority Shi'a (more Catholic-like) version centred in Iran.

Qutb developed his distinctive ideas after the Egyptian Ministry of Education, for which he worked as an official, sent him to the USA in 1948-51 to study American methods of schooling. He returned to Egypt with an uncompromising hatred for the West and all its works. Qutb's rejection of the West was not that of the conservative concerned with preserving his culture's traditions against foreign encroachments, but rather that of the "born-again Muslim" who having adopted or absorbed many modern influences makes a show of discarding them in his search for personal identity and cultural authenticity.

After his arrest, Qutb wrote his famous work, *Signposts*, which is the first clear statement of the aims and worldview of the sects we now think of as Islamist, and is required reading for the cadre of these groups. Qutb defined the regime itself as part of the "infidel" problem. Society was divided into the Party of God and the Party of Satan. The Islamist movement was surrounded by a swamp of ignorance and unbelief (jahiliyya, the term used to describe the society of Arabia before the coming of Muhammed). The creation of an Islamic government was not just a culturally preferable alternative, but a divine imperative. The method of creating it would be jihad, or holy war. (For some Muslims, jihad can mean private spiritual striving, but for Islamist groups it increasingly means, very literally, war.) It is unclear if Qutb himself would have wholeheartedly approved of the modern groups who claim his legacy; but he spelled out the main themes of modern militant Islamism.

As Sadat moved away from Nasserist state-capitalism in the 1970s, the Muslim Brothers re-emerged from their eclipse by repression. Sadat was initially warm towards them. He had broken with the USSR; his new economic policy was unpopular, and opening up dangerous space on his left (both within the regime and outside it). The Brothers were a useful counterbalance. More, Sadat flirted considerably with using Islam as a source of legitimacy as Nasserist ideology was put out to grass: he made much of his own commitment to the faith, and introduced Islamic laws — stoking communal antagonism between Muslims and Egypt's extremely large Christian minority.

The Brothers were still technically illegal, but they grew in the 1970s. And more radical schisms began to emerge. A group called the Islamic Liberation Organisation attempted a coup in 1974, seizing the Technical Military Academy in Cairo. The ILO had links with other Islamist groups abroad. In January 1973 it had published its manifesto, which claims, for instance:

"Liberation is a means, not an end... When we fight for the liberation of Palestine, we do not fight... for the sake of getting back our homeland, but for the glorification of the word of God... We fight to transform every Dar al-kufr [reign of unbelief] into Dar al-Islam, whether its people are Muslims as in Pakistan, or infidels as in India."

A better known group, Takfir wa Hijra (roughly, Atonement and Exile — hijra refers to Mohammed's leaving Mecca for Medina), assassinated a teacher at al-Azhar, Cairo's prestigious mosque-university, who was also minister for religious endowments. When Sadat made peace with Israel, signing a peace treaty in 1978 at Camp David, he had effectively signed his own death warrant. The militant group al-Jihad had formed cells in the army. In 1981, as Sadat was admiring his troops on the anniversary of the 1973 war, Khaled Islambouli shot him dead.

There followed a period of intense upheaval. Islamists in the town of Asyut, where they were strong, attempted an uprising which was crushed. The new regime of Hosni Mubarak began to arrest, imprison and torture Islamists or suspected Islamists in huge numbers — thousands of them — a tradition it has continued ever since.

Chukri Mustapha, an agricultural engineer considered the "emir", or leader, of Takfir wa Hijra, expressed his ideology thus:

"God be praised. He will prepare the land for the group of the just by provoking a war between the two great powers, Russia and America... The war is inevitable, they will destroy each other. God will thus have prepared the land for the Islamic state... Following [this war] the forces of the Muslim nation will be about equal to those of its enemies. It is then that the true Jihad will start."

As the gama'at islamiyya, the militant groups, began to grow, the Muslim Brothers moved more into the mainstream. By the end of the 70s, they had formally declared their abandonment of terrorist activity. By the late 80s, although unable to stand in elections, they formed electoral pacts, first with the Wafd, then with the so-called Socialist Labour Party (getting 17% of the vote in 1987). More importantly, they established a network of schools, clinics, and even banks — a pattern typical of Islamist movements — and made huge inroads into Egypt's professional associations, mainly among engineers, doctors, and by the late 90s, lawyers, winning a majority in the bar association. The Brothers, in other words, sank deep social roots, with cadres in the urban middle class and support from the unorganised poor. In student bodies, too, both moderate and militant Islamists have grown. Now the Brothers are the best-organised and chief opposition to the Mubarak government. In an attempt to curtail their influence, in addition to repression, the state tried to extend its control over mosques; but there are simply too many of these for such control to be effective.

Moderate and legalistic as they now are, it should not be thought that the Brothers are a benign force in Egyptian political life. When the Muslim academic Nasr Abu Zaid put forward a theory that the Qur'an was read and interpreted differently according to historical context, the Brothers declared him an apostate, drove him from the university, and tried, through the courts, to force his wife to divorce him. The couple fled to Scandinavia.

The weight of the moderate, "reformist" Brothers provides the ideological context for the radical variants. Those have grown increasingly violent. In the 1990s, the militant groups made a turn to assassinating tourists, beginning with the murder of some Israelis in Sinai, and tourists near the pyramids. Then in 1997, an attack was launched at the ancient temple of Hatshepsut at Luxor which left 68 tourists and three Egyptians dead. Other murders have been carried out of Coptic Christians; the Nobel Prize winning author Neguib Mahfuz was stabbed; the outspoken secular journalist Farag Fuda was murdered.

Tala'at Fu'ad Qassim, of the Egyptian Islamist group Gama'a Islamiyya, justifies the murder of tourists like this:

"[Tourism]... is a means by which prostitution and AIDS are spread by Jewish women tourists, and it is a source of all manner of depravities, not to mention being a means of collecting information on the Islamic movement. For these reasons we believe tourism is an abomination which must be destroyed. And it is one of our strategies for destroying the government."

Indeed, these attacks have crippled Egypt's tourism industry, one of its chief sources of income and foreign exchange. Qassim's group, like Islamic Jihad, has strong links in Afghanistan; Ayman al-Zawahiri of al-Jihad is bin Laden's supposed "deputy", although there is speculation he is in fact the dominant figure. Al-Jihad seems to be the largest of the militant groups, and has built up influence in slum areas through study groups, distributing literature and audio cassettes with Islamic speeches, providing welfare services, and so on.

A truce was declared between the Islamists and the Mubarak government in 1997. Several thousand detainees were released, although 12,000 or so Islamists remained in prison. After 11 September 2001, though, a new clampdown began.

Secular, or secular-ish, and democratic forces remain alive in Egypt: Islamists are probably still a minority, there are legal left and left-of-centre political parties, and prominent intellectuals who oppose the Islamists. On the other hand, when 52 gay men were arrested on a Nile barge last year – the first time, as far as I know, there has been serious state repression of homosexuals – Egyptian civil rights groups refused to take up their case, probably for fear of Islamist-influenced public opinion.

ii. Iran

The first great victory of the Islamist movements was the Iranian revolution. There is no space here to go into detail. But Iran has shaped and influenced the growth of the Islamist groups, sometimes directly as the "Islamic Republic" trained and funded some of them.

Iran under the Shah had undergone profound social upheaval. The capital, Tehran, for instance, mushroomed in size (although lots of it was unfinished building sites). In the countryside there was radical land reform; and the state led rapid industrialisation. The working class and "new petty bourgeoisie" grew rapidly; old social classes, whether in the countryside or in the bazaar (the market) were squeezed (and heavily taxed, as was the mosque). Iran was the richest, most developed, and most heavily armed state in the region, regarded by the United States as its closest ally along with Israel. But the Shah's rule proved to be far more precarious than CIA experts, for instance, believed. There was widespread opposition to the Shah's so-called White Revolution in the 1960s, when Ayatollah Khomeini first emerged as an opponent of the regime, forced into exile in Iraq, and later in Paris. His speeches on cassette were to become very popular.

The movement which, by late 1978, was challenging the regime, was composed of different social actors with incompatible aims. On the one hand there were the urban poor and the industrial working class, especially but not only in the vital oil industry. A general strike was one of the forces which succeeded in toppling the Shah. There was also a large organised left, although principally in the form of guerrilla organisations – the two most important were the Fedayyin, which was avowedly Marxist (influenced, for instance, by Guevarism), and the radical Muslim People's Mujaheddin Organisation. The pro-Moscow Tudeh Party also played a role, although it soon proved to be one of the most right-wing, pusillanimous "communist" parties on earth.

On the other hand there were the wealthy bazaari merchants, sections of traditional classes rolled back by the White Revolution, and the mosque. These distinct social forces, with distinct aims and interests, temporarily came together for the single aim of removing the hated Shah; but almost immediately the movement fractured into virtual civil war. They came together on a huge scale. Along with the general strike, the mass demonstrations reached a scale rarely seen even in revolutionary movements: millions of people took to the streets, crippling the army's ability to repress them, and indeed splitting the army. The guerrilla organisations fought the army with some success.

For a short period, the working class was centre stage, creating independent workplace organisations, shoras, which could have been further developed in a "soviet"direction, purging managers, taking ever more radical steps in the factories. The chances for working class revolution were very real. The left was strong and confident. Yet the shoras were quickly co-opted by the Khomeini movement; the regime almost immediately turned on the left – and on women, and national minorities – and unleashed a violent, urban mass movement against them. Left-wing organisations had their offices sacked; then the left's stronghold, Tehran university, was physically attacked by the Hizb Allah, a fascistic mass movement. Pasdaran, the "revolutionary guards", attacked demonstrations of unemployed workers. "Islamic laws" were introduced, women forced to wear the veil, "prostitutes" and homosexuals executed; the Khomeini regime introduced a reign of terror. "Imperialism" was declared the enemy, and the left identified as an arm of "imperialism"; the American Embassy was seized in a demagogic display of anti-imperialist fervour. Then, when Iraq invaded an area of disputed territory in September 1980, the two countries embarked on an horrific eight year war.

How did Khomeini and the clergy come to dominate this revolution, and crush its alternative potential? The mosque had been an independent space during the Shah's rule, outside the regime's capacity for repression, enabling the mullahs to emerge as a leadership for a section of the masses. Religious symbols became powerful means of mobilisation (for instance in the timing of mass demonstrations). Khomeini himself, from abroad, was known as a firebrand opponent of the Shah; by the beginning of 1979 he was seen to "personify" the revolution.

Other currents of Islamist thought had also become widely known in the decade or so before the revolution, most importantly that of Ali Shariati. Shariati was a lay intellectual who interpreted the struggle against the Shah in terms of reclaiming an indigenous cultural heritage. His ideas were far from Khomeini's, a sort of populist Islamism which even talked about socialism, and was heavily influenced by the thinking of Franz Fanon. In turn the People's Mujaheddin were influenced by Shariati. Other more moderate clerics were associated with Khomeini (some would form successive governments, subordinated to Khomeini himself and his council of experts; they were purged or resigned). Shariati cannot be held responsible for the Islamic Republic, but for sure the general currency of moderate, or even enlightened and secular-oriented, Islamism created a climate in which the profoundly reactionary variant could win leadership.

Khomeini's Islamism was able to appeal to a number of social groups and classes – to the bazaar, which had historic links to the mosque; to the dispossessed poor; to sections of the intelligentsia; and to sections of the middle class to whom he offered "order". "[T]he basis of the clergy's opposition to the state was a reactionary resistance to the smallest social reforms. Even its struggle against [the Shah was based] only on intransigent opposition to any change that would diminish or undermine its own traditional prerogatives and power." Unlike Qutb and other Sunni ideologues, Khomeini proposed not merely an Islamic state but government by a hierarchy of Muslim clerics. In the end, the Islamic Republic was a hybrid of this proposed theocracy and a truncated parliament, but with the clergy firmly in control. It was never quite a totalitarian state, and opposition, especially from a working class whose economic militancy continued throughout the next two decades, and more recently among students, survived. But the organised left was crushed or driven into exile.

This left, famously, never knew what they were dealing with. From the outset, in the main, they supported Khomeini, accepting his "anti-imperialism" as good coin. Some, like the Tudeh, and what came to be known as the Fedayyin Majority, continued to support him as he suppressed the left, until he turned on them. The Mujaheddin took up arms against Khomeini eventually; but by then it was far too late – and, like the secular left, the Mujaheddin were divorced from the industrial working class. Indeed, the left as a whole had little implantation among industrial workers, and was unable to affect the struggle over the shoras, for example.

But the left's error was not simply that they supported governments or had a tragic misestimation of what governments were about. They fatally misread the nature of the mass movement itself – failed to understand that a section of the mass movement was the regime's brutal battering ram against them. The Iranian revolution, certainly from the viewpoint of the organised left, was lost not in text books or speeches, but on the street.

There was a distinctive Shi'a component to Khomeini-ite Islamism in Iran. The Shi'a are a sect which diverged from mainstream Sunni Islam very early in Islamic history; they are the main sect in Iran, and numerous in surrounding areas (Iraq, Syria, Lebanon, Afghanistan, some in the Arabian peninsula and the Gulf). Unlike the Sunni Islamists, who seek to recreate the centuries immediately following Muhammed's death, which they look to as a golden age, the Shi'a reject the legitimacy of the early Caliphs, and see them as usurpers. Shi'a Islam gives more weight to the temporal authority of the contemporary ulema ("mullahs" in Persian), like Khomeini. The mullahs have historically occupied centre stage in Iranian politics. They were at the heart both of the tobacco protests of 1891-92, and the Constitutionalist movement of 1906.

"[T]he Iranian revolution [was] a direct consequence of the position occupied by the religious leadership... since the 18th century... In addition to acting as tax collectors... the mujtahids and the mullahs... were entitled to a 10 % commission on the waqf properties administered by them. Some of these... constitute very substantial properties."

The Iranian government has particularly supported Shi'a groups abroad, for example in Lebanon. Shi'a or not, though, other Islamists looked to Iran as an example and an inspiration. The most powerful US ally in the region had fallen, and been replaced by an Islamic Republic. It shocked and terrified the West, and testified to the strength of Islam not only as a political force, but a revolutionary one. Almost immediately, Islamist groups turned the inspiration into action – in Saudi Arabia, in 1979, the hajj, or Mecca pilgrimage, saw an Islamist uprising. In the Muslim world and in the West, "Islamic fundamentalism" became not just a lurking danger or promise, but a vital force.

Over 20 years on, the situation in Iran gives cause for some optimism. It is possible that the downfall of Islamism could start in the same country as its dramatic rise, with a popular overthrow of the Islamic Republic. A more moderate president, Khatami, was elected in 1997. His election did not change much, but it did signal a changed popular mood. Much of the Islamist mass movement has cooled and congealed into a government machine, as corrupt and opportunist as any of the regimes which Khomeini used to scorn as "American Islam", and widely despised by young people in the cities. Student revolt broke out in 2000 against repression and censorship. The working class remains militant. And if there is anywhere militant Islamists are unlikely to seize power in the future, it is the country in which they have held it, meting out repression, for two decades.

iii. Afghanistan

In many ways the Taliban and other Afghan Islamists are different from elsewhere – the product of a more backward society, of Russian occupation, of US, Pakistani, and Saudi financial and military-training support. All these factors have

97

created the most virulently reactionary Islamists of all – both among the Afghans themselves, and the non-Afghan forces who have used the country as a base, the so-called "Afghan Arabs"' like Osama bin Laden.

Eighteen years of war between 1978 and 1996 made Afghanistan a veritable cadre school for Islamism. Maybe 100,000 young men from across the Muslim world came to Afghanistan to fight for Islam. They were trained and hardened militarily and ideologically. Many then went elsewhere in the Muslim world – Bosnia, Algeria, or back to their home countries – as armed prophets of the Islamist message.

iv. Algeria

In Gillo Pontecorvo's marvellous film *Battle of Algiers*, a Muslim woman dons Western clothes and make-up for the first time in order to go into the French quarter of the city and plant a bomb in a trendy cafe. Later we see the awful consequences of the explosion. The film dramatises a real event, which at the time, in 1956, seemed to be an epoch-marking terrorist atrocity, leaving three dead and dozens maimed. The Algerian war of independence was a bitterly-fought, bloody business in which perhaps a million people died before the French colonial authorities finally withdrew, in 1962. The war had lasted eight years; colonial rule well over a century.

The new government was formed by the National Liberation Front (FLN), the most important of the nationalist forces. Like others elsewhere, it moved quickly in a state-capitalist direction, first radically under Ben Bella, who was overthrown by Houari Boumedienne in 1965. He was succeeded by Chadli Benjedid, who held power until the coup of 1992. The Algerian revolution was far more thoroughgoing and radical than similar movements elsewhere in the Arab world, but it was more hesitant in its secularism, partly because the mosque played a role in the struggle against the French. The National Charter declared "The Algerian people is a Muslim people... Islam is the state religion."

The FLN formed a one-party state. It was a Muslim state, but far from an Islamic state in the modern Islamist sense. It nationalised religious schools and institutions. Although promises of women's emancipation made in the nationalist struggle were not fulfilled, they were not flatly disavowed either, not for the elite anyway. Of the women who had planted those bombs in 1956, one became the director of Algeria's Ecole Nationale d'Administration, the other the Algerian representative of the cosmetics firm Max Factor.

An Islamist movement began to emerge in the 60s and 70s, although relatively moderate and reformist; it was influenced by the Muslim Brothers. As popular discontent grew, the Benjedid government began to make concessions, promising liberalisation and democracy. In 1989, emulating the ex-Stalinists in Eastern Europe, it ended the FLN's monopoly on power, and moved towards creating a multi-party system. But no safe bourgeois opposition parties on the East European model emerged. The Islamists, grouped together in the Islamic Salvation Front (FIS), a coalition of groups led by the Islamist moderate Shaykh Ali Abassi Madani, became by far the largest opposition group.

The Islamists had won their first core activists among young, educated, urban middle-class men, and, as elsewhere, built their support through welfare work in the communities, among the poor and the middle class, and through the mosques. They had taken over "minor" mosques in peripheral areas. People discontented with the FLN regime, though not necessarily positively committed to Islamist ideas, rallied to the FIS as the most effective opposition.

There were tensions in the FIS between Madani – a Francophone moderate – and Ali Belhadj, an Arab-Islamic militant, originally from Tunisia. Publicly, the FIS sometimes professed itself committed to the multiparty system, to democratic institutions, and to minority rights. But then Khomeini, right up until his victory, had said that what he wanted was the restoration of Iran's liberal 1906 constitution. Many Algerians were afraid of the growth of the FIS. There are a large number who still speak French as a first language; others are Berbers, not Arabs; and the Islamists were stridently Arabist. Algeria's significant feminist movement was alarmed. And many Algerians have strong links with the Arab community in France, "westernised" and often relatively secular, sometimes interested in rap and rai music, which the Islamists condemned.

Unlike other regimes which have permitted political liberalisation, the Algerian government allowed the Islamists to compete in elections. The FIS's programme was relatively moderate; in economics it was positively liberal. But the tensions under the surface would explode over the next few years.

In 1990, in municipal and regional elections, the FIS swept the board. With 65% of the electorate voting, they took 55% of municipal councils and two thirds of the regional assemblies. The FLN did badly – much to their own shock and horror. In all the major cities, the FIS won huge majorities of the vote.

Governmental elections came – to be fought in two rounds. The first were held in December 1991, the first multiparty parliamentary elections since independence. The FLN had gerrymandered as much as possible, but the results were a crushing defeat for the party which had driven out the French. The FLN came third, with just 16 out of 231 seats. The FIS won 188 seats, with almost half the total vote. Second was the Socialist Forces Front, which took 26 seats. Before the second round of elections due, which the FIS was sure to win, the military intervened. There was a coup at the beginning of 1992; the army declared a state of siege, cancelled all elections, banned the FIS and arrested its leaders. More than 10,000 Islamists were held in a concentration camp; their mosques and welfare services were closed. And the country descended rapidly into civil war.

The civil war was to leave as many as 70,000 dead. It was a war, primarily, between the Islamists and the army, with both sides committing terrible atrocities. But many civilians, leftists, secular radicals and intellectuals, trade unionists and others got caught in the crossfire and were identified by the Islamists as their enemies. The Armed Islamic Group (GIA) was responsible for the worst atrocities; but the unofficial armed wing of the FIS itself, the Islamic Salvation Army, AIS, carried out similar attacks.

The Socialist Forces Front condemned both the repression and the Islamists. Many of its supporters fell victim to Islamist attack. At the peak of Islamist violence, women not wearing the hijab (veil) were gunned down at bus stops. Men and women were prevented from travelling on trains together. The rai artist Cheb Hasni, was murdered in 1994; thousands demonstrated in protest in the city of Oran. Large numbers of leftists, feminists and others fled the country, mainly to France.

Not until the late 90s, did the killings subside. In further elections, though the FIS was banned, other Islamist parties, making a bid for a more moderate image, polled well.

As elsewhere, state repression in Algeria had the effect of unleashing the most reactionary elements of, and aspect of, the Islamists. The military's effort to "eradicate" the "fundamentalists", an objective it was keen to show off to western governments – did not, and could not, succeed. The broad left was placed in a terrible position, vulnerable to both the forces of the state and the Islamists. For sure there were divisions among the Islamists. Their leaders sometimes condemned the more extreme actions of the military wings. And clearly the FLN government, and then the army, bears a huge responsibility for the civil war. But the Islamists demonstrated their true character in the way their side of the war was prosecuted. As in Iran, they simultaneously and violently opposed both the government and the forces of genuine progress.

v. Palestine

It was only after the 1967 war that distinct Palestinian nationalist movements emerged. The Palestine Liberation Organisation was taken over by these nationalist movements, the biggest of which was Yasser Arafat's Fatah, and embarked upon armed struggle against Israel. It gained some success in putting the issue on the political map, but made little headway in terms of defeating Israel. After the 1973 war, the PLO — which had declared its objective to be a "secular democratic state for Muslims, Christians and Jews" in all of Palestine — moved towards trying to find a diplomatic solution, although a "rejection front" formed which was opposed to this. Crushed in Jordan in "Black September" 1970, the PLO guerrillas retreated to Lebanon, which soon — partly, though by no means entirely, as a result — collapsed into a devastating civil war. Israeli invasion of Lebanon in 1982 left some 20-30,000 dead and drove the PLO leadership from the country. Then an uprising, or intifada in the occupied territories ultimately forced Israel to the negotiating table. A profoundly inadequate peace deal was signed in 1993, though that collapsed in 2000. At the time of writing, the future of "peace" is very uncertain.

From its emergence as a distinct force, Palestinian nationalism was perhaps more strongly secular than any other Arab nationalism outside Tunisia. There is a significant Christian minority among the Palestinian Arabs, and some of their important thinkers and leaders have come from it. The "secular democratic state" in all Palestine was in effect code for the destruction of Israel, but that the PLO chose that code was testimony to their non-Islamist intentions. In the occupied territories, especially the West Bank, the Communist Party had considerable weight, and controlled a number of municipalities from the 1970s onwards. The PLO had a vocal would-be Marxist (although in truth, ultra-nationalist) left. Partly as a result of the Palestinian people's dispersal and unusually high level of formal (and non-Islamic) education, influence from outside, and Western, intellectual sources was always strong.

Until the intifada of late 1987, the secular nationalists had never considered the Islamists much of a problem or threat. There was an Islamist movement in Gaza, but it had little weight in the more sophisticated (and less poor) West Bank. Among students, for example at Bir Zeit university, the Islamists were a negligible force.

Today all that has changed. Islamists are a growing influence even in the West Bank and among university students. As the post-Oslo Palestine Authority has proved corrupt and repressive, and has failed to bring about meaningful independence, the left has declined sharply, and the Islamists have grown.

The biggest Islamist group is Hamas — the Islamic Resistance Movement. Hamas emerged from the Gaza wing of the Egyptian Muslim Brothers, in the first place concentrating on purely social matters — charitable works, schools, making propaganda for Islamic forms of personal behaviour, the typical fare of the Islamists. For this reason they were looked on favourably, and supported, by Israel as an alternative to the PLO. After the beginning of the original intifada in 1987/8, Hamas took a more political turn. But one of its first ventures into "opposition to Israel" was to effectively initiate, and sanction, a campaign to force Palestinian women to wear the hijab — a campaign which meant unveiled women were stoned in the street. Eventually, the Palestinian leadership condemned this campaign, although making some concessions to the idea that dressing modestly is a patriotic duty. Throughout the first intifada, Hamas remained aloof from the struggle, naming its own days for specific actions, for instance, and focusing on Islamic rather than national or political questions.

With the second intifada in 2000, Hamas did not engage in fighting with the Israeli troops; they left that to the nationalist militias, principally of Fatah. Hamas' contribution was to launch suicide attacks inside Israel. More recently, they seem to have begun commando raids, beginning with an attack on a Jewish settlement in Gaza.

The Palestinian leadership created this space for them. Arafat's Authority has more members in the security forces than it has teachers; and a major aspect to the negotiated deal in 1993 was that Arafat take over policing Arab territories from Israel, which was increasingly unsure of the point of doing it. Much of the repression is necessarily aimed at the Islamists. In addition to its repressiveness, and failure to bring about a just settlement, the Palestine Authority is notoriously corrupt: in the midst of great, and worsening, poverty, officials flaunt the wealth they have gained through corruption; association with these authorities has tarnished the old-style nationalists.

Hamas' evolution, in sum, has been from a deeply conservative social movement into an aggressively chauvinist one which increasingly does nothing but destroy any possibility of peace between Israelis and Palestinians. That Israeli public opinion is today heavily behind Ariel Sharon, the most hawkish leader in its history, is largely a result of Hamas' suicide attacks (and the inability of many Israelis to understand the sources of Palestinian frustration). Clearly, Hamas' actions have quite wide support among Palestinians, who are poor, and desperate, and losing. But that does not change the reactionary character of these actions.

There is, of course, a strong element of straightforward, non-Islamist nationalism in Hamas' growth. But they have redefined the national question in religious terms. If the PLO once wanted a secular state, Hamas wants an Islamic one, in which there is no place for Jews or even Christian Arabs. "The Jews" are intruding on Muslim, not Palestinian, or even Arab, land. Hamas have received financial support from the Saudi regime, which also sees the issue in these terms. It seems likely that images of Palestinian demonstrations holding up Hamas placards and flags exaggerate the real strength of Hamas. Yet they are, unquestionably, a growing force, beginning to eclipse Fatah.

vi. Others

There is no space here to go into detail about other countries where Islamists have been powerful. In *Sudan*, a military coup backed by the Sudanese Muslim Brothers took power in 1989. In Sudan the Brothers had superficially moved in a moderate direction. In practice, they proved as repressive and reactionary as elsewhere. A powerful movement of workers' strikes had gripped Sudan in the late 1980s, and there were moves by the Khartoum government to end the war with the non-Arab, often Christian forces in the south of the country. It was to head off both these developments that the army intervened. The government has been savagely "Islamic" and brutal towards the southern rebels: famine has gripped the southern areas as a result of the war.

In *Lebanon*, Muslims — both Sunni, and (especially) Shi'a — were effectively second class citizens in the sectarian, "confessional" system established after the Second World War. As that system began to break down, and civil war broke out in the mid-70s, the Shi'a Muslims formed a "movement of the dispossessed" with their own party, Amal (Hope). But the civil war — with Israeli and Syrian intervention, crippling action by the various militias, and so on — soon started to reduce the country to rubble. More radical Islamist groups, principally the Hizbollah (Party of God) were backed, both financially and with personnel, by Iran. It was these groups who attacked US marines, kidnapped Westerners, and eventually drove out the Israeli army from the south. Amal remained more moderate and secular; its leader is a bourgeois lawyer who lives in the United States.

In *Syria* there was, from the late 70s, growing conflict between Islamists — primarily the Muslim Brothers — and the Ba'ath government. This culminated in a

101

1982 uprising in the town of Hama, which was brutally repressed; the most conservative estimates suggest over 10,000 people were killed.

Tunisia under Bourguiba was one of the militantly secular Arab states, and also had one of the strongest workers' movements. In 1978 there was a powerful general strike, from which the Islamists, led by Rashid Ghannoushi, stood aside. Later they recognised their mistake, and began to take a more active role in social and political struggles. Although influenced by the Muslim Brothers, Ghannoushi's Islamic Tendency Movement, now known as the Renaissance Party (Ennahda), moved towards a more "Tunisian" identity. Again, state repression has "radicalised" the Tunisian Islamists.

Turkey's governments have been aggressively secular since Ataturk modernised the state in the years after World War One. These governments have been sometimes elected and sometimes the product of coups — though always repressive, for instance towards the Kurdish minority, whose very existence was denied (and in the early days of the post-Ottoman regime, genocidally repressive towards Armenians). In the 1980s, the Islamist Welfare Party led by Necmettin Erbakan emerged — containing within it moderates and militants — which in 1995 won 21% of the vote, and 150 seats in parliament, making it the biggest party. Welfare formed a coalition, with Erbakan as prime minister. In the event, Erbakan proved more pragmatic than many expected: he "did not pull Turkey out of NATO but did turn to the International Monetary Fund for assistance... declared his friendship with the United States and Europe, and described Welfare as the 'guarantor of secular rule'." He also honoured Turkey's agreements with Israel. Secular forces militantly opposed Welfare in power — from the left and from within the state. In 1997 Erbakan was forced to resign, and in 1998 Welfare was banned; it regrouped as the Virtue Party.

3. Why Islamism?

THE nature of capitalist development in the region itself in part accounts for the emergence of Islamism. A huge educated or semi-educated middle class has been created which was promised the fruits of development but has not seen them. The working class is relatively small. A large class of pauperised peasants (not quite peasants, but small farmers certainly) remains. Population growth, and migration from the countryside, has produced overcrowded cities in which there are large numbers of marginalised poor. Pre-capitalist forms of social organisation have survived – the family; the mosque. And as economic crisis has deepened, as the welfare systems put in place by state-capitalist regimes such as Egypt's have disintegrated, these old social structures have proved their worth to millions of people.

The nationalist regimes were experienced as bureaucratic, authoritarian, and repressive. The "socialist" vocabulary of many of them means that in some countries, at least, the population has experienced something of a mild form of Stalinism: socialism is identified with a discredited, failed past. There is now a huge crisis of bourgeois culture: the authoritarian, now mainly pro-Western states, which once, like Egypt, were culturally vibrant, are stagnating. In the last year, only around 300 books were published in Egypt — compared to over 4,000 in Israel, for example.

The left largely identified itself with the state-capitalist project. This is true both of the nationalist left, and the mainstream communist parties: Egypt's disbanded to join Nasser's Arab Socialist Union in the 1960s. Left critics of authoritarian governments have often focused more on economic policy than on questions of democracy or, still less, workers' rights. And of course with the collapse of the USSR, the Stalinist and nationalist lefts have been adrift and in crisis.

Culturally, the Islamists appeal to a sense of past glory; it is relevant that the Islamic, and Arab, pasts are imperial ones. The power of the West is viewed as a source of "humiliation". This is an ideology which appeals in particular to the young educated men who tend to form the activist base of the Islamist groups. Three or four decades ago, on the whole, these men would have been more likely to have turned to the nationalist movements, with their secular agendas. But those older bourgeois nationalisms, whether in earlier forms, or in the shape of the "Arab revolution" of the 1950s and 60s, remained the preserve, to a large extent, of westernised, urban classes. There was a considerable rift between the cultures of these classes and the mass of the population. As the nationalist revolutions ran out of steam, and disillusionment set in, a section of the disappointed petty bourgeoisie began to look to more "indigenous" cultural and political references; to some extent the desire to link up with the dispossessed masses through Islam was an expression of a sort of masochistic guilt on the part of young Western-oriented men who felt detached from "their own people". And those cultural, religious reference points had remained intact, and indeed resilient, throughout the secular nationalist period. Conversely, the secularity of Nasserist and other nationalisms had more feeble roots in popular culture than it sometimes seemed.

One effect of the Arab revolution was what could be called the "de-cosmopolitanisation" of Arab society: the Jewish, Armenian, and Greek bourgeoisie in Egypt were the first targets of the state-capitalist drive in the 1950s; Alexandria, for instance, which had been a "multicultural" city in which up to a dozen languages were commonly spoken, was "Arabised" by the 1960s, diminishing the social weight of non-Islamic communities; large sections of the bourgeoisie had not been Muslim. The effect of this was a narrowing of political life, a loss of pluralist diversity. Even though there is a large Coptic Christian minority in Egypt − perhaps 12 million strong − the Nasser regime was almost completely Muslim in personnel. The Copts had often been seen as opponents of independence and supporters of the British − under whose rule some of them prospered. In the Nasser period they suffered discrimination, but not persecution − though that changed as Sadat flirted with Islamism. But the exclusion of Copts from the centres of power at the height of the secular nationalist period had its consequences.

Elsewhere, nationalists from Christian backgrounds have been important, even central − yet their relationship to the Islamic heritage of the societies in which they live has been deeply problematic for them. Michel Aflaq, founder of the Ba'ath Party (factions of which rule in Syria and Iraq), was a Greek Orthodox Christian, but he wrote in 1943: "Europe is as fearful of Islam today as she has been in the past. She now knows that the strength of Islam (which in the past expressed that of the Arabs) has been reborn and has appeared in a new form: in Arab nationalism." Bernard Lewis, perhaps the leading contemporary Orientalist, argues that the main "Western value" that Christian Arab nationalist intellectuals have succeeded in transmitting to broad popular culture is European anti-Semitism, which is now a core idea of modern Islamism in a way that it never was for Islamic ideologies in the past.

It should not be thought that the growth of Islamism was or is automatic or inevitable. The Islamist movements are disunited and fragmented, and by their very nature are likely to remain so: one person's ideal Islamic state is another's infidel heresy. Energy consumed on issues of dress and suppressing impermissible entertainments has limited power to build mass support. The Islamists not only fail to have solutions to the social and economic problems of the population, they fail even to pretend to offer solutions other than the general and abstract one of a return to an imaginary, harmonious past. Probably most Muslims remain suspicious of or hostile to the Islamists. Outside Algeria, they have not been in a position to win elections. In power the Islamists become − and can be seen by millions to have become — as corrupt, as ineffectual, and even more repressive, than the regimes they replace.

Alternatives do exist. There have been powerful moments of working class action in the history of the region. Iran is described above. It is by no means the only example, though it is the most impressive.

Workers' strikes were a feature of Egyptian life prior to the 1952 coup. Indeed, one of the regime's first actions was to execute the leaders of militant strikes. Later, too, workers played a role: in 1977, it was a combination of rioting and a near general strike which forced Sadat to reinstate subsidies on basic foods. Striking workers and the urban poor united to chant "O hero of the crossing, where is our breakfast?"

In Iraq, a period of intense working class militancy followed the 1958 revolution, and the labour movement's support for the regime was a source of its strength. Its defeat was the foundation of the Saddam Hussein dictatorship which has been in power since 1968. There continues to be a workers' movement in Algeria. Tunisia is often considered to have the biggest and best organised workers' movement in North Africa. It was partly to defeat militant trade union action that the Sudanese military took power in 1989.

It remains true that the Middle East, or the Arab world at least, has never seen working class action on the scale, or of the type, that we have witnessed elsewhere, for instance in South America, South Africa, or south or south-east Asia. This absence of militant workers' movements has shaped political opposition as the bourgeois regimes have gone into crisis. It cannot be stressed enough that just as the victory of the Khomeiniite Islamists influenced the subsequent growth of Islamism, so too did the defeat of the working class alternative which was present in the Iranian revolution. Defeats have their cost. The majority of the population across the region is under 25: they have grown up in a world shaped by the outcome of the Iranian revolution.

4. Socialists and Islamism

The distinction sometimes made is between those Islamists which are "anti-imperialist" and those which accommodate to imperialism and local regimes, with the strong implication that the "anti-imperialist" type is preferable. This raises the question as to what is meant by "anti-imperialism", and whether it is a meaningful guide for a socialist response. In the case of Islamist groups, the more "anti-imperialist" they are, the worse — the more anti-democratic, the more violent towards secular, feminist and progressive opponents, the more chauvinistic towards foreigners, the more repressive they would be in power. "Anti-imperialism" without a positive, democratic and anti-capitalist programme is a reactionary, demagogic force.

The Islamists appeal to a range of social classes, though their membership and cadre tend to come from the urban, educated middle class. They are the product of modern social and political developments, and are therefore in an important sense modern movements. Though Islamism sometimes appeals to old social classes, and certainly gets support from them (from the bazaar, from some sections of the mosque hierarchy, from the Saudi royal family, from landlords and tribal chiefs in the case of Afghanistan), it is wrong to see it as simply the festering sore of pre-capitalist society. It is the product, on the whole at least, of capitalism.

Ideologically, although sometimes Islamists address themselves to "modern" political questions, their answers are backward looking — idealising the early Caliphate, glorifying the Islamic past, resenting economic development which can not be reversed. Many militant Islamists identify with the salifiyya tradition. That school of thought was founded by Muhammed Abduh, one of the early modernising Islamic revivalists. He advocated, for instance, rights for women. But its stress on the salafi — the early followers of the Prophet — has translated, within the modern Islamist movements, into a profoundly reactionary viewpoint.

Politics and ideology have their own weight. There is on the left a type of sociological reductionism which reads the Islamists as "petty bourgeois", and therefore simply a variant of standard petty bourgeois nationalism. This is quite false. There are other movements which seek through extreme violence to recapture some idealised past — the Khmer Rouge springs to mind. But the Islamists' "discourse" is quite different from most nationalist movements, certainly from any which have had progressive, liberatory potential.

In so far as they are violent and reactionary, and especially in so far as they can mobilise a mass movement which, as in Iran, can attack and crush the left and the workers' movement, there are strong parallels between the Islamists and fascism. They are not identical to fascism, but a close enough analogy to be called "fascistic". The significance of this was clear in Iran: relations between the left and the Islamists were of violent confrontation; the left's task was not simply to intervene in an inchoate mass movement and "win it over". The same thing can be seen in Algeria. Often the central issue is day-to-day self-defence.

Other Islamists are more moderate, and concerned with "social reform" rather than violent politics. The Muslim Brotherhood in Egypt has evolved in this direction. Of course, such movements can evolve suddenly in the other direction, as the history of the Brotherhood in Sudan shows. In Algeria, the apparent commitment to democracy of at least a large part of the FIS collapsed when their electoral victory was denied them. European fascism, these days, often professes a parliamentary focus, rather than concentrating on fighting on the streets and burning immigrants alive in hostels; that lesson should not be lost on us.

Even when moderate and reformist, the Islamist groups are best understood as conservative, right-wing movements, concerned with enforcing social conformity, especially on women and "apostates", and a threat to religious and other minorities. The reformist Islamists are less fiercely reactionary than their militant counterparts, but not in any sense progressive.

Military-bureaucratic repression of the Islamists — as in Algeria in the 1990s, or Egypt in the 1960s or since the early 1980s — is no sort of answer the left can support. Even if the repression pushes the Islamists back for a while, it simultaneously pushes back the left, and often only prepares the way for the Islamists to re-emerge, more militant, implacable, and widely-supported than before. The one place where repression seems to have "worked" is Iraq — where the state is even more repressive than anywhere else in the region, and structured quite closely to a totalitarian system.

They have to be defeated "from below". The problem for the left is that where the Islamists, reformist or militant, have built a solid base in communities, the left has not. Even — or, indeed, especially — in student and professional associations where secular nationalists thought themselves impregnable, they have been outflanked. There are energetic organisations across the region attempting to do grass-roots work — civil rights groups, women's organisations, trade unions, of course, and so on. But many of these are wilfully unideological bodies, which simply can't compete with the integrated worldview of the Islamists. The poor, the working class and the middle classes want political answers — the growth of Islamism shows this. So if the left is to compete it needs to be politically clear.

In South Africa, in the 1970s, leftist activists, including many students, played a vital role in starting and building independent trade unions. By the mid-80s these were often strong, militant, and well-organised, and with a firm sense of their own independence from the mainstream nationalist movement, the ANC and its internal surrogates. But as the mass movement rose in the late 80s, the limited political tools of the trade unions proved inadequate to resist the power of the bourgeois nationalists and Stalinists; the trade union movement was largely co-opted by the ANC. That sort of cooption is even more likely to occur in mainly Muslim countries where Islamists have established roots in communities.

Trade-unionist and community activism alone cannot defeat the Islamists. Politics, and socialist ideas firmly based on democratic and egalitarian principles, are not an optional extra in the building of a genuinely progressive movement; as long as no alternative framework for discussing politics develops – alternative to Islamism and old-fashioned nationalism – the Islamists are likely to keep the upper hand. But this is not to say that trade unionism and community activism are not important. One of the sources of the Islamists' strength is their claim to offer an integrated moral system – their critique of the West is a moral one (for example, that Western women are degraded, Muslim women have more dignity, and so on). Trade unionism offers an alternative moral system – a concept of solidarity different to the Islamists'; an alternative, class-based sense of community. It also offers models of genuine, and working class, democracy. The organic process of organisational growth will take time and effort. But it is the essential task now for socialists; insurrectionary fantasies are a hindrance. One measure of the bankruptcy of the "anti-imperialist" conception is that in focusing on the "revolutionary" aspect of Islamism, and presumably imagining the region to be poised on some sort of revolutionary transformation, it ignores the real questions, for socialists, of how a powerful workers' movement can be built.

The state and bourgeois liberal parties are no allies in the struggle to build that movement. But secular and liberal individuals, intellectuals and so on, certainly are, or can be. The strategic task for socialists in Muslim countries is to open the space for working class organisation to flourish and democratic issues come to the fore without losing political independence or subordinating workers' struggle to a schema such as "first bourgeois democracy, then the struggle for socialism".

A central aspect of political rebirth in the Muslim world will be to question hoary notions of "imperialism" and "Zionism", challenging the idea that all social evils are the fault of Western "neo-colonialism", or identifying Israel as the oppressor of all Muslims, or all Arabs, rather than the Palestinians. One element in popular fury against Israel, even if it is not the only one, is that the reactionary regimes have been making demagogic use of the issue for 50 years. A democratic anti-imperialism, the purpose of which is to build international workers' unity, will recognise the rights of the Israeli Jews, and vehemently oppose the anti-Semitic demonisation of them by the Islamists.

Creating a genuine, democratic anti-imperialism, and working-class movements, is an urgent task. Without such an alternative, the immediate future in the Muslim world looks bleak: either the continuation of the existing authoritarian, corrupt and repressive regimes (perhaps slightly modified with US prodding), or Islamic reaction, potentially in a violent and fascistic form, in many countries. The toppling of Hosni Mubarak, for instance, by an "Islamic revolution" led by al-Jihad would not be a blow against imperialism, but a blow against democracy and progress, however awful the regime it replaces. The fall of the Pakistani dictatorship at the hands of friends of the Taliban – giving them access to nuclear weapons – would be an appalling tragedy.

There is hope. The working class of Iran, Algeria, Tunisia, and potentially other countries like Egypt and Iraq, as well as Pakistan and India and further east, holds out that hope. Indeed, Indonesia, which has the largest Muslim population in the world, but so far has seen little militant Islamism, and where an independent workers' movement is beginning to stir, is probably the biggest cause for hope of all.

Our task is to build solidarity with those workers' movements, and with the forces now preparing the way for them.

PLATFORM

Islamism and the left in the Iranian revolution

By Mehdi Kia

I N 1979 Iran saw millions on the streets, and a general strike, in the over-throw of the huge, despotic military and police apparatus of the Shah (king), the USA's strongest ally in the region. It was a great anti-imperi-alist revolution. Or... was it a counter-revolution? Pretty much immediately after the Shah's downfall, the new regime, headed by Islamic clerics, started a drive which soon destroyed the Iranian left by mass executions and jailings; crushed all independent workers' organisations; put the country in the grip of a totalitarian terror worse than the Shah's tyranny; and enmeshed it in an eight-year-long, enormously bloody, war with Iraq.

Here a member of Workers' Left Unity Iran and of the Organisation of Revolutionary Workers of Iran, opens a discussion on the lessons. On some points, readers of Workers' Liberty may question the conclusions. Does our hostility to the totalitarian-Islamic or totalitarian-Stalinist state mean that we can seek a state which is somehow not "politicised" at all? Does our oppo-sition to the clerical-totalitarian "party" of the mullahs, and the Stalinist party model, mean that we need a "new concept" of Marxist party which sees itself as "uniting disparate groups" rather than democratically centralised? After all, the fact that the Islamists used mass street actions to get their way does not make us renounce our street actions. The discussion will continue.

T HE Iranian revolution spewed enough nails on the political road to upend all but the most robust of the left in the country. In the early 1970s the Shah's savage repressive machinery had almost completely broken up the revolutionary left. Those escaping execution were languishing in jail. When the revolutionary waves opened up the prison gates in 1978, the left was small, frag-mented and had been kept isolated from social events for the best part of a decade. During the next two years the Iranian left suddenly found itself the focus for all those who were able to foresee the terrible pit the mullahs were digging for all the democratic slogans of the revolutionary masses. Overnight these small organisations ballooned with literally hundreds of thousands of new-found sup-porters.

Their headquarters were bombarded by workers, students, peasants, and state employees who had taken over control of the factory, office or university, and desperate for direction on where to go from there. In Kurdistan and Turkoman Sahra the left had set up regional administrations and taken over land from absentee landowners and industrial farms. In the universities the left was a major

107

force to be reckoned with. In major cities, hundreds of thousands of votes were cast for candidates from the left in the elections to the first Majles. In the factories left-leaning workers dominated many of the shuras.[1]

Together with the Organisation of the Peoples Mujahedin the left was a major player in the Iranian political scene in the two years following the victory of the revolution. All those who wanted to keep, and extend, the democratic gains of the revolution looked to them for protection against the gathering dark clouds of intolerant Islam and the thugs of the Islamic Republic Party.

Yet by the middle of 1981 the left, (alongside the Mujahedin) had all but been eliminated from the political scene. Undoubtedly the savage repression was a major factor. Tens of thousands were executed and hundreds of thousands spent years behind bars. But to solely blame the repression is to bypass the question: why was the left taken so unawares?

The left, sunk in an ideology soaked in populism, either did not see the storm, or deprived itself of the tools to confront it. It would be foolish to predict in retrospect the relative contributions of outside terror or internal miscomprehension to the demise of the left. The latter, undoubtedly, played a significant role. While state terror is out of our hands, mistakes are not.

The lessons learnt by some on the Iranian left have implications not only for the unfolding of events in today's Iranian scene but also for the left globally. Indeed large sections of the left both inside and outside Iran continue to remain oblivious to these lessons.

Reactionary anti-imperialism

LESSON 1: A regime can be anti-imperialist and reactionary at the same time. The revolution threw out one of imperialism's most trusted allies, and gendarme, in the Persian Gulf and the Middle East. The counter-revolution that rode on the back of the revolution, even if its success was oiled by the scheming of Western governments, upset the carefully laid imperialist jigsaw in the region. The West, and in particular the USA lost a close ally. It took another decade and two wars to re-establish Pax Americana.

The Soviet bloc was openly ecstatic. The Iranian revolution had broken the chain of "containing" states encircling the Soviet block at its most crucial link. The [Stalinist] Tudeh party, always a microphone for the Soviet Union's foreign ministry, had from the revolutionary days endorsed Khomeini. But the Tudeh Party had little support on the ground. It had to win the largest left organisation in Iran, the Organisation of People's Fadai', if its policies were to be actualised. The Fadai', now a large nation-wide organisation, was suffering from theoretical paralysis. In the intellectual apparatus of the left "reaction" and "revolution" were opposites. To combine them was an absolute contradiction [see footnote 2]. The Fadai's deeply ingrained populism told it that a regime coming out of a popular revolution which had toppled the monarchical dictatorship, and was being opposed by every imperialist power, must be progressive. Its eyes, however, told it different.

Any lingering doubts were cast aside when the rulers of the Islamic Republic consummated their anti-imperialist rhetoric by the charade of the US embassy occupation. This and Iraq's invasion of Iran split the left right down the middle. The Tudeh Party used the authority of "brother" parties to break the will of the Fadai'. The process was assisted by the fact that internationally the left in all its hues, all but a tiny faction, had hailed the Iranian revolution and counselled support for the counter-revolutionary regime that had defeated the revolution. The Fadai' split. A Majority fell into line behind Tudeh and Khomeini. The Minority became fodder for Khomeini's repressive machinery.

The theoretical debate over the nature of the Islamic Republic focused on the class nature of the ruling regime. Was it petit-bourgeois, bourgeois, or "affluent petit-bourgeois"? The Tudeh camp went for the former, which through the "non-capitalist road to socialism" was to take the country through to socialism. It was petit-bourgeois – so it must be progressive!

It was left to ORWI, which with a handful of others, pointed to the obvious and observable fact that the new regime (regardless of its class content) was reactionary in its day to day actions and policies. That it was suppressing the working class, destroying the self-governing shuras and systematically taking back all the democratic gains of the revolution. The new ruling cast of Shi'ite clergy was so obviously protecting the capitalist mode of production from the onslaught from below.

It seemed that the left was oblivious to the second part of the central slogan of the revolution: "independence, freedom, Islamic Republic". A significant part of the left shared the disastrous illusion of the revolutionary masses that "independence" flows through the "Islamic Republic". Freedoms were to be put on hold.

Importance of democracy

LESSON 2: Defending unconditional democratic freedoms, even of one's opponents, is for the left a central task for all times. The populist left placed a Chinese wall between the struggle for democracy and that against imperialism. Indeed one was subordinated to the other: fighting imperialism took priority. And anyway the "anti-imperialist Imam" was doing this so well. The battle for freedoms in the streets, in the universities, in the factories – which was a battle against the Islamic rulers – was distracting, nay obstructing, the anti-imperialist struggle, so the argument went. We were to sacrifice everything to a bogus anti-imperialist struggle conducted at the top by the Islamist rulers of Iran.

But even those who did not subscribe to this thesis, in practice, downplayed the democratic struggle. So it was that when women marched in their thousands on that first post revolutionary International Women's Day (March 1979) against compulsory hejab (Islamic covering) for entering government office, the left turned its face away: after all these were "perfumed" women from the more affluent suburbs. The left was again silent when a few month later thugs ransacked the offices of the daily paper Ayandegan. It was "liberal" – nothing to do with us. Within a year progressive newspapers such as the Bakhtar-e Emruz were also shut. And finally the left underground press was annihilated. The Iranian press scene went into total darkness for 15 years.

The left saw political democracy as belonging to the bourgeoisie. At best the era of "bourgeois revolutions" was a ladder to socialism. Personal freedoms, such as the freedom of expression, were "liberal" demands, either to be ignored or tolerated – for the time being – but not high on the agenda. Indeed liberal was used as a pejorative term, a swear word. The "anti-imperialist" mullahs were far preferable. It was thus that the left dug its own grave.

Democracy and political freedoms, including individual freedoms, is the air the left breathes. This air is as necessary while building socialism as when fighting for it [3]. This debate is not confined to Iran. The European left and the left in the Middle East should take heed. Many so-called "bourgeois" freedoms would not have been achieved, nor sustained, without the struggle of the working class. Democratic rights are also a product of the era of proletarian revolutions. As such they form the struts of the future socialist society, to be expanded upon and deepened, not discarded.

A most important element in these freedoms is the freedom to associate. Here too the record of the Iranian left was disastrous.

Non-ideological associations

LESSON 3: Mass-popular associations and organisations must be de-ideologised. Where the left felt itself most at home was helping people to organise. They interpreted this mission, however, as setting up popular organisations as fronts for their own group and organisation. These associations acted as recruiting ground, and a vehicle for realising the "party programme". Women's organisations were set up espousing this or that version of Marxism. Universities were studded by a variety of student bodies. The left would have extended this ideologo-centric vision of popular associations to trade unions where they able to organise these. They indeed, did split the Shuras along ideological lines.

So when the scimitar fell on women, they had already been fragmented along ideological fault lines [4]. And when the mullahs purged 60,000 teachers they faced not one, but several teachers associations who could hardly resist. And when in April 1980 thugs, supported by security forces, and hailed by president Bani-Sadr, attacked and closed Iran's universities as part of the "Islamic cultural revolution" there were almost as many student organisations as there were political groupings[5]. After putting up a valiant and bloody fight they capitulated with many dead and wounded.

The Iranian left had inherited the tradition of the left everywhere to set up front organisations, mere appendages of the parent body. Thus where it came to defending the common interests of the social group which they were nominally representing, they found themselves locked in ideological battle with their counterparts as to what ideologically correct path to take. Social groups were fragmented into supporters of this or that interpretation of Marxism.

"Maoist" women confronted "Trotskyist" women. And in Iran, women supporters of this version of Islam lined up against women defenders of that version of Marxism. Nowhere did women as women stand together. Not even secular women against the encroachment of the Islamist state. When women's groups called for unity they implied capitulation of one group to the conditions of another [6].

Mass-popular organisations and trade unions, should by their very nature remain above ideology. They unite people on basis of their immediate and direct democratic demands. They should combine over what unites them — trade, profession, gender, ethnicity, sexuality — rather than what divides them — ideology. Political groupings need to operate within these structures, formulating demands and arguing for changes in policy and direction, all within the framework of the raison d'etre of the mass organisation. Ideological issues, whether political, religious or cultural, must be kept out unless it has direct bearing on the purpose of the association.

Civil liberties and trade union rights can, and often will, come into conflict with the interests of the state and of political parties. The independence of these institutions of civil society from both political parties and the state are vital if the struggle for democratic rights is to have any concrete meaning. This applies as much to after, as before, the revolution. There is certainly much work that needs to be done to unravel the relationship between the party and mass-popular organisation and the relationship of both with the state.

The Iranian left tragically mirrored the Islamic rulers who split all institutions of civil society. The mullahs went on to amalgamate civil society into the state.

Non-ideological state

LESSON 4: The struggle for a non-ideological state is inseparable from that for socialism. The Iranian left experienced the disaster of the ideological-state and the party-state twice over: once in the Islamic Republic and again in the collapse of the Soviet bloc. The Islamic regime had annulled civil society, physically destroying what it did not like, and amalgamating the rest into itself. All institutions and organisations were "Islamised". None were allowed to exist outside the state. The Works Shuras, the Islamic Societies, women's organisations, the myriad cultural, charitable and economic bonyads (foundations), are all part of the state apparatus.

Once the bloody repressions of 1981-3 had achieved this goal, the ideologically "homogenous" state found itself splitting along ideological lines — this time over this or that interpretation of Islamic rule. The ideological state was behaving true to form. This kind of state defines itself by its beliefs. It is exclusive by excluding all non-believers. It is divisive and fragile because it fragments the "self" through different interpretations of the ideology — the "self/non-self" debate going on to this day.

And paradoxically it is all-inclusive: by placing an ideological block to social participation, the state expands to encompass the whole of society in a frenzy of bogus ideological posturing. Anyone wanting to enter university in Iran will have to take a religious exam, which they will memorise parrot fashion. Everyone who wanted a job in the old Soviet Union claimed to be a Marxist and joined the party. Dishonesty and corruption becomes institutionalised and engulfs the whole state apparatus.

A further tragic consequences of politicising the state is the corruption of society. It is not only that dishonesty is sanitised and "normalised" — that kids will brazenly lie when asked by teachers if they have a [banned] video at home. The total politicisation of society, including the politicisation of culture, has two damaging effects on the longer term health of society.

Firstly it moves the battle between above and below into the cultural arena. Listening to jazz in the former Soviet Union or to pop music in today's Iran, or having a satellite dish, or exposing a few strands of hair becomes an act of defiance against the government. But paradoxically it fragments society in that opposition becomes an individual act, or at best that of a small group such as family and friends.

Second, by saturating and exhausting society in a constant political combat which reaches into the recesses of the home, it can wear society down. An exhausted de-politicised society is the paradoxical potential consequence of the total politicisation of an ideological state. We see this happening in the former Soviet bloc and to some extent among the youth in Iran today. The long term damage to society and social cohesion can only be guessed at [7]. The experience of ideological states in the 20th century has been unequivocal: it corrupts the state apparatus and erodes society.

Much work needs to be done in understanding the relationships of ideology, embodied in the party, and the rule of class(es) embodied in the state, the party and the class it claims to represent, and the triangle of the party(ies) the state and mass-popular organisations.

The left and the working class

LESSON 5: The left's commitment to the working class must go beyond lip-service. The left everywhere acquires its identity through its self-identification with the working class as the "historic class" — the class through whose self-emancipation the whole of society is emancipated. Yet the seeping of populist ideas into the left's world-view meant that often this allegiance was no more than a lip-service. Time and again the working class was turned into an appendage of other classes. This is particularly true in countries with either a small working class or one that had not entirely cut its roots from the village. Iran was a good example.

The Tudeh spectrum had no doubts: the working class should support the anti-imperialist Imam and his government. Production was to be at the service of an "anti-imperialist" government on the non-capitalist road to socialism hand in hand with the international proletariat. The latter was idealised into an abstract entity: the socialist bloc.

The revolutionary left, deeply imbued with the populism of the Tudeh tradition[8], had spent years arguing why it should not organise the working class even while it was forcefully rejecting the reformist path of the Tudeh party in the 1960's. Even when it witnessed the central role played by the working class in toppling the Shah[9] the revolutionary left went about organising almost every class but the class with which it self-identified. When it recruited workers, it was to organise them outside the factories – selling papers, demonstrating, speaking at street corners. For much of the left trade unions, or fighting for immediate working class demands, was out and out reformism.

The Islamic revolution has more than one lesson here: what had triggered off the revolution was a deep social-political-economic crisis which shook the apparently impregnable monarchy to its foundations[10]. The slogans of the revolution had been freedom and independence. Indeed the Islamist movement in the Middle East had been the direct response to the profound crisis of Iranian and other Middle Eastern countries were undergoing in the 1970s. In societies with such deep crisis – where the international division of labour had marginalised an increasingly larger section of society, newly won political freedoms, even by revolutionary means, cannot be consolidated without a corresponding move towards economic equalisation.

For this reason it is obvious that lasting democracy in Iran requires that the direct producers have a stake in their produce. In short, a revolution with democratic slogans cannot be consolidated in the context of Iran today, without a tangible move toward a workers' state. For individual freedoms to last it is necessary to move towards self-rule at the point of production.

Pluralistic workers' state

LESSON 6: A workers' state is the government of the workforce in its totality. In Iran today, as in most countries of the world, the working class – defined not just as the industrial proletariat but as all those whose labour contributes to the production of surplus value (all wage-labour) – are a majority. The state the left should be fighting for is one in which this majority exercises its self-directed rule. The shape of this self-government can be open to debate, and indeed a number of models have been tried since the Paris Commune of 1871.

Perhaps the most important lesson of the last two decades for the left, including the Iranian variety, is the concept of pluralism. I will refer the reader to the article by Shalguni for a detailed expose of this point [footnote 2].and will confine myself to a summary:

The working class becomes a "class" only through the active participation of the entire workforce. Yet the working "class", like the "people" is not homogeneous and has to be understood by the totality of its individuals and groupings. Class solidarity is achieved by incorporating the normal differences and dissensions among workers. These differences are expressed in a plurality of political parties, labour organisations and associations. No political current has the right to claim special rights as the bearer of the "historic" consciousness or the interpreter of the "historic" will of the proletariat.

The workers state has therefore to be understood as just that: the state of the social forces of production working for society in its entirety. Hence this state will be pluralistic. The shape of this state, the relationship between its forces, its classes, etc are open to debate and to experimentation. There are no ready-made golden answers.

Left party

LESSON 7: New concepts of the party need to be developed. Pluralism in the working class inevitably means pluralism within the left. The fragmentation of the left in Iran has made it imperative to find a model of working together. Events today make this even more urgent. The largest class is being sidelined in the momentous developments of the country.

One model designed to unite disparate groups and the large number of left individuals is that adopted by the Workers' Left Unity. Organisations and individuals collect around the principles of the programme. Each grouping within this block maintains its autonomy and the right to expound its programme while uniting to work for the agreed goals[11]. We believe that this and similar models are applicable to the non-Iranian situation.

Any model should simultaneously address (a) the need for plurality (b) the need to have a common will – an ability to make decisions (c) ensure the autonomy, and right to agitate for their views of the individual constituents of the whole is not compromised, (d) a structure that can combine open activity, which is essential for organising the working class, with clandestine underground, work which is essential for survival in a repressive state.

International solidarity

LESSON 8: The international left must create its own grass-root human rights movement. Iranian revolution showed the importance of international solidarity. 20 years on, the unipolar world has lost some of the international levers that allowed revolutions to breathe. Pax Americana is being imposed by a blatant militarism using various international institutions such as the UN, Nato, international courts etc. under a carefully selected use of the banner of human rights.

US imperialism has hijacked the slogans that properly belong to the left to punish "rogue" states. We need to pull the rug from under its feet. The Iranian left has taken the first step in proposing to launch a campaign to try the rulers of the Islamic regime for crimes against its own people. This is a plea for a grass-roots movement organised on a global scale to stop crimes committed by states against their own people [12]. It is a movement of the same nature as the green movement, the feminist movement and the trade union movement. It aims to destroy the legitimacy of criminal states such as the Islamic Republic of Iran. It also aims to erode the legitimacy of the highly selective human rights concerns serving the new world order.

We hope to get support from all progressive forces for this campaign. We also hope that similar moves can be made for other criminal governments. Again the theoretical and practical aspects of this campaign need debate on a world scale. We open our pages to this, and related debates.

Finally the lesson of the Islamic Republic of Iran and that of the last 80 years is that you cannot drag people against their will even to paradise.

Notes

1. Shura: factory, work-place and university committees, in places with management function. See Asef Bayat *Workers and revolution in Iran*. Zed Books 1987.
2. Mohammad Reza Shalguni: The Iranian left in an era of breaks and transition, *iran bulletin* 21-22, Spring-Summer 1999.
3. See Shalguni ibid.
4. Etahade Melli Zanan (National Alliance of Women), Sazman-e Democratik-e Zanan-e Iran (Democratic

Organisation of Iranian Women), Sazman-e Rahi-e Zan (Organisation for Women's Emancipation), National Democratic Front (women's section), Women's Solidarity Committee and many others.

5. At one stage there were over 50 left organisations. The most important, not counting such "national" organisations as the Kurds, Turkoman and Arab were: Ettehade Chap, the Fadai' Organisation (which split into majority and minority – the former later splitting in two), Fadai' Guerrillas, Razmandegan, Sazman-e Peikar, Rah-e Kargar (later ORWI), Tudeh Party, United Communists (an alliance of five organisations), The Union of Communists, Vahdat-e Komunisti.

6. Eg Women's Solidarity Committee. See for example Parvin Paydar. Women and the political process in 20th century Iran. Cambridge Middle East Studies 1995 p249-256.

7. For a more detailed exposition of these and other effects of radical Islamism on society see Ardeshir Mehrdad in iran bulletin.

8. Tudeh means "mass" and the party began life during World War II as a party of "popular" classes.

9. The mass street demonstrations had apparently reached a stalemate, when at the instigation of the universities a mass general strike was initiated which culminated in the crippling strike by oil workers. It was this that finally broke the back of the Shah's regime. See Asef Bayat ibid.

10. See Fred Halliday, *Iran: dictatorship and development*. Penguin Books 1979; Nikkie R Keddie. *Roots of revolution*. Yale University, 1981; Ervand Abrahamian, *Iran between two revolutions*. Princeton University Press 1982.

11. Workers' Left Unity invites organisations and individuals to join it on the following platform: For the struggle to overthrow of the Islamic Republic Regime in Iran; for the overthrow of capitalism and the formation of a workers' state relying on the self governing organs of workers and toilers; for the establishment of the socialist alternative capable of expanding democracy in all political, social and economic spheres; for the establishment of social ownership relying on the self rule of producers; to defend unconditional political freedoms, as an integral part of the struggle for socialism; for organising workers' struggles on the basis of the confrontation between capital and labour. http://www.etehadchap.com.

12. See *iran bulletin* no 20 Winter 1998 and 21-22 Spring-Summer 1999.

two nations
two states

SOCIALISTS AND ISRAEL/PALESTINE

a workers' liberty pamphlet £2/£1

From Workers' Liberty – a discussion of the history and the politics of Israel and Palestine. £2 (£1 unwaged) plus 44p post from AWL, PO Box 823, London SE15 4NA

Catalogue for "Entartete Kunst" - "Degenerate art" - an exhibition mounted by the Nazi regime between 1937 and 1940. Four million Germans and Austrians saw an eclectic collection of pieces seized from museums and galleries, designed to inoculate them against art that was 'anti-German', 'confusing' or simply 'badly executed' - like the mask shown here. The artists derided in the exhibition included George Grosz and John Heartfield, dadaists who had criticised the German bourgeoisie, militarism and Hitler.

115

Taking the piss? Or,

Whatever happened to the avant garde?

By Gerry Byrne

"**H**E'S taking the piss." We are looking at the Turner Prize nominees at the Tate, and have come to Martin Creed's A Light Going On and Off. A big bare gallery room that could house a whole exhibition and he's got a light going on and off, and that's it. He's taking the piss. Later, looking at the Channel 4 film, we see Martin in another gallery, surrounded by suited curators and flunkies, carefully arranging a small piece of masking tape on a wall: he stands back, studies its placing, runs up to it, measures, re-sites it a few centimetres higher, stands back, looks, and nods approvingly. The gallery folk stand rigidly to attention – this is the artist at work, they are not allowed to laugh. We can, though, and do. Serious piss-taking. Piss-taking raised to high art.

Interestingly, the reaction to Martin Creed winning the Turner Prize has been most positive among the least "arty" people I've spoken to: "I may not know much about art, but I recognise a good laugh when I see one." He cannily declined to explain the meaning of his work, so any interpretation from post-modern high art waffle to piss-take is equally valid. But it does make me want to question: Is that all that's possible? Is there no role for radical modern art? Whatever happened to the avant garde?

The weekend the Turner Prize was announced, the *Guardian* magazine ran an article on the claim by the heirs of Kasimir Malevich for compensation for the billion dollar collection of his works in Amsterdam's Stedelijk Museum, allegedly looted by the Nazis. MOMA (the American Museum of Modern Art) has already settled out of court for its Malevich collection, and returned one painting, which sold for $15.5m. Malevich was the Martin Creed of his day. In 1915, his minimalist Black Square caused a scandal and the police had to be called. Now his works are selling for incalculable sums. What happened?

Malevich's Black Square and Martin Creed's Light Going On and Off seem to sum up a century of Modern Art. Is there no role, as the Post-Modernists would claim, for an avant garde? Is such an idea necessarily elitist? When did modern art become big money, and how has that affected the artists? Has Charles Saatchi bought and butchered the best and brightest (or just the most noisy)?

At the start of the Twentieth Century, political radicalism and artistic experimentation seemed indissolubly wedded. Modern artists were at war with bourgeois conservatism. They were out to shock, provoke and also have a good laugh. They were in love with the energy of mass production – speed, noise, the angular, mechanical, shiny, discordant, breathless, chaotic newness of everything. For some, like the Italian Futurists, this led them to militarism, misogynism and fascism; most, though, allied with the Left and, after the Russian Revolution, with Communism.

Post-revolutionary Russia saw an explosion of artistic creativity. In the midst of Civil War and invasion by foreign armies! The avant garde flocked to the service of the Revolution. The poet Mayakovsky joined ROSTA, the Russian Telegraph Agency: "It meant telegraphed news immediately translated into

The First International Dada Fair opens in Berlin in 1920, beneath a flying dummy with the face of a pig and a German army uniform

posters and decrees into slogans. It was a new form that spontaneously originated in life itself. It meant the men of the Red Army looking at posters before a battle and going to fight not with a prayer but a slogan on their lips." With a largely illiterate population, graphics, theatre and film were vital to get the message across. With scarce resources, ingenuity and functionality were a spur to originality and developing new media. For a brief period, the dream of total creative freedom, experimentation, and a mass popular audience, was realised. Perhaps the crowning artistic achievement of this period (and of the century, film being the quintessential medium of the twentieth century) was Eisenstein's 1925 film *Battleship Potemkin.*

By 1927, when Malevich exhibited in Berlin, the atmosphere had changed sufficiently that he felt it necessary to discuss disposal of his works in the event of his death or long imprisonment. Lenin was dead and a massive struggle was underway for control of the Party and the country. Populism took on a new soul-deadening meaning. Propaganda in the sense we understand it today, turgid, bludgeoning repetition of hollow slogans, replaced spontaneous creativity. Malevich, in common with all the modernists, was denounced for excessive formalism, inaccessibility, elitism. In 1929, a week before the opening of his massive spectacular celebration of the 1905 Revolution, Mayakovsky, who had said of 1917, "there was no doubt, it was my revolution", killed himself in despair at the direction of events. The love-boat was wrecked on the rocks.

Outside of Russia, especially after the adoption of the Popular Front strategy, when Stalin directed communist Parties to woo liberal, democratic intellectuals, and set himself up as the defender of culture against the threat of fascism, Communism or its fringes seemed the natural home for modernism. Senator George Donderoe from Michigan declared "Modern art equals communism". A view echoed by Hitler. The best attended exhibition of avant-garde art of the century was, ironically, the Munich Exhibition of Degenerate Art, 1937, organised by the Nazis to demonstrate how the Weimar Republic had squandered precious national resources on Jewish/Bolshevik/Negro-inspired art, which mocked and vilified the German national spirit. 16,000 works were confiscated from German museums. The exhibition included works by Gaugin, van Gogh, Kandinsky, Klee, Matisse, Mondrian, Picasso. It's mind-boggling to imagine the value of all those works in today's art market. Goebbels felt that all these works should be burned, but the most saleable were auctioned off to swell the coffers of the Third Reich, and some found their way into the personal collections of Nazi leaders, such as Göring.

The Spanish Civil War underlined the identification of Communism with mod-

117

ernism, democracy and progress. Picasso's Guernica, another defining modernist work of the twentieth century, was painted in response to the atrocity bombing by the Fascists of that small town.

The fact that the Stalinists in their turn were slaughtering Anarchists and Trotskyists, the Moscow Trials were in full spate, and the avant garde inside Russia suffered the same fate as anyone with a critical thought in their heads — exile, imprisonment, death — did not immediately break this link. There was debate in the international art movement. The Surrealists split (and split again and split and splintered, echoing the splits in the political movement). Breton, one of Surrealism's prime movers, allied with Trotsky, as did Diego Rivera, the Mexican muralist, who was influential on the young American avant garde. They produced a manifesto "Towards a Free Revolutionary Art", which held out artistic freedom combined with political engagement, as an alternative to the stifling dogma of Stalinist "Socialist Realism".

"Some day it will have to be told how anti-Stalinism which started out more or less as Trotskyism turned into art for art's sake, and thereby cleared the way, heroically, for what was to come." (Clement Greenberg)

Clement Greenberg, who "discovered" Jackson Pollock, became the spokesman for depoliticised art for art's sake. So how did it happen? The focus of modern art shifted to New York, and the internal economic and political conditions of the US did the rest. There was a mass exodus of avant-garde artists from Germany to the United States, after the Degenerate Art Exhibition, to be followed by a second wave from occupied Europe, when War started. Stalin had obliterated the Russian avant garde. Initially the modern art scene focussed on the European exiles, but then young American artists started to organise themselves to take advantage of the "picture boom".

Pearl Harbour accomplished what a decade of the New Deal had failed to do, reviving American capitalism and redirecting class struggle into patriotism. During the first six months of 1942 the government placed $100 billion worth of orders with the private sector (as opposed to $12 billion the previous six moths) and 17 million new jobs were created. By 1945, Americans held $140 billion in savings and war bonds, three times the entire national income of 1933. A lot of money just waiting to be spent on luxury goods, including art. Upmarket department stores, like Gimpels and Maceys, started selling art, beginning with Old Masters but moving on to the modern. In this situation, American artists, no longer supported by New Deal funding, needed to address themselves to this new market.

The Federation of American Painters and Sculptors, originally a Trotskyist-influenced split-off from the CP-dominated Congress of American Artists, set itself the task of increasing the public visibility and therefore sales potential of modern American artists. In the process they succeeded in a complete transformation of the concept of an artistic avant garde. The immediate post-war years were a time of intense debate and cultural restructuring, which set in place many of the structures and attitudes which are still with us today.

With Europe devastated and the working class on the verge of, or actually, insurrectionary, the US found itself economically dominant but culturally disoriented. From the political isolationism of the thirties, American capitalism had to become totally interventionist to counter "Soviet" expansionism and the threat of working class revolt. It had to back up its military and economic with cultural dominance. Art was part of this programme. Economic aid was tied to cultural and political conditions. European markets had to be opened up to American products, including those of "the cultural industries". The French film industry was destroyed, for example, as part of the aid package, to make way for the total dominance of Hollywood. As a part of all this, New York had to main-

Otto Dix's "Kriegskrüppel" — "War cripples" — painted in 1920. The Nazis would ban Dix from teaching and painting, and included his work in the "Degenerate art" exhibition.

tain its new role as the centre of modern art.

The project of the American modern artists therefore dovetailed with the needs of US (and world) capitalism. The newly rich American middle classes were given a crash course in the appreciation of modern art. Avant-gardism became a species of commodity speculation: spot the art that's too advanced for today's taste but will be worth tons in tomorrow's market. The Federation orchestrated the debate in the press about the need for a specifically American, vital (largely abstract) art which reflected the uncertainty of the times but secured American dominance. Both the Nazis and the Stalinists, the two enemies of "freedom", had denounced abstraction and modernist experimentation and dogmatically insisted on their versions of Realism, therefore the Free World should embrace the new art and repudiate realism. American artists returning from the War were shocked at the complete transformation of the art world in their absence.

It would be wrong to see the Federation and the Abstract Expressionists, Rothko, Pollock and de Kooning, e.g., who came to dominate the modern art scene, as simply cynically selling out to American cultural imperialism. They were as affected as anyone else by the Post-war intellectual shell-shock. The impact of the Nazi death camps and the atomic bombing of Hiroshima and Nagasaki, had to be assimilated. "After Auschwitz there can be no poetry". There was a pervading sense that, in an age of industrialised slaughter, realism was almost pornographic. They were suspicious of the prostitution of art to politics by the Stalinists. Abstraction, individualism, and the total removal of art from the diktats of politics, seemed the most honest approach. One side effect of the focus on individual genius, permeated by Cold War ideology, was the exclusion of women artists from a leading role. Pre-war European avant-garde art had been as much about New Woman as New Man. The Russian movement, particularly, represented women artists in equal numbers with men, though their role was obscured in later histories. Surrealism too involved many women artists: Meret Oppenheim's Fur Breakfast became almost iconic of Surrealism. Now women were returned to their pre-twentieth century role in art, as models and enablers for men of genius.

There have been many attempts to challenge the commodification of art, and the imperialist and masculinist domination of culture, most recently Post-Modernism, which succeeded only by reducing everything to "discourse". You could see Martin Creed's work in this light, teasingly refusing to "discourse" at the same time as obliquely commenting on the state of modern art.

Some critics, echoing Adorno, have said, "after September 11th there can be no irony", which pretty much spells the death of Post-Modernism. New York is the centre of the world culturally and it suffered a direct hit. Perhaps the aftershocks are sufficient to shift the cultural centre of gravity, as happened after World War Two. It's certainly true that Grand Narratives, Good and Evil are back in a big way. Will this be the spur for a twenty-first century avant garde?

Subscribe to workers' liberty

- UK subs: £25 or £14 (students, unwaged) for 8 issues, £15 or £8 for 4 issues. Cheques to "AWL"
Send to Workers' Liberty, PO Box 823, London SE15 4NA

- European subs: £34, sterling cheque, for 8 issues, to London office.
For details of how to pay in euros (55 euros), contact the London office

- US subs: $53 for 8 issues, $28 for 4
Cheques to "Barry Finger"
Send to Barry Finger, 18 Cragswood Road, New Paltz, NY 12561

- Australian subs: $63 for 8 issues, $35 for 4
Cheques to "Workers' Liberty"
Send to Workers' Liberty, PO Box 313, Leichhardt, NSW 2040

Other areas, please contact the London office. Or you can subscribe via the website at www.workersliberty.org.

Pamphlets from workers' liberty

An injury to one is an injury to all: writings of a socialist railworker, by Rob Dawber
£1

Two nations, two states: socialists and Israel/Palestine £2

How to beat the racists £2

How solidarity can change the world (book) £3.95

Our demands are very moderate: we only want the earth. Global capitalism and the environmental crisis. £1.50

The fight for a workers' government 60p

Radical chains: sexuality and class politics £1

Socialism and feminism £1

Why you should be a socialist 50p

Socialists answer the New Right £1.50

Globalisation: special issue of Workers' Liberty (no.63) £1.95

How do we get left unity? Special issue of Workers' Liberty (no.52) £1.95

Lenin and the October Revolution 50p

New problems, new struggles: a handbook for trade unionists 95p

Send cheques, payable to "Alliance for Workers' Liberty", to AWL, PO Box 823, London SE15 4NA. Postage is free on orders above £10; others, please send 20% extra (minimum 20p).

Toussaint L'Ouverture, leader of Haiti's revolution against slavery

The Haitian revolution and Atlantic slavery

By Colin Waugh

Toussaint, the most unhappy of men!
Whether the whistling Rustic tend his plough
Within thy hearing, or thy head be now
Pillowed in some deep dungeon's earless den; -
O miserable Chieftain! where and when
Wilt thou find patience? Yet die not; do thou
Wear rather in thy bonds a cheerful brow:
Though fallen thyself, never to rise again,
Live, and take comfort. Thou hast left behind
Powers that will work for thee; air, earth, and skies;
There's not a breathing of the common wind
That will forget thee; thou hast great allies;
Thy friends are exultations, agonies,
And love, and man's unconquerable mind.
William Wordsworth (*Morning Post*, London, 3 February 1803)

THE Haitian revolution of 1791-1804 is arguably comparable in importance to the American Revolution of 1776 and the French Revolution of 1789. Just one of its effects, for example, was that Napoleon abandoned his plan to seize north America, with the result that in 1803 he sold "Louisiana" (i.e., about one third of the present USA) to the US for £3 million. It illustrates also why to understand the world we must take into account "black history" – that is, history from which most people are not left out. Thirdly, it is a prime example of history from below, illustrating how it was "slaves who abolished slavery".

Unlike the forms of slavery internal to African societies or the trade between sub-Saharan Africa and Egypt, the Middle East and across the Indian Ocean, Atlantic slavery was an aspect of what Marx termed the "so-called primitive accumulation of capital" in Europe and North America. Based on the "triangular trade" – the movement of manufactured goods from northern Europe to West Africa, of slaves from there to the Americas, of agricultural produce to North America and Europe, and of items like clothing, tools and salt fish from North America to the Caribbean and central South America – it involved the enforced transportation of perhaps fifteen million people from Africa between the early 1500s and late 1800s.

122

Hispaniola, the largest Caribbean island after Cuba, is close to Cuba, Puerto Rico and Jamaica. Haiti (called St-Domingue till 1804) is the western third of Hispaniola. In 1492 Columbus claimed Hispaniola for Spain. Seeking gold, the Spaniards reduced a Taino-Arawak population of perhaps a million to about 200 by 1532, although we shall see that Arawak culture was not so easy to kill. Black slaves were imported from Spain itself (i.e., rather than directly from Africa) in the 1520s and the Muslims amongst them at once led a rebellion (1522), with the result that maroon groups were established in the mountains, which reach 8,000 feet. (This episode caused slavers to avoid Muslims in future.) Of a further 15,000 Africans imported in 1577, 7,000 also escaped to the mountains. Even in 1751 there were thought to be 3,000 maroons there.

Under Spain, Hispaniola remained thinly populated, with few plantations, and there were never more than 15,000 slaves in the Spanish section of the island (now the Dominican Republic). However, during the 1600s, pirates, most of them French, established a base in the off-shore island of Tortuga, and from about 1670 many of these became planters on St-Domingue itself, which was granted to France under the Treaty of Ryswick (1697).

The development of these plantations made St-Domingue the most lucrative piece of land on earth. By 1789 there were about 800 sugar plantations concentrated on the northern plain around the town of Le Cap Francais (now Haitien), as well as about 2,000 coffee plantations. St-Domingue now produced more sugar than the entire British West Indies, exporting 163 million pounds in 1791, along with 60% of world coffee (68 million pounds in 1791), 930,000 pounds of indigo, and over 6 million pounds of cotton. This bonanza depended on slavery.

From the late 1600s the French crown, through an arrangement called the exclusif, compelled the St-Domingue planters to trade only with France or with other French colonies in the Americas, and to do so via a single private company designated by the crown itself. Taxes on this trade went to the royal treasury. When France lost Canada in 1759, the exclusif became even more burdensome, because all imports to St-Domingue had now to come from France itself, further enriching the merchants and shipowners in Bordeaux, Nantes, Marseille – cities which had grown wealthy by processing tropical produce and exporting it across Europe. By 1789, 80,000 people were engaged in the overall trade between France and St-Domingue, of whom 15,000 were sailors involved in the slave trade specifically, in 600 ships.

In St-Domingue itself, the crown was represented by a military governor and and a civilian intendant. Strife was endemic between, on the one hand, the French merchants and crown, and, on the other, the St-Domingue planters, whether resident in the colony or not, and other whites there. For example in 1722 the colonists imprisoned the governor in protest at the trading company's privileges, whereas in 1760 the intendant dissolved the planters' militia. However, in the first phase of the French Revolution the France-based planters, organised in a political club called the Massiac, set up partly to counter growing anti-slavery sentiment, combined with the mercantile bourgeoisie in a struggle against the privileges of the feudal nobility.

The Haitian population in 1789 included 30-40,000 whites, comprising about 500 employees of the French crown plus the resident planters who dominated the colonial assembly (local parliament) and the "small whites" – plantation overseers, book-keepers, lawyers, priests etc. The "free coloured" population (i.e., descendants of slave women and white men, then often termed "mulattos") also numbered 30-40,000 by 1789. Even people whose only black ancestor was seven generations back were still counted within this group. Many had become wealthy, with plantations and slaves, while others were entrepreneurs. There was a strong tendency amongst this group to look down on the blacks. Nevertheless they suffered high levels of discrimination, being excluded, for example, from the franchise for the colonial assembly and from carrying arms, while in 1768 the colonial assembly forbad marriages between mixed race women and white men. This hurt all the more because in France itself they were treated much better, and many had also fought as volunteer officers on the American side in the War of Independence.

The overwhelming bulk of the population consisted of slaves, split between two distinct groups. First, there were slaves born in St-Domingue or elsewhere in the Caribbean, referred to as creoles. On the plantations, this group monopolised such functions as domestic service, building crafts, sugar boiling, looking after cattle and horses, driving carriages and acting as chargehands over field gangs. Secondly, there were those — the vast majority — born in Africa, and used as fieldhands. There were 250,000 slaves in 1779 and 480,000 in 1791. At the time of the revolution, then, a very high proportion of slaves were fieldhands recently imported from Africa. The history of slave revolts and maroonage across Central America and the Caribbean shows that the single factor most likely to precede an outbreak was the concentration of such imports. A majority of these Africans were male. Because of this, because of overwork, poor feeding and lack of medical attention, and because of measures taken by women to restrict their fertility, the birth rate was low. As early as 1685, the French government had decreed measures — the Code Noir — aimed at stopping individual planters from jeopardising the common interest by excessive ill treatment of slaves, but in practice there was ferocious repression. Because it was easier to import new slaves than to breed from the existing ones, the practice was to work them to death.

The slaves came from a coastline stretching from present-day Senegal to Angola, but especially from Benin (formerly Dahomey), and from as far inland as the savannah areas beyond the rainforest. Most were either debtors or prisoners of war. The disruption of African societies on the southern fringe of the Sahara caused by the growth of trade by ship along the Atlantic coast rather than by camel train across the desert produced a ready supply. The slaves were traded by the ruling class of the coastal nations.

Because of the 1522 revolt and because Muslims were forbidden to enslave other Muslims, the majority of these slaves would have held traditional beliefs, which in St-Domingue developed into voodoo. The word voodoo itself comes from the Fon people in Dahomey. The religion underlying voodoo is a polytheistic system, in which spirits, in Haiti called loas, comparable to, say, the Greco-Roman gods, take possession of worshippers in a manner often likened by participants to a rider mounting a horse. It reflects a social order based on peasant agriculture with surpluses allowing the growth of trade, cities, states, armies, intellectuals (for example priests and scholars), and skilled artisans. Versions of it existed across West Africa, sometimes alongside, sometimes beneath, sometimes in synthesis and sometimes in struggle with Islam. A mixing amongst these different traditional religions took place in Africa itself, especially under the destabilisation caused by the slave trade, and was then accelerated in colonies like St-Domingue.

In St-Domingue, this mixing of beliefs underwent three further influences. First, the fieldhands were baptised into — though not systematically instructed in — the French version of Roman Catholicism. Eventually each loa came to be linked to a Christian saint, while the Christian cross was reinterpreted to stand for the intersection of the horizontal plane of everyday life with the vertical plain of spirit possession. Secondly a synthesis also seems to have taken place with the Taino-Arawak religion, with the result that voodoo could be celebrated both in the relatively sedate Dahomeyan manner (called Rada) but also in a much more rebellious and explosive Arawak style (called Petro). The latter especially would have allowed the fieldhands to feel that in the end they were more powerful than the creole blacks, the mulattos and the whites. Thirdly, although the former house slaves, slave craftspersons, etc., who eventually came to lead the revolution were opposed to voodoo and when in power tried to suppress it, they acted as a channel through which, for example via overheard conversations, the ideas of the French revolution found their way to the − overwhelmingly nonliterate − fieldhands. These ideas too became synthesised with voodoo.

Francis Macandal was a slave born in Guinea, who worked on the Lenormand plantation near Cap Francais. After losing his arm in a sugar press when the ox that was turning it staggered, Macandal became a maroon, and in 1757 organised a conspiracy to poison whites across St-Domingue, the first systematic attempt to destroy slavery rather than just escape from it. Caught and burnt alive in 1758, Macandal's legend grew amongst the slaves at precisely the moment when the importation of Africans rose sharply.

Following the onset of the French Revolution with the convening of the Estates General in 1789, Vincent Oge, a wealthy, educated person of mixed race who was living in France and attracted to revolutionary ideas, bought arms in the US and in October 1790 tried to start a revolt amongst the mixed race population of St-Domingue. Because he ignored the advice of one of his associates to draw in the blacks, Oge was easily defeated. On conviction, his elbows and knees were crushed with hammers and he was then tied to a wheel and left face upwards in the sun to die. That this method of execution, routine for a slave, should be used on someone like Oge provoked horror amongst enlightened opinion in France.

The spread of Jacobin ideas amongst sections of the petty bourgeoisie and sans culottes in France − that is, the movement of the French Revolution to the left − was now paralleled by events in St-Domingue. Boukman Dutty, a chargehand field slave imported from Jamaica, convened on the night of 14 August 1791 at the Lenormand plantation (i.e., that from which Macandal had fled 34 years earlier) a meeting cum voodoo ceremony attended by 200 slaves delegated from plantations across the northern plain, at which he made in Kreyole the following statement:

"The god who created the sun which gives us light, who rouses the waves and rules the storm, though hidden in the clouds, he watches us. He sees all that the white man does. The god of the white man inspires him with crime, but our god calls upon us to do good works. Our god who is good to us orders us to revenge our wrongs. He will direct our arms and aid us. Throw away the symbol of the god of the whites who has so often caused us to weep [a reference to crosses that the slaves wore round their necks CW], and listen to the voice of liberty, which speaks in the hearts of us all."

On 22 August, as a result of this meeting, 100,000 fieldhands rose in revolt across the northern plain, burning plantations and killing the owners, overseers, etc. One hundred and eighty sugar and 900 indigo and/or coffee plantations were affected. Soon, led by their houngans and mambos (male and female voodoo priests) the rebels, armed only with machetes and other agricultural tools, took on and defeated a substantial force of the heavily armed Marechausee (colonial militia) and crown troops. Twenty thousand of them then withdrew into the mountains near the Spanish border, from which they conducted warfare across a large part of St-Domingue. Boukman himself was killed in November 1791, either in action or immediately after being captured.

From this uprising of the fieldhands there now emerged a layer of creole black and mixed race generals who threw in their lot with them − initially Biassou, Jean Francois and Jeannot, and soon afterwards a black man then called

Toussaint Breda (after the plantation where he was born). Of Dahomeyan descent, Toussaint as a child was treated well, learnt to read and in 1777 became a coach driver. He is thought to have read at some time a book by the French anti-slavery campaigner the Abbe Raynal published in 1781 which included the passage:

"If self-interest alone prevails with nations and their masters, there is another power. Nature speaks in louder tones than philosophy or self interest. Already are there established two colonies of fugitive negroes, whose treaties and power protect from assault. Those lightnings announce the thunder. A courageous chief is wanted. Where is he, that great man whom Nature owes to her vexed, oppressed and tormented children? Where is he? He will appear, doubt it not; he will come forth and raise the sacred standard of liberty. This venerable signal will gather around him the companions of his misfortune. More impetuous than the torrents, they will everywhere leave the indelible traces of their just resentment. Everywhere people will bless the name of the hero who shall have reestablished the rights of the human race; everywhere they will raise trophies in his honour."

Toussaint, who later acquired the name "L'Ouverture" (the opener), identified with this predicted figure. Two weeks after the start of the fieldhands' revolt he joined it, initially as a medical officer subordinate to the main generals.

As the French revolution entered the phase of revolutionary war against Britain and Spain, in which the king of France surreptitiously aligned himself with the anti-revolutionary powers, the black generals in St-Domingue, recognising that the revolt in its present form could go no further, offered (November 1791) to lead the slaves back onto the plantations in return for their own freedom and that of 400 of their followers. But out of a racist unwillingness to negotiate with such people, the colonial assembly rejected this offer. In the meantime, France declared war on Britain (January 1793) and on Spain (March) and both of these countries then invaded St-Domingue. The British government's aim was to destroy French colonial wealth, and this led the prime minister William Pitt to sponsor moves by the MP William Wilberforce to get parliament to legislate the end of the slave trade (i.e., with a view to wrecking St-Domingue). In this situation, the black generals and their armies allied with Spain and Britain against the planters as a way of continuing the struggle against slavery. In July 1793 the Spanish commissioned these leaders, including L'Ouverture, as generals in their own army.

However, the French Revolution now moved still more decisively to the left, with first the Girondins and then the Jacobins taking power, one effect of which was that anti-slavery sentiment gained ground in France. In December 1793 the French assembly decreed all slaves in St-Domingue free, and sent a commissioner, the leftwinger Leger Felicite Sonthonax, to St-Domingue, among other things to enact this.

Secret negotiations took place between Sonthonax and L'Ouverture, who was emerging as the dominant black general. He had already issued in August 1793 the declaration:

"Brothers and friends. I am Toussaint L'Ouverture, my name is perhaps known to you. I have undertaken vengeance. I want Liberty and Equality to reign in San Domingo. I work to bring them into existence. Unite yourselves to us, brothers, and fight with us for the same cause, etc. Your very humble and obedient servant. (Signed) Toussaint L'Ouverture General of the armies of the king, for the public good."

And in May 1794, as soon as Sonthonax freed the slaves in the area under his jurisdiction (i.e., that part of St-Domingue not under British or Spanish control), L'Ouverture crossed over to the French with his army, which he was rapidly building into a force capable of taking on European regular troops. A layer of black generals, including the former slaves Henri Christophe and Jean-Jacques Dessalines and Toussaint's nephew Moise, came with him. His army then recaptured the north of St-Domingue from Spanish forces under Biassou and in February 1795 attacked the British across the whole of the north and west of St-Domingue. By early 1798 the British forces were collapsing, partly under the impact of the black offensive and partly from disease. By the time they withdrew in November of that year, at least 20,000 out of 30,000 British soldiers had died – said by military historians to be the biggest defeat ever suffered by the British army.

However, the anti-slavery alliance between Sonthonax and the black generals provoked the mixed race slaveowners against him, and even as L'Ouverture and Sonthonax were cementing their alliance, the French Revolution itself had begun to move to the right, starting with the overthrow of the Jacobins in July 1794, thus undermining Sonthonax's base in France. During the anti-British war, Sonthonax proposed to L'Ouverture that they kill all the whites in St-Domingue and establish a black republic allied to revolutionary France. He also told the rank and file black soldiers that if a moment ever came when the French called upon them to hand in their weapons, that would be the time to use them. However, L'Ouverture considered that the former slaves needed the expertise of the former plantation owners to maintain a viable sugar industry in St-Domingue, and refused Sonthonax's proposal. To remove Sonthonax from St-Domingue he then organised the latter's election to the French assembly (May 1797), and when Sonthonax delayed leaving, deported him (August). Sonthonax was replaced as commissioner by Hedouville, who proposed that the army built by Louverture be used to invade Jamaica (belonging to Britain) and Louisiana (belonging to Spain). Louverture refused this plan too, instead taking on and defeating the mixed race forces under Andre Rigaud. By 1800, he was effectively the ruler of St-Domingue, and in January of that year his forces seized San Domingo from Spain and freed the slaves there, such that the whole island was under his control. At all stages, however, he saw himself as acting on behalf of revolutionary France.

The continuing war between France and Britain allowed L'Ouverture to consolidate his regime. He introduced a constitution, one term of which was that he should be president for life. (He was now in his late fifties, old for a former slave then.) He protected whites and their property, encouraging the planters who had fled to return, and negotiated a trade deal with the US President. He aimed to keep the plantations together, because he saw these as the only basis for an independent economy. He therefore enacted laws to keep the former slaves, now labourers, on the plantations, in return for a guaranteed quarter share of the crop, a shortened working day and no whipping. Roads were built across both St-Domingue and the former Spanish zone. People were able to travel in security and the cities such as Le Cap and Port au Prince were rebuilt. He aimed also to construct a civilised society, and this included the building of mansions for the generals and the revival of the French culture that had existed in these cities before the uprising. However he was still a revolutionary. For example, he conceived a plan to invade Africa and attack the slave trade at its roots, and in the meantime he stockpiled arms in readiness for the attempted restoration of slavery that must come once the war against Britain ended. Moving constantly amongst the rank and file of the army, he would often hold up a musket and tell them: "This is your freedom!" But he failed to explain each turn of policy fully enough to them. In particular he failed to get across the necessity for treating the whites well, and this became the basis of a rebellion by his nephew Moise (November 1800). L'Ouverture had Moise and 2,000 of those who rebelled with him executed.

At all stages, L'Ouverture saw himself as the first consul ruling St-Domingue on behalf of revolutionary France, but the first consul in France itself from November 1799 was Napoleon Bonaparte. In the autumn of 1801 France signed a peace with and Britain and Spain. Napoleon's economic policy entailed the restoration of slavery in St-Domingue, which he openly acknowledged would entail killing all the blacks currently there and restocking with new slaves from Africa. This was part of a longer term plan to use St-Domingue as a base for invading north America via Louisiana, which had been returned from Spain to France as part of the peace treaty. He assembled for the first wave of the invasion of St-Domingue a fleet of 86 ships and an army under his brother-in-law General Leclerc. Leclerc's wife, Pauline Bonaparte, travelled with the expedition, with an array of dresses she intended to wear at the balls that would be held in Le Cap once the rabble of ex-slaves caught sight of the French army and surrendered.

As the first ships dropped anchor off Le Cap and Leclerc issued a call to surrender, the general in charge, Henri Christophe, set fire to his mansion with his own hands and, in line with Louverture's orders, supervised the burning of virtually the entire city (4 February 1802).

There followed a war between the two armies, in which the rank and file French soldiers, the most feared in Europe, were astonished at the discipline shown by the blacks, and in particular began to question their role when, at the siege of a fortress called Crete a Pierrot, they heard the black soldiers inside singing French revolutionary songs. The black armies fought the French, by this time beginning to succumb to disease, to a standstill.

The black generals did not see St-Domingue as having a viable future in isolation from revolutionary France. L'Ouverture retired to a plantation which he owned, but then he was captured by a trick and deported to France. The other generals crossed to the French side and for a time their forces were used to hold down a ferocious resistance from below which now sprang up in the form of a guerrilla war conducted by women as well as men across the whole of St-Domingue, a war which the French on their own were clearly losing. Despite this, Leclerc now attempted to arrest the other black generals and disarm their troops. Led by Dessalines and Christophe, along with the mixed race generals and their forces, the black regulars now finally turned on the French. Leclerc himself died in November 1802 from the disease that was wiping out his army. In a despairing letter to his brother-in-law he wrote: "Here is my opinion. You will have to exterminate all the blacks in the mountains, women as well as men, except for children under 12. Wipe out half the population of the lowlands and do not leave in the colony a single black who has worn an epaulette."

The general (Rochambeau) who succeeded Leclerc tried terror tactics. For example, he laid on public entertainments for the colonists in which captured black soldiers, their abdomens opened with sabres, were eaten alive by dogs imported from Cuba. But this could not halt the effects of disease on his army nor did it weaken the forces lined up against him. L'Ouverture died of deliberate neglect in prison in the Alps in April 1803, but in May war resumed between France and Britain, and on the 18th, at a conference in Arcahaye, Dessalines produced a red and blue flag (ie a French revolutionary tricouleur with the white removed) and with the words "Liberty or Death" replacing "RF" ("Republique Francaise"). On 16 November the black and mulatto forces under Dessalines concentrated for a final assault on the remnants of Rochambeau's army, now bottled up in Le Cap. When Dessalines threatened to bombard the city with red-hot shot (28 November), Rochambeau surrendered, and the next day, along with his remaining 4,000 (out of an original 30,000) troops and 4,000 French civilians, he was evacuated by British ships to Jamaica.

The departure of the French forces was followed by the partition of St-Domingue into a south under mixed race leadership and a black north, where Dessalines was in power. Massacring the remaining whites, he declared St-Domingue independent of France in 1803, giving it in 1804 the name Haiti (from the Arawak meaning land of mountains) and having himself crowned as emperor. Dessalines was assassinated in a mixed race plot in 1806 and eventually succeeded (1811) by Christophe. Christophe took measures to provide schools but he also used forced labour to build a massive palace and citadel for himself, and was eventually overthrown in 1820, when a mixed race president, Jean-Pierre Boyer, took power. In 1825, Boyer did a deal with France in which Haiti's independence was recognised in return for a 150m franc indemnity for the losses to French citizens during the revolution This settlement ensured that Haiti would remain in debt to French financiers for most of the 1800s and was followed in 1826 by the Code Rural — a set of laws forcing agricultural workers to stay on the big estates. Boyer fled in 1843, to be succeeded by a long series of other mixed race dictators till 1915 when, following the absorption of Haiti into the US economy as a source of agricultural produce and cheap labour, the US occupied the island until 1934. The first black ruler after Christophe, Jean Claude (Papa Doc) Duvallier, was elected to power in 1957, but soon turned into an even worse dictator, creating a reign of terror based on the so-called Tontons Macoutes and on a debased parody of voodoo arguably standing in a similar relation to the original as Stalinism to Marxism. When Duvallier died in 1971 his son (Baby Doc) succeeded him, only to flee in 1986, when he in turn was succeeded by a military regime under General Namphy. Jean Bertrand Aristide was elected president with popular support on June 1991, overthrown by a military coup on 30 September but then restored by US forces in 1994, remaining in power till now. Haiti has the lowest per capita standard of living on earth, and has undergone severe ecological damage, partly dating from destruction during the revolution and partly as a result of farming methods used since by the corrupt elite. The population, which rose sharply under Dessalines and Christophe, is now about seven million, but there is a very large immigrant group (probably about 800,000 people) in the US, many of whom are educated people that Haiti needs.

The Haitian revolution did not end Atlantic slavery: cane sugar production shifted not only to India, Natal, Mauritius, Fiji, etc., but also to Cuba and Brazil, while Napoleon's sale of "Louisiana" to the US opened the way to the expansion of inland cotton production by slave labour which continued till the American Civil War. On the other hand, Haiti did spread terror throughout slaveholders across the Americas. For example blacks in Bahia, Brazil who rebelled in 1805 wore amulets with images of Dessalines. It was a major turning point in the 400 year struggle in which slavery was abolished primarily by the slaves themselves and only secondarily by reform movements amongst those who profited from it.

Main sources used:

Robin Blackburn, *The Overthrow of Colonial Slavery 1776-1848* (Verso, 1988), *The Making of New World Slavery: From the Baroque to the Modern 1492-1800* (Verso, 1997)

Alejo Carpentier, trans. Harriet de Onis, *The Kingdom of This World* (Penguin Books, 1975)

Basil Davidson, *The African Slave Trade* (Back Bay Books, 1980)

Maya Deren, *The Voodoo Gods* (Paladin, 1975)

C.L.R. James, *The Black Jacobins: Toussaint L'Ouverture and the San Domingo Revolution* (Vintage Books, New York, 1963)

Wenda Parkinson, *"This Gilded African": Toussaint L'Ouverture* (Quartet Books, 1978)

Roger Plant, *Sugar and Modern Slavery: A Tale of Two Countries* (Zed Books Ltd, 1987)

Ronald Segal, *The Black Diaspora* (Faber and Faber, 1995)

James Walvin, *Black Ivory: a History of British Slavery* (Fontana Press, 1992)

OUR HISTORY

French Trotskyist magazines from the 1930s, where they hammered out ideas before the test of World War Two.

The 'Third Camp' in France

YVAN Craipeau, who died at the end of 2001, aged 90, was the first Trotskyist to argue systematically that the Stalinist USSR was not a degenerated workers' state, but a new system of class exploitation. He had been convinced since 1934 that the USSR was no longer a workers' state, and in 1937 he had debated the question with Trotsky in writing. In the myth-ridden orthodox histories of the evolution of Marxist thinking on the USSR (including academic accounts, and Isaac Deutscher's well-known biography of Trotsky), Craipeau's ideas are typically attached to Bruno Rizzi, a maverick and

eccentric who repeated some of them in 1939.

Jean-René Chauvin and Paul Parisot were among his close comrades in the leadership of the French Trotskyist movement, the Parti Communiste Internationaliste (PCI), in the 1940s. They spoke to Martin Thomas about the struggles and debates of that time, and their lessons for today.

Parisot became active as a student socialist in 1934, and joined the Trotskyists in September 1935; Chauvin joined the Trotskyist movement at the end of 1936, from the Gauche Révolutionnaire, a left current in the Socialist Party.

France has long been a central country for the Trotskyist movement. There were quibbles, squabbles, departures, though — even more in France than in other countries where the hard-pressed Trotskyists organised. In 1935 there was a large split. Raymond Molinier, long suspect in the eyes of many of his comrades as a businessman and a political "entrepreneur", full of schemes but short on theory, took a contingent off around a supposedly broad-left paper, La Commune.

Actually La Commune was never anything "broader" than any other Trotskyist paper, and Molinier soon recognised that. But the split was lasting.

During World War 2 the Trotskyists were divided into two main groups. The Molinierists (minus Molinier, who was now in South America) organised the CCI, and denounced the other group, the POI, led by Craipeau and Marcel Hic, for its efforts to integrate concern for the national rights of the French people under Nazi occupation into socialist politics. In February 1944 the groups were reunited; between then and 1948 the Trotskyist movement, called PCI, grew from some hundreds to maybe 1000 strong, and had more impact than it had had before or would have again until 1968.

But the political situation, in France and internationally, was one difficult to orient in, and there were sharp arguments among the Trotskyists. The wing led by Craipeau was regarded as "right-wing" by the other wing — led by some ex-Molinierists, such as Pierre Frank, Jacques Privas, and Pierre Lambert, and some ex-POIers — whom they in turn regarded as sectarians and phrasemongers.

The Frank wing held the leadership until September 1946, and the Craipeau wing from then until November 1947. In 1948, the PCI, buffeted by the Cold War and the Communist Party's demagogic turn to the left, fell apart. Most of the Craipeau wing left in search of broader political frameworks; by mid-1952 the PCI was down to about 150 members, and then it split again. Only small groups were left to struggle through 1968 — which they did, though accumulating much baggage of political confusion on the way.

P: In the 1940s there was a majority in the French Trotskyist movement, undeclared and unorganised, who questioned the theory which Trotsky had continued to defend. We were not convinced, especially after the publication in France of The Revolution Betrayed [by Trotsky, in 1937] that one could talk of a degenerated workers' state in the USSR.

There was no longer any element of a workers' state. What served as the argument for the thesis of the degenerated workers' state was that private property in the means of production and exchange had been replaced by the collective property of the Soviet bureaucracy, so we were divided among supporters of the ideas of state capitalism, or bureaucratic capitalism, or bureaucratic collectivism.

I am still of the same opinion as Craipeau on that subject — that none of these formulations amounts to a programmatic basis. What mattered was our daily activity in France, especially in relation to the Stalinist party. That is why in 1946 we did not push for a debate on the USSR. We wanted to remit the question of the characterisation of the USSR to a serious scientific inquiry. There was one person who did something in that direction — not conclusive, but interesting studies — and that was Charles Bettelheim. Later he became a Maoist [and a very prominent academic figure] but he nevertheless developed a serious critique.

For us the formulation on the USSR was not decisive. What was decisive was to push the Communist Party, first not to disarm the "patriotic militias", and not to accept the deal which De Gaulle [post-war president of France], and then to push the CP and the left of the Socialist Party to support working-class struggles, to which they were very hostile until the episode of spring 1947 of the Renault strike. The CP did not support the strike at first. The Socialist Youth supported it, and the real cause for the expulsion from the Socialist Party of the leading comrades of the Socialist Youth was their support for the strike. Guy Mollet, who had just taken over the leadership of the SFIO [the Socialist Party] expelled them on the pretext of "factional activity by Trotskyists inside the Socialist Youth".

In the end, the split of the Socialist Youth, supported by the Trotskyists, pushed the Communist Party to change its position and to support the Renault strike. The consequence was that Ramadier threw them out of the government and the Communist Party remained excluded from the direction of the country for 34 years. All that did not contribute at all to bringing the Communist Party closer to a revolutionary tactic. On the contrary, it became stuck in an ultra-Stalinism, violent in the forms of struggle — on some demonstrations they took placards made of iron so as to bash the police with them — but with a politics which consisted of trying to get back into government in one form or another.

J-R: In the period that followed, the

Communist Party still considered itself as a party of government. The Russians were not content to see the French Communist Party marginalised. They hoped to do in France what they had done in central Europe — to gain control of the state machine, to colonise the state machine in one way or another, rather than to base themselves on the masses. Where they had control, in Toulouse, it was like Poland.

[Given the character of the Communist Party, was it right for revolutionaries to call for the seizure of power by the Communist Party at that time? In 1944-7 the Communist Party was a big force, facing a bourgeois state machine that scarcely existed. The Trotskyists demanded a Communist Party/ Socialist Party government. But if we look at the countries where the CP took power, it was not good for the working class].

J-R: At the time I agreed with that slogan. But on reflection it was a mistake. I was sceptical even at the time as a result of the experience I had had in the concentration camps with Russian prisoners. They had political commissars, and their conduct had nothing in common with socialist politics. I discussed with those of them with whom one could discuss, and they thought that the revolution in France — in Europe, more generally — would happen thanks to the Red Army, without reference to the masses of the people. Of course, I was not able to have very deep discussions with them, and besides I was in the same block as those political commissars only for a short time.

P: On this particular point, I would say that we were making a gamble — if the Communist Party had put itself on the side of the workers' demands, if it had taken the risk of entering into conflict with De Gaulle and a whole section of the bourgeoisie and the petty bourgeoisie around that great centre-right regroupment which was the MRP [the main Establishment party of the time], then the Communists risked creating a situation in which a differentiation would develop even inside the CP. We thought that the mass movement after the war was sufficiently powerful to provoke breaks between Stalinism and the authentically working-class forces. That was the basis for our gamble.

To go back further, what characterised our current and what we did in 1946-7 was an argument which went back right to the start of the war, in 1940, at a time when we were the majority of the little group which would become the Parti Ouvrier Internationaliste (POI). That majority was led by Marcel Hic with the support of David Rousset and a series of very young comrades. The debate between the two groups which subscribed to the Fourth International, the POI and the CCI — essentially, the Molinierists — was about where or not there was a national question in France due to the German occupation. The Molinierists said no, and they pushed their own logic far enough to have comrades doing entry work in a fascist and collaborationist party, the RNP of Déat [originating from a right wing of the Socialist Party]. I should say in fairness that inside the CCI Lambert differentiated himself from their disdain for the national question.

On the other hand, we thought that we should constitute, inside the nebulous current of the Resistance, a group which was working-class and revolutionary but also fought against the occupation. All the discussion just after the Liberation revolved around this argument, and one other problem. Pierre Frank developed a theory according to which capitalism following the Second World War would be incapable of reconstructing Europe, and thus, becoming stuck in impotence and crisis, it would create new revolutionary opportunities. We. on the other hand, saw that the reconstruction had actually begun, not only in France but across Europe, including Germany.

If one speculated on rising difficulties for capitalism and consequent revolutionary opportunities, one would follow the Molinierists; if on the contrary one put that estimate in question — that was at the centre of the congress where we took the majority [in 1946] — then one turned more to the tactic of the united front. It was like the situation the Bolsheviks faced in 1921-2, when Lenin and Trotsky pointed out that there was a certain stabilisation of capitalism — it would not last for ever, but it was there for the moment — and thus one could no longer reject all alliances with social democracy. Radek put it one way when he said to the Germans yes, we must sit at the same table as the assassins of Rosa Luxemburg and Karl Liebknecht. We thought we should follow the ideas of the Third Congress of the Communist International. We had close relations with Shachtman's group at the time. Shachtman stayed in France for a while. He was a remarkable speaker, who could speak in four or five languages, and he won a lot of sympathy among us. In 1945-6, three American leaders came to France, first Shachtman, then Cannon, then Goldman.

While we were the leadership, the party's official position was still that the USSR was a degenerated workers' state. The open, proclaimed break with what had been Trotsky's old doctrine was made by the group which became *Socialisme ou Barbarie*, especially

Claude Lefort and Cornelius Castoriadis. Our opinion was that it was best not to have an official party doctrine, but to continue the discussion.

J-R: Although we were interested by what Castoriadis said theoretically, on the political level he represented quite ultra-left positions. It was difficult to work with his group. They contented themselves with being a group of intellectuals. Later on they posed to themselves the question of activity in the workplaces, but it did not get very far. They remained a group of intellectuals; they developed some interesting ideas but it led to nothing. We knew about the hypothesis of Burnham, which assimilated the extension of the Soviet bureaucratic regime to the growth of managerial layers in Western capitalism. We did not follow that view. We saw Stalinism as something in evolution. It was showing itself even more reactionary when it destroyed the workers' movement in the so-called People's Democracies [of Eastern Europe]. We had a moment of hope at the time of the split between the USSR and Yugoslavia [in 1948]. We thought that maybe in Yugoslavia there was a regeneration of the communist movement. I went to Belgrade as a correspondent for *France-Observateur*. We were well received as Trotskyists by the upper circles, but in the population it was different. There was strong opposition. There were a certain number of discussions in the Yugoslav Communist Party, but when Djilas came out with his critical views, it was all stopped, and the bureaucratic control was reconstituted.

There was industrial self-management, but it was self-management on paper.

P: What decides the character of an economy is not the economic relations, but, in the last analysis, the social relations. The social relations that existed in a country where a small group — or, at the limit, one person, like Stalin — could dispose of all the productive forces define a regime which is not far from capitalism.

We had discussions on Palestine, too, starting in the PSOP [before the war]. In 1945 it became an issue in the organisation that I had spoken in a meeting in defence of a Zionist who was threatened with being hung by the British in Palestine.

J-R: We were for a binational state in Palestine. After we were excluded from the PCI [in 1948], we produced a magazine called *Confrontations Internationales*. It lasted for four issues. The Shachtmanites were involved, and Maximilien Rubel, one of the best French editors of Marx's writings.

P. Craipeau bore the burden of being the artisan of the fusion with the Molinierists in

1944. Later I think he recognised that he had made a serious mistake. At the time of the Liberation [of Paris from the Nazis] the main thing was to get a newspaper. All the groups, large or small, seized a newspaper. But the Molinierists would not do it. They were sectarian.

J-R: The Molinierists had an almost religious position on the USSR as the workers' state...

[But in 1937 they had officially renounced the view that the USSR was a workers' state, returning to it only at the start of the war].

P: It was just an immediate reaction to the break between Molinier and Trotsky.

J-R: Everything was really decided in the course of the Resistance. After that, those groups that did not have arms were marginalised. There had been an underestimation of the national-liberation character of the fight against the Nazis.

P: The Molinierists had a position of rejecting any kind of alliance — neither Washington nor Moscow nor London nor De Gaulle nor anyone at all.

Our tendency failed, essentially, because we were defeated by the Molinierists. The Molinierists conducted a factional struggle everywhere, based on a naive belief in the imminent collapse of Stalinism. The international leadership was on their side. Our tendency was considered to be rightist, because it was a working-class tendency which tried to play a role in the trade unions as they actually were.

The Molinierists were a caricature of Bolshevism — all the faults of Bolshevism with none of the merits.

J-R: After *Confrontations Internationales* I was active in the RDR [Rassemblement Démocratique Révolutionnaire, a "third camp" group launched by David Rousset, Jean-Paul Sartre and others].

P: Everyone went their own way. We were for quitting the nebulous Fourth International, and everyone integrating themselves into the broader workers' or trade-union organisations. I joined up with a newspaper called *Franc-Tireur*, put out mostly by former Communists who had broken with the CP but also including members of Souvarine's circle and an old leader of the PSOP, Jean Rous. We went into the SFIO [Socialist Party] until the Algerian war, then I joined a little group which later became one of the components of what would become the PSU [a left split from the Socialist Party].

J-R: After the RDR, I made contact with the editorial board of *Franc-Tireur*. Then I was in the Nouvelle Gauche, the Union de la Gauche Socialiste, and the PSA, then the PSU.

The sailors' mutiny at Kiel in November 1918, as Germany faced defeat in World War 1, sparked revolution. Workers' councils spread across the country, and the Emperor had to flee. But the sailors, new to politics, listened to the Social Democrat leader Gustav Noske (speaking above), although he had supported the war.

Marx and Engels on war

By Hal Draper

Marx and Engels commented on many conflicts and wars between the great powers of 19th century Europe. In this article Hal Draper demonstrates that their political attitude towards those conflicts was consistently based on advancing, not whichever of the established five great powers seemed the "lesser evil" or more progressive, but what Engels called "the sixth great power... the [workers'] Revolution".

Draper's account is here abridged from appendices in his book, *War and Revolution: Lenin and the Myth of Revolutionary Defeatism* (edited by Ernest Haberkern: Humanities Press, 1996). It forms the second part of a feature, the first part of which was an abridgement from the body of the book which we carried in WL2/1. In that first part Draper discussed Marxist attitudes in World War 1, and showed that the idea that Lenin's polemics of that time establish a new standard Marxist response to wars involving imperialist powers — "revolutionary defeatism" — is false. (A third part of the feature will follow in WL2/3).

The gist of Lenin's stance in World War 1 was that socialists should refuse to support any imperialist camp in the war. They should promote working-class struggle; they should advocate socialist revolution as the way to win a peace without conquests or annexations. Other revolutionaries, such as Rosa Luxemburg and Leon Trotsky, argued essentially the same view without the confusing terminology of "defeatism".

At the outset of the war, Lenin sought to state his opposition to Russian socialists offering any support to Russia's war effort by declaring that the defeat of Russia by Germany would be a lesser evil than Russian victory. He preferred defeat of Russia by Germany. But, then, should the German socialists prefer victory by Germany over Russia? Seeing the snare, Lenin successively redefined "defeatism" until, finally, it meant no more than that Marxists should not let their socialist struggle be limited or restrained by the risk that it might bring on the defeat of their own country. True enough: but quite different from preferring defeat.

After the end of 1916, Lenin dropped the term "defeatism", and it disappeared from Marxist discourse — until it was revived after Lenin's death, by Zinoviev and others, then allies of Stalin, as part of their campaign against Trotsky.

In his polemics during World War 1, Lenin took as good coin the claims of the pro-war, or equivocal, socialists that their line was a continuation of an attitude taken by Marx and Engels, who supposedly decided their stance in wars according to which great power's victory they calculated to be probably the lesser evil. He sought to refute them by claiming that the world had changed since Marx and Engels wrote, mandating the new policy of "revolutionary defeatism". Draper shows that the pro-war socialists' claims were false. The world had indeed changed, but in their time Marx and Engels had advocated the same fundamental independent working-class approach as Lenin himself would advocate in World War One.

WL

The Franco–Prussian war, 1870

ALL authorities have taught for a very long time that a "special Russian position" on the war question was established by Marx, who suffered from a phobia against Tsarist Russia (or maybe just Russia). It is quite true that Marx regarded the Tsarist regime as the main focus of reaction and counterrevolution in the world, and that he thought the Tsarist state had to be fought harder than any other. But it is not true (though repeated a thousand times in authoritative works) that the mature Marx made this anti-Tsarist (or anti-Russian) position the be-all and end-all of his political line on war and peace.

In many cases these authorities are concerned mainly with expressing horror over the call by Marx and Engels (and the German Democratic movement in general) in 1848-1849 for revolutionary war against Russia; for they are evidently unaware that this was explicitly a call for the revolutionary overthrow of the alliance of the Prussian absolutism with the Russian Tsarist knout, and that at that very time Marx used the words "war" and "revolution" interchangeably for this demand.[1] Indubitably Marx would have supported this "war", for it was also the revolution toward which they were oriented.

But while gross incomprehension of Marx's line in the 1848 revolution frequently surfaced in the 1914 debates between pro-war and anti-war socialists, it is important to see how much further the social-patriots went in their concoction of a fable about Marx's war position. We are concerned here to see it through Lenin's eyes, to see how it entered into his thought at the time.

The first article in which Lenin confronted the argument-from-Marx was a polemic he started writing in early 1915 (but did not finish) against the pro-war Menshevik A. Potresov, "Under a False Flag". Here Lenin quoted Potresov's account of what Marx's policy was, and *accepted* it, arguing only that it was no longer valid in the new era of imperialism. Repeatedly it was asserted in this way (assertion and quotation by Potresov, conceded by Lenin) that Marx's basic criterion for support of a war was "the success of which side was more desirable," slightly modified by Lenin only to say "the success of which *bourgeoisie*...". This, asserted Potresov, was how Marx went about it even when both sides were "highly reactionary", and therefore "Marxists too are at present

obliged to make a similar appraisal". In Marx's day, Lenin agreed, "*no other* question could not have been posed at the time..."[2]

In the first article that Lenin published on this subject, in May 1915, he added another facet to this picture of Marx's war policy, as taken over by him from Potresov's and Kautsky's writings, in justification of the pro-war line. Marx, repeated Lenin from these teachers, took sides with one of the belligerents when, despite the will of the socialists, war had become a fact. "That is the main contention and the chief trump card in Kautsky's pamphlet. It is also the stand of Mr Potresov..."[3] This too was accepted as historical fact by Lenin, whose political reply was only this: "The sophistry of this reasoning consists in a bygone period of history being substituted for the present." So the movement was educated to believe, in retrospect, that confronted with two belligerents, however reactionary, Marx and Engels always supported one or the other, on the stated basis. The subsequent generations of Leninists, real or alleged, found Lenin's reply so satisfactory that no one ever asked just where Marx or Engels laid down these categorical principles of war policy, and likewise never asked why no one had ever quoted them.

Indeed, Lenin never asked this. Though he was always concerned to find support for his views in Marx's and Engels' writings (unlike Trotsky, for example), not once and nowhere did Lenin ever purport to cite a source for these magisterial expressions of Marx's views. He never reported that Potresov or Kautsky (or Plekhanov, et al.) had offered such evidence. He simply accepted. The whole structure of what in 1914 was called "Marx's position on war" rested upon a series of unsupported assertions, which no one has ever found in Marx's own work.[4]

But while these alleged principles of policy cannot be found in Marx and Engels, it is not difficult to find numerous examples of how the two thinkers followed courses basically different from these that have been alleged. Instead of the fable that has Marx always asking "the victory of which of the warring bourgeoisies would be better for socialism", we find again and again that Marx asked a very different question: "How can this conflict, before or after war has been declared, be turned to promote or hasten *revolution?*" (More or less the same basic princi-

137

ple that was laid down by the resolution on war of the Stuttgart Congress of the International in 1907, and again at the 1910 Congress.) And again and again Marx or Engels declared against supporting *either* belligerent in a war – even when they specifically recognised one side or another as more "progressive".

There is no doubt that at the outbreak of the Franco-Prussian War in 1870, Marx was pulled in different directions; but the frequent statement (by Lenin among others) that at least in the first period of that war Marx supported the German side as a war of defence against Bonaparte – this is an inaccurate exaggeration. It is based almost solely on the "Address on the War" which Marx wrote for the First International; but it is seldom understood that this address (public statement) was not only ambiguous but was intended to be ambiguous; for it was naturally not put forward as Marx's personal opinion but as the official stand of the International, to be accepted by the French and German sections as well as the British.

Alongside this ambiguous statement were two far more definite ones. The best known of these was Marx's position, stated at the time and subsequently, enthusiastically approving the stand taken in the German Reichstag by Bebel and Liebknecht, refusing to vote for the war credits – precisely in the first period of the war. The significance of this stand can be appreciated especially when one realises that Marx and Engels had to go through a change of mind to get there. Certainly Engels at first condemned the Bebel-Liebknecht vote,[5] perhaps Marx momentarily also. But soon, and for the rest of their lives, Marx and Engels proudly endorsed the anti-war vote, precisely with reference to the first period of the war.

On July 28, still in the first period, Marx wrote on the subject to his daughter, Laura, and her husband, Paul Lafargue, who were active in the French movement. He sounded very "neutralist" indeed: meaning that he refused to give political support to either side. Marx remarked that the war was considered a "national war" *in Germany*, and wrote about that view with acrid cynicism, without a word of approval; "on both sides", he grunted, "it is a disgusting exhibition". The only consolation was "that the workmen protest in Germany as in France". This war "will produce results not at all expected by the 'officials' on both sides". Bebel and Liebknecht "behaved exceedingly well in the Reichstag". And finally (writing in rough English):

"For my own part, I should like that both, Prussians and French, thrashed each other

alternately, and that – as I believe will be the case – the Germans got ultimately the better of it."

Even this mild preference was not motivated by the claimed principle about progressive bourgeoisies. What Marx stated as the reason had solely to do with the dialectics of defeat and revolution: "I wish this, because the definite defeat of Bonaparte is likely to provoke revolution in France, while the defeat of the Germans would only protract the present state of things for 20 years." In England, Marx told the Lafargues, the workers "hate Bonaparte", but –

"At the same time they say: 'The plague on both your houses'... For my own part, I do everything in my power, through the means of the International, to stimulate this 'Neutrality' spirit..."[6]

There it was: refusal to vote war credits, mutual defeat, "neutrality", and "a plague on both their houses" – but the only sentiment usually quoted is the completely overshadowed preference that Germany "ultimately" defeat France because of its objective consequences. *But for Marx this was not the equivalent of a statement of political position*; it was exactly what it said it was, namely, a statement about objective consequences regardless of political policy.

So even as early as 1870, and in regard to a war with some "national" coloration in its early days, Marx's considerations turned out to be: not based on "progressive" bourgeoisies, but on the revolutionary calculus; not based on a choice between belligerents, but on the mutual defeat and revolutionisation of *both* sides.

We only want the Earth

Global capitalism and the environmental crisis

£1.50 plus 44p postage from AWL, PO Box 823, London SE15 4NA

The Crimean war, 1854-6

BUT Marx's real "phobia" is alleged to have been Russia, and especially in 1914 the crux was, naturally, defencism in a war alleged to be for democracy and civilisation against Tsarist absolutism. We are told, indeed, that Marx simply yearned to support war, any war, against Russia – just as Scheidemann and Ebert did in 1914; and Lenin's only reply was (in effect) that times and politics had changed. To this day, the Authorities' books are full of this myth.

Well, by 1853, Marx had a splendid opportunity to support a war against Tsarist Russia. This war was mainly fought by the most advanced and "progressive" governments in Europe, namely England and France, against that most hateful of autocracies. Marx and Engels wrote voluminously about it for two years and more in the *New York Daily Tribune* articles and in letters. Here is the place to find Marx definitely supporting a war against his bête noire...

But this cannot be found, because it never happened. Marx did not support the war of the Western powers against Russia in the Crimean War. He wrote this down repeatedly, but has not succeeded in getting any of these statements quoted by the Authorities. Instead they cite his usual imprecations against Tsarist crimes and turpitude. Also, Marx and Engels were always willing to explain, in the columns of the *NYDT*, why the English bourgeoisie, from the standpoint of its interests, should stiffen its opposition to Russian policy. But in no case did this mean they were promising their support (or that of the working class) to a war fought for said interests.

"England cannot afford to allow Russia to become the possessor of the Dardanelles and Bosphorus," Engels told his *NYDT* readers, as military analyst (which was the capacity in which Marx sent these articles to editor Dana in his own name). But at the end of this same article, Engels (writing for Marx) stated his own views. Today, he stressed, the chief antagonist of the Russian regime is not any of the Western Powers.

"We mean the European Revolution, the explosive force of democratic ideas and man's native thirst for freedom." This Revolution will roll over both war camps. There are now "in reality but two powers on the continent of Europe – Russia and Absolutism, and the Revolution and Democracy".[7]

This concept – counterposing the European revolution to the European war, in a way not emulated by the Second International until the Lenin-Luxemburg-Martov amendment was added to the main resolution on war in 1907 and 1910 – was repeated by Marx and Engels in article after article throughout the year 1853.[8] In early 1854 the language became even more dramatic. One of Engels' analyses of the military strength of the Powers ended with the counterposition of the Revolution to all the Powers:

"But we must not forget that there is a sixth power in Europe, which at given moments asserts its supremacy over the whole of the five so-called "great" powers and makes them tremble, every one of them. That power is the Revolution. Long silent... awaking from its slumbers... A signal only is wanted, and this sixth and greatest European power will come forward... This signal the impending European war will give..."[9]

There was not a word compatible with the notion that workers should support the war of the established Powers against Russia. Perhaps one should support the war by Turkey? Marx left no room for the thought: in the case of Turkey too only the Revolution was a viable choice.

"The Sultan holds Constantinople only in trust for the Revolution... The Revolution which will break the Rome of the West will also overpower the demoniac influences of the Rome of the East."[10]

If anyone had the idea of ranging Turkey among the bearers of civilisation, that country would itself have to be remade, transformed, and this too would mean nothing less than the Revolution.

"Can any one be credulous enough to believe in good earnest that the timid and reactionary valetudinarians of the present British Government have even conceived the idea of undertaking such a gigantic task, involving a perfect social revolution, in a country like Turkey? The notion is absurd."[11]

Marx was most brash and direct in repudiating any support to the war against Russia by the advanced bourgeoisies of Britain and France. In an article of 24 June 1854, Marx criticised a speech by Kossuth. For one thing Kossuth had threatened that Hungary might ally itself with Russia if England allied itself with Austria. This obviously was sure to draw Marx's fire.

And then Marx attacked a bisymmetric error: it was equally a mistake [by Kossuth] to describe the war against Russia as a war between liberty and despotism.

"Apart from the fact that if such be the case, liberty would be for the nonce represented by a Bonaparte, the whole avowed object of the war is the maintenance of the balance of power and of the Vienna treaties – those very treaties which annul the liberty and independence of nations."[12]

Here Marx applied to the war the same methodology that Lenin worked out in 1914: namely, what politics was this war a continuation of? What was the war being fought for – not in slogans but in socioeconomic fact?

An article by Marx of 27 April 1855 brings us back to our starting point, Marx's starting point: the "sixth power" or third camp – the Revolution. Reviewing the war, he explained that the British bourgeoisie had begun by being enthusiastically in favour of the anti-Russian war, but cooled down considerably as it began to affect their purses. As against these motivations of the ruling classes he counterposed the social alternative: power to the working class.

"With regard to the political positions taken by the working class in Britain and France – the main point, with them, is this: that this war, coinciding with a commercial crisis... conducted by hands and heads unequal to the task, gaining at the same time European dimensions, will and must bring about events which will enable the proletarian class to resume that position which they lost, in France, by the battle of June 1848 [the "June uprising"], and that not only as far as France is concerned, but for all Central Europe, England included."[13]

No-one has ever documented a word of political support by Marx to the alliance of the Western Powers against Tsarist Russia in the Crimean War; but on the other hand, we have by no means touched on all the aspects of Marx's statements of an opposite character. Marx's line on the Crimean War was 100% in line with the 1907-1910 anti-war resolution of the International, including the Lenin-Luxemburg amendment. Through it all, Marx noted now and then something that was ABC in terms of revolutionary politics:... things are clearly seething and fermenting and we can only hope that great disasters in the Crimea will bring them to a head.[14] Or as it was also put frequently enough: defeats facilitate revolution.

Engels' last words on looming world war

The last years of Engels' life – for convenience we can consider the dozen years by which Engels outlived Marx – coincided with a period of rapid growth of the imperialist tensions that were going to lead to the first world slaughter. It grew clear to all that a great world war was looming in the near future; and there was no-one who warned against the coming catastrophe as often and as cogently as Engels. The following, written by Engels, is perhaps the best known:

"And in the end, for Prussia-Germany no other war is possible any longer except a world war, and indeed a world war of an extensiveness and fierceness undreamt of up to now. Eight to 10 million soldiers will be at each others' throats and thereby strip all Europe bare as no swarm of locusts has ever done. The devastation of the Thirty Years War... famine, pestilence, general degeneration of civilisation... irremediable disorganisation of our artificial machinery... ending in general bankruptcy; breakdown of the old states and their traditional state wisdom, such that crowns by the dozens will be rolling in the streets and no-one will pick them up; absolute impossibility of foreseeing how all this will end and who will emerge the victor... general exhaustion and the establishment of conditions for the ultimate victory of the working class. This is the prospect... And when there is nothing else left for you except to start the final great war dance, that will be all right with us. The war may perhaps push us into the background temporarily; it may take away from us many positions we had previously won. But when you have unleashed forces that you will never again be able to get under control, then let events take their course: at the end of the tragedy you will be ruined and the victory of the proletariat will either have been achieved or anyway will be inevitable."[15]

A couple of weeks after writing the above passage, and indeed about the time it was coming off the press, Engels spelled his views out so that no one could make a mistake. The new Romanian socialist movement had asked him to write for its new magazine, *Contemporanul*, published in Jassy, and as usual Engels complied. He sent a survey of the state of Europe as it faced world war. Before citing the conclusion of this survey-letter, we must make perfectly clear that it was as toughly anti-Tsarist as ever; there was not the slightest evidence of any increasing softness about the Russian autocracy: "Since Russia enjoys a strategic position almost

German and Russian troops fraternising during the First World War. Revolutionary socialists in both countries debated how best to oppose the war effort.

impervious to conquest, Russian Tsarism forms the core of this alliance ['the old Holy Alliance of the three assassins of Poland'], the great reserve of all European reaction. To overthrow Tsarism, to destroy this nightmare that weighs on all Europe – this is, in my eyes, the first condition for the emancipation of the nationalities of the European centre and east." And a good deal more of the same, such as he had written all his political life.

Did this mean, to Engels himself, that workers should give political support to war by the "progressive" Allies against this reservoir of world reaction? Not a bit. The statement ended with the following political conclusion, in view of the fact that war seemed "imminent":

"I hope that peace will be maintained; in such a war, one could not sympathise with any of the combatants; on the contrary one would wish them all to be beaten if that were possible."

We are back, or still with, the "plague on both their houses" approach of 1870, and, before that, with the support given only to the "sixth power" or third camp in the Crimean War. Engels' statement ended with a repetition of the idea that the war would be terrible, but it would lead in the end to the socialist revolution.[16]

The idea of the defeat of all sides in a war was going to be mooted in 1914; but no one quoted Engels' trenchant epistle to the Romanians of January 1888. It was in effect buried, and has remained effectually buried for a century, while Authorities filled books with assertions that the Marx-Engels view was its opposite.

But this demonstration of Engels' war-and-peace politics of the last period is not yet complete; and there was another facet that seemed to look in a different direction. This was the large loophole that Engels – along with the entire socialist movement – left for support of war by one's own government: in case of invasion or attack by a predatory power, socialists had to be concerned with the defence of the nation in the name of national self-preservation. (This knotty problem was not adequately analysed from the standpoint of Marxist politics until Luxemburg did so in her Junius Pamphlet of 1915.) In 1891-1892 Engels published, in both France and Germany, a statement that attempted to cover this question in the light of the looming war, through an article titled "Socialism in Germany".[17] Whereas the main facts about Marx's and Engels' war policy have met with much silence and suppression, this article by Engels was well publicised in the movement, and lives on – in selected quotes – through the works of the "marxological" Authorities.

This is not the place to detail the background and content of the article, but there is no difficulty in understanding how it could be used in 1914 to vindicate "defencism". Yet it could be so used only by maintaining silence and suppression about two features of his explanation which Engels tried in vain to make clear and unmistakable.

1. Very far from Engels' thinking was a "defence of the nation" in which the socialists declared the class struggle suspended, as was the universal interpretation of the defencists of 1914, in the concept called *"Burgfrieden"* (civil peace). Engels' idea, as he made very clear more than once, was just the reverse: the socialists could really defend the nation "only by the application of revolutionary measures". But it was not the present government that would "unleash the

revolution". It was the Social-Democratic Party's job to see that this was done, either by forcing the present government to take revolutionary steps, "or, if need be, [it] can replace it". Thereupon Engels referred to the great historical example of what he had in mind: "The splendid example that France gave us in 1793." Engels' concept was that, *in the very course of taking the lead in the nation to save it against the hated autocracy,* the socialist movement would force the carrying on of the war as a revolutionary war.[18]

2. This "defence of the nation" repudiated the idea that socialists should wish for victory by any of the present ruling classes. Engels stated this so expressly that no one could misinterpret, and so his statement is not usually misinterpreted — it is simply not quoted. What he wrote was this, as part of a pithy summary laying down his position in ABC terms:

> "No socialist, whatever his nationality may be, can desire the military triumph either of the present German government or of the French bourgeois republic, least of all that of the Tsar, which would mean the subjugation of Europe."[19]

The reader must recall that the revolutionary precedent of 1793 not only urged socialists to take over the reins of power, but also taught the great lesson that "defeats facilitate revolution". That principle was much older than 1793, as a matter of fact, and so when we run into it again, we must not think it was a new invention called defeatism.

The idea that war's stresses made for revolt by the people was as old an idea as any in the socialist movement. When Lenin referred to it on the eve of the First World War, in 1913, it was uncontroversial. He was writing to Gorky about the probable position of the Polish Socialist Party (PPS, a right-wing Social-Democratic party opposed to Luxemburg's):

> "The PPS are undoubtedly for Austria and will fight for her. A war between Austria and Russia would be a very useful thing for the revolution (throughout Eastern Europe), but it's not very probable that Franz Josef [the Hapsburg emperor] and Nicky [the Tsar] will give us this pleasure."[20]

1. Instead of citing a long list of articles of this period by Marx and Engels, we select one for quick confirmation: Marx's "The Revolutionary Movement", published in Marx's paper on the first day of 1849, as a summary of the situation; in MECW [Marx-Engels Collected Works] 8:213-15.
2. Lenin, "Under a False Flag" (not published until 1914), LCW [Lenin Collected Works] 21:139-40, p. 148.
3. Lenin, "The Social-Chauvinists' Sophisms", pub-

lished 1 May, 1915; LCW 21:185. For a similar passage, see the pamphlet (by Lenin and Zinoviev but mainly Lenin) *Socialism and War*, in LCW 21:308.
4. What Kautsky and others did, by and large, was offer their accounts of the wars of the nineteenth century that Marx discussed, work out their interpretations, and then assert that these interpretations were Marx's. Here I am interested only in stressing what went to form Lenin's thinking on the war question in the early stages of the war.
5. Engels to Marx, 15 August 1870, in MEW [Marx-Engels Werke] 33:39-41.
6. Marx to Paul and Laura Lafargue, 28 July 1870; original, in Marx's rough English, is here transcribed from Marx: *Lettres et Documents de Karl Marx*, pp. 177-79.
7. Engels: "The Real Issue in Turkey", *NYDT*, 12 April 1853, in MECW 12:13, p. 17.
8. See especially the following five articles which, for the sake of space, are here identified by their initial pages in MECW 12:22, 93, 101, 209, 421.
9. Engels: "The European War", *NYDT*, 2 February 1854, in MECW 12:557.
10. Marx: "Financial Failure of Government...", *NYDT*, 12 August 1853, MECW 12:231.
11. Marx: "The Greek Insurrection", *NYDT*, 29 March 1854, in MECW 13:72.
12. Marx: "Reorganisation of the British War Administration...", *NYDT*, 24 June 1854, in MECW 13:228.
13. Marx: "Prospect in France and England", *NYDT*, 27 April 1855, in MECW 14:145.
14. Marx to Engels, 3 July 1855, in MECW 39:541.
15. Engels: Introduction to Borkheim's pamphlet *Zur Erinnerung für die deutschen Mordspatrioten, 1806-1807*, in MEW 21:350f; dated by Engels 15 December 1887.
16. Engels to Nadejde, 4 January 1888, published in *Contemporanul* (Jassy), January issue, translated into Roumanian by the magazine. Engels had sent it in French; extant is his (first?) draft in French. The German translation in MEW 37:6 was made from the Roumanian text checked with the French draft; my English translation is based on the French draft checked against the MEW version; but no substantive differences are visible among any of these versions. I am indebted to the Institute of Marxism-Leninism in Berlin (GDR) for sending me copies of both the *Contemporanul* publication and a typescript of the French draft.
17. The article was first written (October 1891) and published (December 1891) in French, in an almanac of the French party; then somewhat enlarged for German publication next February. The German version can be found in MEW 22:245-60; there is an English translation, not always reliable, in the appendix of Henderson's *Life of F. Engels*, 2:796+.
18. Note that this was not the same as the conception of Karl Liebknecht in 1914 (adopted by Lenin), tagged with the slogan "Turn the imperialist war into civil war!" even though in both cases the objective of the socialists was to utilise the war crisis to take power. Whether Engels' perspective was feasible, in 1891 or any other time, is a subject for debate. But this debate would have nothing to do with the myth that Engels' kind of "defencism" was akin to that of the prowar social-democrats of the First World War.
19. This passage can be read in MEW 22:256; the preceding quote, about 1793 (etc.), is on p. 255.
20. Lenin to Gorky, written after 25 January 1913; in LCW 35:76.

FORUM

One way forward: one state

I AGREE with and have learned much from the analysis of Zionism and anti-Semitism in the *WL* pamphlet *Two Nations, Two States*. However I do not think that the two state "solution" (or even interim solution) is the necessary political consequence of the analysis. I would make the following points in the spirit of contributing to a debate:

You are right in arguing that the exceptionalism with which most of the left treats the Israeli state is anti-Semitic. The grossest example of this are the pickets of Marks and Spencer on account of its assumed Jewish ownership. However, Zionism, the ideology which justifies the state, is genuinely exceptional.

I know of no other ideology which possesses an internal contradiction of such magnitude whereby it encompasses its own polar opposites. Zionism is both racist and anti-racist. Hence the reason it understandably provokes such extreme reactions on both sides.

It is, at least in its triumphant form, undoubtedly racist towards the Palestinians. Even within the pre 1967 borders Palestinians are manifestly second class citizens. At the same time Zionism is anti-racist in that it presents itself as an answer, the answer, to centuries of pogroms culminating in the holocaust. As Marxists we would have wished all this otherwise and (as a few did) fought accordingly. We would have wished and fought to try and ensure that the European labour movement had smashed Nazism and prevented the holocaust. We would have wished and fought in Palestine for combined action by Palestinian and Jewish workers against their own reactionary leaderships and the British mandate authority. However though we can learn from history we cannot roll it back or pretend it never happened. The result today is the Zionism of contradiction.

In my view the creation of two states – formed not through workers' solidarity but through the coming together of Bush, Blair, Sharon and Arafat – would in all likelihood simply increase, if that were possible, this contradiction. Far from being a bridgehead for workers unity it would cement the existing divisions between Jew and Palestinian. It would be a recipe for perpetual war (the analogy with Pakistan and India is apposite). This would not only fail to roll back history. It would repeat it with a vengeance.

I think *WL* is absolutely correct in supporting in retrospect the right of Jews fleeing the impending holocaust to have had right of entry into the then Palestine ("the law of return"). Any other position would have meant siding not only with the reactionary Arab leadership and the British mandated forces – it would in effect have meant siding with the Nazis.

To argue, as is sometimes argued today against Zionism and Zionism alone, that it is somehow an absolute principle of socialism that the oppressed should remain and fight in their place of oppression – even after defeat – would in fact result in the denial of support for all asylum seekers whatever their origin and whatever their country of destination. To use such an argument against Jews fleeing Nazism amounts not so much to immigration control as a bizarre form of emigration control. It is exceptionalism. It is anti-Semitism.

However, once it is acknowledged that Jews had and have a right to enter Palestine/Israel, then it seems to me politically and morally obvious that Palestinians should have exactly the same right. Such a Palestinian law of return is already denied by the present state of Israel. This denial would be consolidated and enshrined by the creation of two states.

Workers Liberty's denial of this Palestinian right is completely illogical. You state that "...the proposal for the Arab 'right of return' is a proposal for people who have never lived there to 'repossess' Israel from people born there". However the original Zionists had far less connection (in fact they had no connection) with Palestine/Israel than the majority of today's Palestinians many of whom, and most of whose families, were indeed born there.

I guess *WL* would argue that the situation of Jews fleeing Nazism would not be the same as that for Palestinians once an independent Palestinian state exists – as the Palestinians would not be refugees fleeing persecution. However this raises a far broader question – that of immigration controls.

WL is opposed to all immigration controls. I agree. However opposition to all controls means refusing to accept any distinction between refugees and other migrants or immigrants. No controls means freedom of movement for all. Otherwise you end up accepting the reactionary distinction between "genuine" and "bogus" entrants.

Actually within the context of the proposed two states WL substitutes another equally invalid and parallel contradiction – namely that between the right of "individual" Palestinian immigration into Israel, which you support, and the right of "collective" immigration – which you oppose on the grounds this would undermine the Jewish Israeli "common identity". Leave aside for now the highly problematic notion of what is meant, if anything, by a "Jewish nation" with a "common identity". The point here is that this allegation about the undermining of identity is exactly the same as that used by racists in this country to oppose all immigration.

If WL genuinely believed immigration controls against a "collective" Palestinian right of return to be progressive in the context of the new partitioned Israel then the logic would be for your comrades and supporters to help police the borders of the two states and act as immigration officers (or more realistically as army officers). Count me out – I'd go AWOL.

The logic of your emphasis on a "common identity" for Israelis and thus your support for two states has some pretty horrific consequences. First, it would presumably require forced population movement – which would make the present involuntary dispersal scheme under British asylum law seem benign by comparison. I was shocked to read in your pamphlet that the Israeli left is prepared for a "negotiated" number of Palestinians to be "resettled" in Israel. You say "such measures are surely desirable".

In my view they are absolutely undesirable. What about the Palestinians whom the left in its wisdom and arrogance decides not to "negotiate" for resettlement? It seems to me what you are supporting here is a Middle Eastern equivalent of "fair" immigration controls – which is hardly fair to those remaining subject to controls.

Second, any "settlement" based on demographics is both reactionary and doomed. What in your view would happen to the two state solution (and the Israeli "common identity") if the Palestinian birth rate in Israel itself lead to a Palestinian majority? I guess the Israeli right would propose expulsion or forced sterilisation.

There are many other arguments against the creation of two exclusivist states. Not the least of such arguments is the physical separation of Gaza and the West Bank – look what happened to the attempt to form a similarly exclusivist entity out of West and East Pakistan.

I do not underestimate the huge problems in forging the political alliances necessary to create a single state which would allow for a socialist alternative to the present impasse. However there is something quite bizarre about the whole two state notion as far as the Palestinians are concerned. It is like a person being deliberately blinded in one eye (1948) then in the other eye (1967) and now being offered blurred vision as a compromise.

Steve Cohen

The politics of the Grand Vizier

ONE of the things which I find attractive about WL is its insistence on the importance of what it calls independent working class politics and I call a class line. All too often, however, this perspective disappears when it is applied to practical questions of war and peace. Instead of independent working class politics, we get Grand Vizier politics. I will discuss the Forum article on East Timor by Roger Clarke from WL 2/1, written as a criticism of the WL position on East Timor, because it is a textbook example of the problem. I believe, however, that the WL position itself shares a similar flaw.

"Grand Vizier politics" is a term I've chosen for the phenomenon of an organisation in the workers' movement using its visibility (such as it is) to advise a government, usually the one of the country in which it is located, what it should do to solve a problem which the organisation sees. Whatever mobilisation of the working class may be involved in this approach is, at bottom, merely to allow the Grand Vizier to advise the correct policy to the ruler more compellingly. It is very far removed from independent working class politics. Instead, it sees the State as a relatively uncomplicated instrument which can be used by the working class for its ends provided sufficient pressure is applied.

This is not to say that we should not make any demands on the ruling class at all. This would be a retreat into the sterile politics of "revolution and nothing but". Rather, we need to make a distinction between demands which serve independent working class politics and those which do not. The distinction is basically between demands for the State or the ruling class to perform (or not perform) certain clearly defined acts which leave the working class with greater freedom of action and demands for the State to adopt a different policy. Further, demands for specific acts should be avoided if it can be clearly seen that these actions, if conceded by the State, would be performed as part of a reactionary policy of its own. Examples of appropriate demands are "Troops out of the West Bank" or "6% rise with no trade offs". An example of Grand Vizier demands would be "Double the foreign aid budget".

In his article, Roger makes a number of problematical points, but probably the most important was when he agreed with the statement:

"This is not advice. Socialists should simply say what we want done."

Certainly we should say what we want done. The crucial question, however, is "By whom?" Are we revolutionaries speaking to the working class and arguing for a working class solution to the problems we see, or are we the Grand Vizier, telling the ruler what he should do? Independent working class politics require that it be the former, but Roger's article is all about the latter — and could not be otherwise, given his advocacy of sending Australian military forces to East Timor.

A working class response to the East Timor crisis would have recognised the concrete situation and what the various capitalist states and parties were doing and/or would do and then sought to mobilise the working class for its own solution. Given that the forces we would mobilise for this were very small and our influence was thus very limited, we had an added responsibility to advance our solution in a way which did not affect the machinations of the capitalist states and parties so as to increase the probability of a worse outcome than if we had not acted at all.

There were four broad outcomes to the East Timor crisis of 1999 which were possible at the time:

1. The workers of Australia and Indonesia unite around a program of recognising the result of East Timorese self determination and, by strikes, demonstrations and boycotts, compel their respective governments to do likewise. The labour movements of both Australia and Indonesia rise to a new plane.

2. The Indonesian government, bowing to international pressure and unstable in its own right, accepts a UN-authorised military force (in the circumstances, inevitably dominated by Australia) to supervise Indonesian withdrawal and clean up the remnants of its militia. East Timor effectively comes under Australian domination. Any demand that the "peacekeepers" act as allies of the East Timorese rather than overlords is a particularly deluded fantasy born of Grand Vizier politics at its worst.

3. The Indonesian army and its puppet militia continue their rampage in East Timor until the entire country is terrorised into silence and submission. In the course of achieving this, Dili and many other places would be sacked and burnt.

4. The Australian government invades East Timor without approval either from the UN or Indonesia. The worst fears of insecure Indonesian nationalists are apparently confirmed and a wave of nationalist fervour sweeps the country. The Indonesian military seizes its chance and takes control, proceeding to round up and shoot the Left. A bloody war in East Timor ensues, with Australian military training and hardware confronted by much more numerous Indonesian soldiers and shorter Indonesian supply lines. The death toll (both in Timor and within Indonesia) hits five figures, maybe six.

As can be seen, the scenarios are set out in descending order of desirability. Working class revolutionaries should have been advocating #1, since it is the only scenario consistent with independent working class politics. In the course of our agitation, we would, like the rest of the Left, have taken opposition to #3 as our starting point, but should also have fought vigorously against #4 and put our opposition to #2 on the record. On the other hand, Roger's article indicates that revolutionaries should have advocated #2. Since he was willing to accept an Australian invasion in the event of #2 not eventuating, #4 would have followed in those circumstances. #1 doesn't even enter into his calculations.

It can also be seen that arming the Timorese (a call a version of which was adopted by WL) was not mentioned. This is because even with all the guns they could handle, Falantil was never going to be a match for the Indonesian military. The disproportion of forces was just too great. Further, this demand begs the question, not only of *who* was going to arm them, but of *how*. Timor is, after all, an island, and half of it is undisputed Indonesian territory. Nobody except the Australian military was in a position to arm the Timorese and transferring any more than a minimal amount of weaponry would have been impossible to keep secret. Military confrontation with Indonesia was therefore probable and we would have been on the road to scenario #4, albeit in a way from which it would be easier to pull back.

Was an internationalist working class campaign possible? Yes. Not only was it possible, but it happened. Australia Asia Worker Links, an organisation of individual members and affiliated unions, agitated in the labour movement in Australia, Indonesia and across the Asia Pacific region for workers' action to compel the Indonesian government to withdraw their troops. As well as encouraging the unions in Australia to take the strongest possible action and publicising the action they did take, AAWL worked with the independent union federations in Indonesia to build support for the campaign there.

Both significant independent union federations in Indonesia, SBSI and FNPBI, were calling for an Indonesian withdrawal and the entry of a UN force. Further, support for East Timorese self determination was a touchstone on the Indonesian Left and was a key issue separating the political elites (including their "opposition" members) from the grassroots opposition, which included the workers' movement. By building support for this campaign in both countries, AAWL was contributing to making scenario #3 unsustainable, while also maximising the small chance that East Timor could be rescued without falling into the clutches of Australian imperialism. If other working class organisations had also seen the Indonesian workers' movement as our key ally in this campaign (i.e. they had been *internationalist*), the chance of success would have been somewhat greater than it was.

In this context, three arguments in Roger's article need disputing. They are that Australia was not acting as an imperialist country in its intervention in East Timor; that the wishes of the East Timorese leadership should have been respected; and that there was no realistic prospect of war between Australia and Indonesia.

In the first place, Australia does not become any less of an imperialist country when it changes its policy on East Timor. Rather, both the alliance with Indonesia at the expense of East Timor and the decision to intervene in East Timor were driven by imperialist dynamics. Australia and Indonesia, being significant countries and next door to each other, cannot bypass each other like ships in the night. They must be either friends or enemies, and there are advocates of both camps within the capitalist class in Australia.

For most of the time since Indonesian independence, the dominant opinion in the Australian bourgeoisie has been in favour of an alliance with Indonesia. This has entailed turning a blind eye to the murderous appetites of the Indonesian military in East Timor, West Papua and Aceh, as well as providing active assistance to the genocidal slaughter of the Left in 1965. The benefits have been considerable, with the Timor Gap Treaty of Gareth "Blood for Oil" Evans being only the most visible. Probably more important has been the fact that, with Indonesia onside, Australia is virtually impregnable from a military perspective. Only the United States would have the capacity to threaten Australia militarily.

The contrary opinion, however, also has its adherents within the capitalist class. These people decry the thuggish behaviour of the Indonesian military and want to take the government to task over human rights. Amongst the working class, this attitude is entirely healthy, but a different logic is at work in the bourgeoisie. The bourgeois critics of Indonesia in Australia are the war party. Because their only way of gaining concrete results from their criticisms is by exerting the economic and military might of Australian capitalism, the logic of their policies leads to ever-deepening confrontation. As a sign of what lies at the end of this road, a prominent broadsheet newspaper article at the time of the East Timor crisis blithely proposed that Indonesia be dismembered to stop the Javanese-chauvinist Indonesian military oppressing the other ethnic groups across the archipelago. The author did not explore the method by which this dismemberment might be achieved and the suggestion went, to my knowledge, unremarked.

Secondly, Roger attaches great importance to the fact that the East Timorese leadership requested UN troops. *Of course* they would – you can't expect petit bourgeois nationalists to call for a working class response, at least these days. It should also be remembered that during the 80s the Left was purged from the leadership of the East Timorese resistance, most probably at the insistence of the Catholic Church. The working class, on the other hand, must not tail these forces. If we come to the aid of a struggle for self-determination, we must do so on our terms and using our own methods of struggle. And, as a final argument on this point, I can't imagine the East Timorese liberation movement disowning a struggle, in the event that it occurred, linking the Australian and Indonesian working classes in support of Indonesian military withdrawal. To the extent that AAWL's work had any impact, it was to hurry the Indonesian withdrawal and also reduce the reliance of the East Timorese movement on Australian imperialism.

The final disagreement I have with Roger's article is on an even more significant matter. He drastically downplays the prospect of war in the event that an Australian force invaded East Timor in the face of opposition from the Indonesian government. Indeed, he even says "How to face down Indonesia and avoid a war was the government's problem". This is not so much the politics of the Grand Vizier as of Pontius Pilate!

In fact, the Howard government is probably the least likely candidate for managing a crisis with Indonesia since that country became independent. And a war would definitely have been the most probable outcome, since it would have served the internal purposes of the Indonesian military to a tee.

Twice already they have attempted the physical liquidation of the Left, in 1948 and 1965, and both times it has been done amidst cries of treason.

In 1999 the military were deeply discredited and retreating in disarray, but the nationalistic fervour which would have gripped Indonesia if Australia invaded East Timor (and remember that most Indonesians outside the Left knew little or nothing about how it was acquired, so would have had no basis for seeing through the official lies) would have catapulted the military back into command. Once in command, of course, they would have taken their bloody revenge. Whatever the intentions of the working class forces advocating an invasion, the result would have been a bloodbath. It was the worst possible outcome.

"A bloke I met"

The medium and the message

I AGREE with John Cunningham (WL 2/1) about many of the points he makes about cinema: that particular techniques have been misrepresented as progressive, and that attempts to create an alternative "political" cinema have been failures. However, he is completely missing the point about "modes of perception".

His account is based on confusing perception (the way in which the world seems to a particular person) with sensation (the physical input of images through the senses). These are related, but separate; perception is not reducible in any mechanical way to sensation.

John's claim that "There is no evidence that the way we perceive the world changes other than by a slow, evolutionary process" is simply wrong. He has a point if we limit the discussion to sensation (though even here, senses such as sight, sound and touch are now frequently modified by technology; cinema for instance allows us to look at a flat screen yet nevertheless see a three-dimensional image). But there is another dimension to perception.

The evidence John asks for comes from cross-cultural psychological and anthropological studies of perception, i.e., how things seem to people. To take a few examples: one study around the turn of the last century found that the ability to see a specific image in a two-dimensional photograph is cultural-

ly specific. People in some isolated areas of Switzerland were unable to recognise themselves in photographs. The reason for this is that seeing an image of a face in a photograph is not merely a matter of sensation (seeing the physical photograph), but also involves a process of interpretation ("translating" the small two-dimensional image into a representation of a larger, three-dimensional face). This ability is not inherited or evolved; it is learnt, and therefore varies between cultures.

Another study examined an African tribe who lived exclusively in enclosed environments (forests), so they rarely saw anything from a distance: the trees around them obscured anything which was not physically close to them, so they did not have to assess their distance from an object. This study found that members of the tribe did not acquire the ability to perceive distance. For instance, when taken out of the forest, they thought distant objects were near, and reached out to touch them; and they thought approaching vehicles were actually growing larger before their eyes. People who have learnt distance perception do it so automatically that it seems natural to them, but it is actually a learnt form of perception (not sensation), specific to some cultures and absent in others.

Another set of examples come from the Gestalt school of psychology. These studies found that, if you show someone a picture which is incomplete, they "imagine" it to be a complete picture. For instance: if you draw a face as a circle of dots which are not joined to each other, you see it as a face, even though all that it physically coming in through your senses is a number of unconnected dots. Then there are studies such as that by Carmichael and others: these researchers found that people's memory of an image was different depending on how the image was captioned.

In anthropology, this leads to something called the "Sapir-Whorf hypothesis" which states that we don't directly perceive the external "real world" at all; each culture sees it through its own spectacles, as it were, so that what each culture sees differs from that of others. It is as if we are inside a house with stained-glass windows: what we perceive relates to something outside us, but that "something" is always distorted by the particular assumptions we hold. This does not only include explicit assumptions, but a lot which come as second nature to members of a particular culture. Our language, systems of meaning, and technologies serve as our particular "stained-glass window": they put a particular slant on what we see, so no perception is ever purely sensation and nothing ever precisely reflects "objective reality as it really is".

In this sense, therefore, there is no problem on principle with saying that a form of technology, such as film, can alter our "mode of perception" in a relatively short space of time.

It is also likely that technology alters ways of viewing the world – hence the development of revolutionary movements and different "modes of production". The 'primitive' idea of a magical world beyond human control could not survive the development of technologies to control the world; the medieval Christian assumption that all human beings believe in God could not survive the rise of technologies such as writing and practices such as global trade which led to sustained contact with other cultures. The French Revolution came hot on the heels of the spread of the printing press; it is no coincidence that the revolutionary ideas came from mass-produced books and were disseminated in printed pamphlets and illustrations. Also, the evidence for the effects of film and other new technologies are the changes in social life in the 20th century. For instance, 20th-century political movements (whether Bolshevik, Thatcherite, social-democratic, Blairite, Nazi or whatever) have depended on new technologies to constitute themselves as movements. There is a large difference between a political movement which is run through face-to-face contacts, and one which relies on cinema, radio or TV to mobilise a following which may well be geographically fragmented.

To take an example: the modern TV election is a quite different affair to the older kind of election which relied on grassroots mobilisation (in this case, a change for the worse). It is unlikely that Blairism could have 'achieved' anything as a movement were it not for the technology of television. It is no coincidence that the debate about Socialist Alliance campaigning focused around the use of face-to-face or massified means of communication (i.e., canvassing versus leaflets).

Thus, technology is far more than merely a 'technique' for getting across the same basic message; it fundamentally changes the messages which can be delivered. As Marshall McLuhan put it, "the medium is the message". When new technologies – especially communication technologies – spread across society, this can change not only the ease with which existing practices occur (e.g.,. speed up communications): it can alter the way people see themselves and their world. I agree with John that this does not necessarily make film progressive; but I think film has been influential in some ways on perception. For instance: many of the figures of speech George W Bush is employing against "the terrorists" are drawn from cinema. In action films, "terrorists" are always motiveless evildoers, and they are defeated by strong, ruthless, male heroes. It now seems the present crisis is being assessed through these same assumptions. Medieval politics was viewed through images drawn from the technology and culture of its day. For instance, many dissident movements relied on religious beliefs and ways of thinking drawn from experiences of the church, which was then a major focus of communication. Though not a technology, religion involved a "way of seeing" which altered what people thought and perceived.

The relationship between medium and message is important for revolutionary politics because it completely falsifies the bourgeois account of history. In both fact and fiction, bourgeois authors write as if human history was always made up of basically the same kind of people as today. Actually, the way people perceive the world has changed fundamentally through history – and that means that it can change again. It also means that the development of new ideas, technologies and techniques can alter people's perceptions in a progressive direction.

Andrew Robinson

Decline of reality, or decline of theory?

In *Workers' Liberty* 63 I wrote an article ("New Forces and Passions") against the commonplace Marxist idea that capitalist development has been "in decline" or "reactionary" since about World War 1. Like it or not, capitalist development has generally been — and still is — *advancing*; socialists should not be waiting for the "decline" to become sheer free-fall, but instead organising and promoting the working-class "new forces and passions" which capitalist advance generates as its inescapable subversive counterpart. Instead of casting around for ways to "stop" capitalist globalisation, our perspective should be (in the phrase of Michael Hardt and Toni Negri) for "the multitude, in its will to be-against and its desire for liberation, [to] push through Empire to come out the other side".

My polemic has brought four replies — Paul Hampton in WL 64-5, Hillel Ticktin in WL66, and Bruce Robinson and Clive Bradley in WL 2/1.

Some of these writers suspect me of preaching a bland confidence in the capacity of capital to "augment the raw materials for socialism in a linear manner", or even giving credence "to the support of the bourgeoisie as a progressive force". In fact, I borrowed the words of Rosa Luxemburg from 1915, about the "brutal victory parade of capital... bear[ing] the stamp of progress in the historical sense only because [it] create[s] the material preconditions for the abolition of capitalist domination", in order to make the point that I was no more recommending complaisance towards modern globo-capital than Luxemburg was cheering on the imperialism of the First World War. I wrote that: "The thought here is certainly not... that things get better, evenly, steadily, bit by bit, all the time". I described capitalist development today as "saturated with violence, robbery and infamy... cruel, disgusting and crisis-ridden".

I also tried to make clear that I would not choose "progressive" as a summary descriptive term for capitalist development today. To do that, I wrote, would be "incongruous or even politically false".

In left-wing discourse for most of the 20th century, "progressive" usually signified "naive or venal enough to support Stalinist swindles". The word does not come down to us with a sharp, clear meaning. Even in his time, Marx preferred the adjective "revolutionary" when he wanted to refer to capital as a social force pushing forward

rather than stagnating or falling backwards.

But the conventional view against which I was contending is that capitalist development was "progressive" until about World War 1, and then has been "reactionary" ever since. My argument was that capitalist development today is "progressive" in broadly the same sense as the conventional view deems it to have been before World War 1. I did not wish to obscure or soften that point by burying it under a side-argument, however valid, about "progressive" generally not being the best adjective to convey a Marxist view, either now or then.

The basic argument against me from Paul Hampton and Hillel Ticktin is that through monopolies, state enterprise and regulation, and so forth, capitalist economy diverges more and more from "the law of value which is its fundamental law of motion". And that divergence *is* the decline of capitalism.

Here I'm embarrassed. Over the years I have read dozens — no, hundreds — of books and articles asserting or assuming that the law of value is the basic defining law of capitalism. It still makes no sense to me, and possibly that's just my slow wits. For now, though, assume that we can formulate a proposition, the law of value, which encapsulates a theory of how a capitalist economic system works, and we establish that the divergences between capitalist reality and that theoretical model become greater and greater.

Why must we read this as showing that capitalist reality is increasingly not up to the mark, rather than as showing that the theoretical model is increasingly not up to the mark? Maybe the Hampton-Ticktin theory of capitalism is "in decline", rather than us having to label the world around us as "in decline" because it increasingly departs from the model in Paul's and Hillel's heads?

So far as I know, the only extended discussion of the term "law of value" in the Marxist classics is Engels' supplementary note to volume 3 of *Capital* entitled *Law of Value and Rate of Profit*.[1] Engels nowhere states a "law" of the format that we are used to with, say, Newton's Laws of Motion, or the Laws of Thermodynamics. Instead, by "law of value", he seems to mean the rule by which the value of commodities is determined by the social labour-time of their production, and the exchange of commodities is determined by their values.

That is no closer to being "the law of

motion" of the whole system than the proposition that water boils at 100°C is to being "the law of motion" of a steam engine.

Engels argues that in "simple commodity production" — an economy of small producers, each owning their own (small) means of production — the rule operates more or less directly. "Prices, on average, approach to within a negligible margin of values". In capitalist production, however, the rule operates much more indirectly. Prices diverge systematically from being proportional to values, even apart from the discrepancies due to cheating, short-term variations of supply and demand, monopolies, and so on.

Engels quotes Marx: "The whole difficulty arises from the fact that commodities are not exchanged simply as commodities, but as products of capital, which claim participation in the total amount of surplus-value proportional to their magnitude..." Thus, commodities produced by capitals with a high proportion of constant capital (equipment, buildings, raw materials, etc.) to variable capital (living labour) systematically have prices above those proportional to value, and commodities from capitals with more "labour-intensive" production systematically have prices below proportionality, so that capitals receive surplus-value in proportion to their total size as capitals, not in proportion to the living labour they use.

On this account, actual prices moving further away from direct "law of value" proportions — because some capitalist industries become highly automated, while there are always some remaining "labour-intensive" — is a sign of capitalist *advance*, not decline. What would truly signal a catastrophic decline of capitalism would be a closer and more direct approximation to the "law of value"!

For Paul Hampton, I think, what brands capitalism as knackered is not so much these divergences of price from value-proportions, due to differing compositions of capital, but others due to monopoly, state subsidies and so on. He could also mention sales taxes, I guess.

As Bruce Robinson indicates (WL 2/1), it is not certain that divergences of that sort are in fact increased in modern capitalism. In any case, if those divergences did increase, why would it signal "decline"?

Paul also mentions "the rise in unproductive labour... arms production... the growth of finance capital". These are important tendencies, but they have nothing directly to do with how much prices diverge from value-proportions. The thought seems

to be that the capitalist norm is an atomised ultra-free-market economy, all small enterprises, with their cash kept under the owners' mattresses and a minimal state, and any departure from that indicates "decline".

Hillel's notion, cited by Bruce, that nationalisation, planning, and large bureaucratic apparatuses of any sort are "inherently anti-capitalist", is in the same line of thinking.

But doesn't that mean relabelling the *whole* development of capitalism out of small-scale commodity production — growing power of fixed capital, concentration and centralisation, development of credit, increased economic role of the state, etc. — as "decline"? How does that help understanding?

To be sure, the advance of capitalism always has a sort of "decline" built into it, in that it enlarges the contradictions and the scope for crises, and augments the subversive potential of the working class. But "decline" built into advance is different from decline, full stop.

Hillel states that: "Its [capitalism's] overthrow is not a voluntary process, but one conditioned on the internal decline of capital itself". Paul is horrified that I imply that "capitalism will go on and on, unless the working class intervenes (or the system destroys the planet)". But, yes, the capitalists will "go on and on" unless someone acts, "voluntarily", to change things! History is human action, and unless their adversaries act the capitalists will have their way. There is no superhuman force — no person doing the same job in world history that Anne Robinson does in the TV quiz show — to tell capitalism, "You are the weakest link. Goodbye", while the working class watch from our sofas.

When Trotsky, for example, wrote about the decline of capitalism in the 1930s, he had a much less abstruse idea of it than Paul and Hillel. "Mankind's productive forces stagnate. Already new inventions and improvements fail to raise the level of material wealth... the proletariat grows neither numerically nor culturally". Even in that sort of "decline" Trotsky did not believe that capitalism would be overthrown without a "voluntary process". And the sort of decline-within-advance which is endemic to capitalist development certainly requires working-class action if it is to become a factor in stopping the capitalists "going on and on".

Is the idea behind Paul's and Hillel's argument that capitalism has a system of self-regulation proper to it — the free market — and that if it moves away from that then it becomes increasingly unable to manage? If so they are wrong. Markets do have some self-regulating mechanisms, but the notion that a comprehensive free market provides an ideal system of regulation for capitalism is an ideological myth concocted by late 19th century bourgeois economists in their attempts to do down socialism. Actually, even capitalism – let alone a better system – requires, and has developed, large measures of non-market regulation.

I agree with pretty much everything Bruce Robinson writes, including about the destructive tendencies in capitalism today. But I do not see how his conclusion follows: that our overall assessment of capitalist development today must be indeterminate, neither advance nor decline.

Is the industrial development visible in several ex-colonial countries today a real capitalist development (accompanied by great horrors and crises within itself, and vast pauperisation on its edges), or is it just a "fake" industrialisation, as some radicals say? Does capitalist globalisation represent an advance in global communications and interlinking (together with all sorts of villainies), or is it just a matter of the USA going out to plunder the rest of the world because normal capitalist profit-making has hit a dead end? Is there a real expansion of the productive forces outside national limits involved in the European Union, or is it just a political gambit by the German ruling class to control workers across Europe?

We can answer yes – the industrial development is real; we have to aim to push through capitalist globalisation rather than stop or reverse it; and so on – without becoming apologists in any way for the IMF, the European Commission, or the capitalists of countries like South Korea. To give an indeterminate answer – "don't know", or "a bit of one and a bit of the other" – is unhelpful. In fact I suspect Bruce would answer yes to all those questions. Isn't there a common underlying question that he should also answer yes to?

Clive Bradley has a different objection, centred on a question I mention in passing in the article.

"What", I wrote, "about Lenin's insistence, in his wartime writings, that his revolutionary anti-war position was based on identifying the current period as 'the epoch of the reactionary, obsolete bourgeoisie' whereas a different attitude was correct in 'the epoch of the progressive bourgeoisie'? (_Socialism and War_. I think Hal Draper gives the right answer to this question in... his book _War and revolution: Lenin and the myth of revolutionary defeatism_. Despite myths promoted by opportunists in World War 1

and taken for good coin by Lenin, the basic approach of Marx and Engels on wars in their time was the same as the internationalists' in World War 1)".

Clive is bothered that my argument might suggest that "advanced capitalism is not necessarily imperialist". Almost all ruling classes are "imperialist" in the general sense of seeking to expand their power, privilege and revenues. The advanced capitalist ruling classes are "imperialist" in that sense. We can identify the mechanisms – IMF plans, trade agreements between unequal economic powers, demands from big investors on host countries, extortionate interest payments, the role of the dollar as world currency, royalties from high technologies, and so on – through which they pursue their specific sort of imperialism, and a horrible business it is too.

But if the word "imperialist" is taken in the narrower sense of the imperialism of great rival colonial empires, dominant in 1916 when Lenin wrote _Imperialism_, then in fact advanced capitalism is _not_ necessarily imperialist. In recent decades the big capitalist ruling classes have concluded – partly under the impact of repeated colonial revolts – that market and para-market mechanisms provide a much cheaper, more reliable, and less risky way for them to profiteer world-wide than military conquest and colonial rule over weaker nations.

The problem with making the proposition "advanced capitalism is necessarily imperialist" into an axiom – and then, effectively, redefining "imperialism" as "whatever advanced capitalist states do" – is that we end up with a politics which combats advanced capitalism not so much because it is capitalist as because it is _advanced_. The more advanced, the worse! In the original article I tried to spell out the destructive implications of this stance for socialist politics.

Chris Reynolds

1. Many writers hold that this text is yet another example of bad old Engels bowdlerising Marx's ideas. However, as far as I know Marx never discussed the term "law of value" in any extended way, least of all in any text he readied for publication.

Correction: Susan Carlyle's and Sean Matgamna's article on Sylvia Pankhurst in WL2/1 stated that "in Germany [before World War 1] the Reichstag was elected on an unequal suffrage – the vote of a worker had less weight than other votes". The Reichstag was in fact elected by universal male suffrage, though it had very limited power; it was the Prussian state parliament that had a "three-class" voting system.

POLEMIC

The left and 'reactionary anti-imperialism'

The theory of accommodation: falsifying the history

The Prophet and the Proletariat: Islamic Fundamentalism, Class, and Revolution, by Chris Harman. Socialist Workers' Party pamphlet.

IN Manuel Puig's novel *The Kiss of the Spider Woman*, two men confront each other in a prison cell, somewhere in South America. One is a trashy movie-loving homosexual; the other a revolutionary, a guerrilla. The book is concerned with the nature of liberation; Valentin, the political activist, learns that Molina, his cellmate, for whom at first he has nothing but contempt, deserves freedom and respect. Valentin is a terrorist, if you like, a member of a militant guerrilla organisation not unusual in the Latin America of the 1960s and 70s, influenced by the Cuban revolution and Che Guevara.

The methods of such guerrillaism, whether urban or rural "foco", proved disastrous, provoking repression and resulting in the deaths of many revolutionary militants. But their "discourse" was one of freedom. Valentin has waged war on the military dictatorship of his unnamed country in the name of freedom; and so he is able to learn, locked in his prison cell, that his notion of freedom was too limited. Molina, in the name of love, sacrifices himself for Valentin's cause. However distant they seem to be, Valentin and Molina are speaking, ultimately, the same language. They have the same aim.

You can imagine a version of *The Kiss of the Spider Woman* set in a jail perhaps in Egypt, in which one of 52 recently arrested gay men is confined with a member of Islamic Jihad. Perhaps, fictionally, by the end of it, the Islamist — let's say he's one of those responsible for the slaughter of tourists at Luxor a few years ago — has come to love his cellmate, as Valentin does. Or perhaps our Egyptian Molina finds himself ready to die for the Islamist cause. But such an ending involves quite a different kind of understanding than that in Puig's novel. In this case there would be no fused, common language. Either "Molina" accepts that his sexuality is a crime against God, and the tourists with whom he has, no doubt, enjoyed liaisons in the past are "abominations" deserving death; or "Valentin" realises that the project to which he has devoted his life is wrong. There can be no cross-fertilisation, no rejuvenated, single concept of liberty, only a mortal clash of world views in which one or other must win.

It is this specific character of contemporary Islamism which Chris Harman fails utterly to register in *The Prophet and the Proletariat*. On the contrary, the gist of his argument is to see Islamism as no different, in essence, to other "contradictory", "petty bourgeois" movements elsewhere in time and place. Against the views that Islamism is "automatically reactionary and 'fascist'" and that it is "automatically anti-imperialist", Harman argues that it is the product of "a deep social crisis which it can do nothing to resolve". He concludes that, politically, socialists need to be "with the state, never; with the fundamentalists, sometimes."

Harman says that "the Islamists are not our allies" and "socialists cannot give support to" them. (p53). But we can't "simply take an abstentionist, dismissive attitude to the Islamists", because the "feeling of revolt" of those who suffer under world capitalism and who have turned to Islamism, "could be tapped for progressive purposes." There is a lot of verbal ambiguity here ("not support" rather than "oppose", "not allies" rather than "enemies"; who, after all, wants to be abstentionist? And what does "dismissive" mean?) Harman confuses an assessment of why sections of the "suffering classes" turn to Islamism with an analysis of the movements as such. His ambiguities hide behind an apparently rigorous Marxist study of social classes and "contradictions".

To begin with, the dichotomy Harman presents, the two views of Islamism he sets out to attack, is not a fair one. It is true that many leftists in the Middle East from Stalinist or nationalist backgrounds, and intellectuals in the West, advocate support for "liberals" or the state against the Islamists. It is true that some commentators describe these movements as "fascist" without qualification. Fascism is, largely, a European phenomenon, in its full-blown sense, which (as Harman notes) aims to smash powerful working class movements. Islamism exists in countries without such movements.

But you can very well consider Islamism analogous to fascism without going on to ignore its differences with classical fascism and without supporting state repression against it. Instead of dealing with the substantial arguments about the important similarities between Islamist movements and fascism, with qualifications, Harman tries to discredit them by association with the political conclusion – support for state repression – which he suggests must follow from recognising those similarities. Islamist movements, which are organised political forces, are the enemies – the violent enemies, more often than not – of workers, trade unionists, socialists, feminists, women generally, non-Muslim minorities, oppressed nationalities, and so on. This is a fact. It is also a fact, increasingly, that they express their violent hostility through the mobilisation of a mass movement. It is, indeed, a mass movement with its own contradictions; socialists, with tactical skill, could hope to break individuals from these movements; and with success in building powerful workers' organisations hope to influence the mass base of the Islamist groups and marginalise them.

But for the most part imagining ourselves, as Western socialists, as engaged in a tactical battle with the Islamists against a common enemy is a fantasy. Our first job is to "say what is".

It is instructive to see what Harman means when he says that the Islamists are not "automatically anti-imperialist". Analysing Algeria, Sudan, Egypt and Iran, he argues that being, fundamentally, petty bourgeois in nature, the Islamist movements are pulled in two directions. Essentially, one wing – representing conservative classes – is pulled into an accommodation with capital, imperialism, and so on. The other – representing other layers of the petty bourgeoisie, students for instance, and the poor – becomes dissatisfied with such accommodation. As far as it goes, this is true. But in attempting to subsume Islamism, effectively, into old-fashioned nationalism, Harman misses the point dramatically. Because even where Islamist groups take a "radical", violently oppositionist stand,

this does not demonstrate that their notion of anti-imperialism has anything in common with ours.[1]

Arguing for support for some Islamist actions, such as demonstrations against the Gulf War in 1991, Harman writes: "But even then we continue to disagree... on basic issues. We are for the right to criticise religion as well the right to practice it... We are against discrimination against Arab[ic] speakers by big business in countries like Algeria – but also against the Berber speakers and those... who have grown up speaking French... as well as defending Islamists against the state we will also be defending women, gays, Berbers or Copts against some Islamists." (p 56).

We "disagree", "defend against"... The language here is all as if fictional SWP members in Algeria or Egypt are engaged in some united front with confused reformists, or some version of the Anti-Nazi League. When Algerian women who won't wear the veil are gunned down by passing Islamists on motorcycles, are we merely "disagreeing"? When supporters of the Iranian Islamic Republican Party abroad used thuggery against leftist opponents, were we merely "disagreeing"? Perhaps Harman has in mind people, mainly youth, in Britain who are influenced by Islamism, and the pamphlet is aimed at engaging with them. Whether this is a method which succeed strikes me as questionable.

Harman's anxiety to understand the social discontents feeding Islamist movements is laudable. But not if it means a failure to understand the concrete reality of these movements in relation to actual, currently existing, real progressive forces, or to see their reactionary programme merely as something to argue with them about (over Turkish coffee in the suq, no doubt).

Harman's one comment on Hamas, for example, is to remind us of "the arguments [in Hamas]... about whether or not they should compromise with Arafat's rump Palestinian administration – and therefore indirectly with Israel..." (p 54) "Compromise" with Israel, for Harman, is the symbol of capitulation; as long as Hamas does not compromise, it is expressing genuinely radical aspirations. The nature and consequences of its political programme are less important than the fact of its "militancy" and refusal to "compromise".

In other words, when Harman says the Islamists are "not automatically anti-imperialist", he means that while some (bad) Islamists are not anti-imperialist, other (better) ones are. The task of socialists, therefore, is to sort out which Islamists are anti-imperialists and which are not. The substance and nature of their anti-imperialism is a secondary matter.

These movements plainly — nobody is seeking to deny it — articulate social grievances of the masses, the dispossessed poor, layers of students and petty bourgeois, and so on. But they are not merely expressing "progressive" struggles with a reactionary programme, which is Harman's train of thought. They have channelled struggles which could, under some circumstances, be progressive, in a reactionary direction, mobilised them in a reactionary movement. Anti-imperialism without a democratic programme, without freedom for women, and national minorities, without the space for the working class to develop its own ideas and organisations, this is not inconsistent and limited; in the world as it is today, it is not anti-imperialism at all.

Harman's analysis enormously downgrades the role played in the formation of the Islamic Republic by the old exploiters, who had suffered under the Shah's land reforms, the bazaari merchants (though he mentions this), and the mosques who had been taxed by the state, and the extent to which, therefore, the revolution in the first place brought together social forces with quite contradictory aims. Of course the Islamic Republic was not merely this: but the dominant social and political forces represented by Khomeini were traditional ones, mobilising a popular base, and of course in the contemporary world having no choice but to "be capitalist" once in power.

It also downplays the practical, as opposed to abstract-strategic, failures of the Iranian left. Khomeini mobilised a mass movement physically to destroy the left. Harman refers to this but seems to draw no conclusion from it other than a descriptive one. The problem for the left was that it didn't recognise that this mass movement was its homicidal enemy until it was too late. Perhaps even if they had, they would have been too weak to defeat it. But it was not only the government in which the left had illusions. The violent attacks on them took them by surprise. Harman underrates the problem presented by the Islamists "on the street", imagining it is all a matter of how to win them over, since they and the left share a common anti-imperialist objective (although in their case inconsistently). The Iranian revolution shows that the problem was rather more severe than that.

Harman refers to the impasse in Middle Eastern societies, the failures of post-war nationalism, such as Nasserism. He explains the rise of Islamism as a consequence of the social crisis in which this political history is embedded. But he fails to answer the question why an alternative to such failed ideologies and movements would be sought in radical Islam, rather than something else. If it was simply the weight of religion in these cultures, it would be a mystery that nationalisms which were fundamentally secular had emerged at all, now to be increasingly eclipsed. He does refer to the consequences of capitalism on traditional societies, exacerbated by global trends in the world system more recently. But he does not adequately register the fact that the defeat of popular movements, especially in Iran but also elsewhere, has played a vital role.

And what is missing from Harman's account is any sense that the growth of the Islamist movements is any cause for alarm. On the contrary, the gist of his case is that since they are "contradictory", sometimes progressive, and express a "feeling of revolt" that could be mobilised for progressive ends, the rise of the Islamists is an opportunity rather than a threat. Sure, they have some unpleasant ideas we "disagree with" and would "defend" various people against, but if the workers' movement can move in the region, it will all be all right. This view, of course, informs the SWP's recent agitation on the war in Afghanistan — that imperialism is the only enemy, not "fundamentalism", and so on. This pamphlet was written in 1999; but one assumes that were it written now, its main argument would be that the upsurge in Islamism provoked by imperialism was only to be expected, and still not much to worry about. For any sane socialist, on the other hand, the prospect, for instance, of Islamists coming to power in Pakistan is worth worrying about very much indeed.

The rise of Islamism is depressing and dangerous, from a socialist point of view. However "contradictory", there can be little doubt that the Islamists will be an anti-working class force where the working class does move. We don't have to guess about this. It was proved in Iran.

Edward Ellis

Notes

1. Harman piles on further confusion by referring to the Iranian People's Mujaheddin, who by 1979 were Marxist-influenced, as if they are part of the same phenomenon as the regime they later took up arms against. They were not. While it is right to distinguish different kinds of Islamism (some of which are moderate; there is a type of Islamism running through Arab nationalism from its inception, although mutedly), it is not helpful to throw into the discussion examples which can only obscure the issue, and the movements, at hand.

The practice of accommodation: poisoning the new anti-capitalists

No to Bush's War. Socialist Workers' Party pamphlet

IT is hard to see how the Socialist Workers Party's recent pamphlet *No to Bush's War* could convince anyone not already "on side" to oppose the war in Afghanistan. It seems not to have been written for that purpose, but instead to concoct a story to "make the links" for activists in the "new anti-capitalist" milieu. Its subtitle is: "The military wing of globalisation".

If its message is swallowed, rather than criticised, it will turn the new left into a caricature re-run of the Stalinist "old left".

That "old left" was morally compromised and politically crippled by "power-bloc" thinking. It saw a world of two "camps" – the "imperialist" camp of the USA, and the "socialist", or at least "anti-imperialist", camp of the USSR – and its first duty as supporting the "anti-imperialist" camp.

There is no "socialist camp" any more. But the SWP is busy building up a picture of a new "anti-imperialist" camp and urging us to rally to it. The main forces in their "anti-imperialist" camp are the various regional powers which may clash with the USA – "sub-imperialist" states, as Marxists have called them – such as Iran, Iraq, and Serbia at various times; and the whole jihadi-fundamentalist movement is, they insist, part of it too.

The SWP criticises these "anti-imperialist" forces – just as within the old left, at least from the 1960s onwards, criticism of the USSR was permissible and even sometimes vigorous. But for the SWP the criticism is always subordinate to fundamental solidarity with the "anti-imperialist" camp – just as, for the old left, the criticism was always within the limits of basic solidarity with the USSR.

The SWP used not to think like this. In the South Atlantic war of 1982 it opposed both Britain and the allegedly "anti-imperialist" Argentine dictatorship. For the first seven years of the Iran/Iraq war of 1980-8 it opposed that war on both sides. Then in 1987 it swung round to support Iran in the Iran/Iraq war, on the grounds that the USA's semi-support for Iraq made Iran's cause "anti-imperialist". It has subsequently backdated that attitude to the war's start in 1980 and extended it into a whole world view.

The new pamphlet is constructed round three main ideas. First, that world politics is shaped by a relentless "drive for global economic and military dominance" by a nebulous force variously named as "the world system", "globalisation", "imperialism", "the West", or "the USA". Second, that other forces in the world are mere "products" of that drive. Either they are examples of the rule that "barbarity bred barbarity", "barbarism can only cause more counter-barbarism", or they are "terrorists the West has created".

Everything reactionary and horrible in the world is a mere reflex or creation of "the West" – and yet, magically, even the most regressive of such forces can be progressive and deserving of socialist support if it clashes with the USA, no matter what about.

That is the third idea – that we should side with the "counter-barbarism" against the "barbarism". We should even side with the "terrorists the West has created", such as Osama bin Laden, when "the US's drive to dominate... turn[s] him and others (for example, Saddam Hussein's Iraq) against the West".

This third idea is not stated forthrightly. Despite frequent references to the Gulf War of 1991, this pamphlet nowhere repeats what the SWP wrote at the time – that Saddam's "call for Israel to 'get out of the occupied territories of Palestine' will increase his standing among those Arabs who have supported the intifada... So, the more US pressure builds up, the more Saddam will play an anti-imperialist role... This means he will increasingly have to rely on one of his few remaining strengths, the Arab masses' hatred of imperialism. In all of this Saddam should have the support of socialists... Socialists must hope that Iraq gives the US a bloody nose and that the US is frustrated in its attempt to force the Iraqis out of Kuwait" (*SW*, 18 August 1990).

But the message in the new pamphlet is clear. It is the same message as in 1990. The SWP talks freely about how "horrifying" the 11 September attacks in the USA were. It does not condemn them. The SWP has insisted that it will not condemn the attacks, though it has not explained why not in its public press, or in this pamphlet.

The SWP's scheme of "barbarism" and "counter-barbarism" begs several questions. Even though the Taliban had US support in the mid-1990s, it is bizarre "conspiracy theory" to blame its barbarism on "the West". In fact the Taliban is more regressive than even the worst advanced-capitalist powers.

And, in any case, why side with the "counter-barbarism" rather than the "barbarism"? Because "barbarism can only cause more counter-barbarism", so supporting "counter-barbarism" is the only way to fight "barbarism"? Then how will we ever get socialism?

In the SWP's pamphlet, every adverse comment on the Taliban, bin Laden, or similar forces, is immediately followed by an excuse — "but the West is really to blame..."

"The American government denounces the Taliban regime as 'barbaric' for its treatment of women." A true denunciation, or untrue? The SWP doesn't say. Its answer is: "It was the Pakistani secret service, the Saudi royal family and American agents... that organised the Taliban's push for power".

Bin Laden was behind the 11 September attacks? "It was because of the rage he felt when he saw his former ally, the US, bomb Baghdad and back Israel."

"US leaders condemn the Afghan government..." Does it deserve to be condemned? No answer. The SWP quickly assures us that evils in Afghanistan are all down to the fact that "the superpowers stepped in and poured petrol on the flames".

The SWP, though you wouldn't guess it from this pamphlet, used to refuse (rightly) to side with the USSR against the USA. It called for "Neither Washington nor Moscow, but international socialism". In this pamphlet's account of Afghanistan, however, the USSR's 1979-89 war to try to subjugate the country, which killed a million Afghans and drove six million to flee as refugees, gets only a passing mention. "Russia sent troops into Afghanistan in December 1979 to prop up its client government." No comment. The SWP's condemnations are reserved for something else: "The US threw its weight behind the assorted Afghan forces ranged against the Russians... flooded the country with arms." Not the would-be conquerors, but those who (for their own reasons) aided the resistance, are the chief villains.

The SWP explains "Islamism" as "a variety of movements that... express some of the bitterness of masses of people in predominantly Muslim countries... enormous resentment against the West and the local despots allied to it".

Fascism, too, and British working-class racism, often express "resentment" against the upper crust. But for the SWP the fact that Islamism expresses "resentment against the West" is sufficient for it to deserve the solidarity of socialists.

That it "can take a religious form, Islamism" does not bother the SWP. To them this is no more than a natural result of the fact that "the majority religion in the region is Islam". Why then in Latin America doesn't revolt take the form of some sort of Catholic

holy war against the Protestant US elite? Political movements are more than just a photographic-negative image of what the US does in this or that region.

The "terrorist methods" of the Islamists do bother the SWP. Why do the Islamists adopt such bad "tactics"? The SWP cites "rage at the suffering imposed by the world system" — but also, here, for once, allows itself to suggest that its "anti-imperialist" allies have done wrong for a reason other than being "driven to it" by "the West". Where the Islamist movements "have had a mass character", as in Algeria around 1991, they have wrongly "turned their backs on the strategic power of urban workers" and thus found themselves reduced to "small groups", "embittered" and "desperate".

If only the Algerian Islamists had "turned their backs on the workers"! In fact they turned their knives and guns on the workers, massacring hundreds of trade unionists.

The difference between the Islamists and socialists is not that we socialists pursue working-class action, while they "turn their backs on the workers" and choose less effective methods to the same goal — but that they have utterly different goals. Their reactionary goals of defeating the "infidel" world; banishing women's rights, democracy, secularism, sexual self-determination, and individual liberty; and bringing "death to America" and "death to Israel", cannot be achieved through working-class action! Action by Islamist workers for these goals is no more progressive than action by fascist-led workers in Britain, France or Germany.

Moreover, the Islamists are unfortunately far from just "small groups". They run the country in Saudi Arabia, in Iran, and (still, to a large degree) in Afghanistan! They have mass support in other countries.

To dismiss fascism as just "a product of the capitalist regime", so Trotsky wrote in 1934, "means we have to renounce the whole struggle, for all contemporary social evils are 'products of the capitalist system'... Fatalist prostration is substituted for the militant theory of Marx, to the sole advantage of the class enemy.... The increase in the misery and the revolt of the proletariat are also products of capitalism..." Politics is about which "products of capitalism" we base ourselves on in their conflict with which others. To dismiss Islamism as just "a product of the world system" is to evade politics. To adopt anything other than an attitude of mortal hostility to it is to disarm politically.

Karl Marx criticised the German socialist leader Ferdinand Lassalle for his claim that everyone other than the working class was "one reactionary mass". "The bourgeoisie", Marx pointed out, "is... a revolutionary class – as the bearer of large-scale industry – relatively to the feudal lords and the lower middle class"; moreover, sections of the lower middle class could be won over by the workers "in view of their impending transfer into the proletariat".

The SWP has a curious inversion of this idea. Advanced capitalism (aka imperialism, aka "the West", aka the USA) is reactionary, and everything else, everything that comes into conflict with it, is progressive! Even the most extreme Islamists, like the Taliban, who, as one Afghan Stalinist rightly put it, plunged Afghanistan's cities "into a black hole, 500 years back in history", are progressive compared to the 21st century!

The SWP's approach whitewashes the Islamists, Saddam Hussein – and any local despot who comes into conflict with the USA. It is also atrociously metropolito-centric and condescending in its attitude to the people of the world's poorer countries.

The socialists and democrats of those countries, who fight with great courage against the Islamists, are painted out of the SWP's picture. The SWP sees the people of those countries as capable only of "rage" and "despair", not of thought. When the 11 September attacks in the USA drive the US government to war which kills innocent Afghans, then the US government is to be condemned. But if people in Muslim countries feel "driven" to kill innocent Americans (and also – though the SWP does not mention it – socialists, democrats, trade unionists and national minorities in their own countries), then the SWP shrugs. "Regrettable, but what can you expect?"

The only way out of this cycle of "rage" and "despair" which the SWP can see is... for the new anti-capitalist movement, from its main bases within the West, to grow and hand down "hope" to the benighted masses of the poorer countries!

Certainly we must wish for the new anti-capitalist movement to grow both numerically and politically; and the stronger the socialist movement here, the greater the help we can give to (and receive from) socialist movements in poorer countries.

But that begs the question of politics. The first plank of the pamphlet's argument is the claim that world politics is shaped by a relentless "drive for global economic and military dominance" by a nebulous force variously named as "the world system", "globalisation", "imperialism", "the West" – or, to come down to specifics, "the USA".

The US government has done many evil things; US-based corporations and banks do many evil things; decisions by the US-based IMF are responsible for great misery; and Britain is an ally of the USA. All that is true; and on a quick skim-read, it may seem that the SWP pamphlet is only reasserting these facts, with a bit of permissible polemical exaggeration here and there.

In fact the pamphlet's picture of the world pulps Marxism. The USA's giant corporations and banks dominate the world not through governor-generals, but primarily through capitalist market forces.

To combat the growing inequality, misery and cruelty of the world today, the first thing any serious socialist must understand is that these are fundamentally the product of the capitalist market system, not of any particular government's urge to tyrannise. A large part of the theoretical work of Karl Marx, in his day, was about arguing with radicals that they should no longer see their struggle as one of the virtuous people against the vicious aristocrats, but should contest the fundamental economic relations on which they stood.

To regress from Marx's insight, and to see the whole of world politics as a matter of the unaccountable propensities to tyranny of George W Bush and his friends, or of the USA, is particularly disorienting at the present time.

The "new anti-capitalists" have come out on the streets against the policies of the IMF, the WTO, and the US government. What many of them are not so sure about is whether they should be fully anti-capitalist, or whether they just object to a distortion of capitalism by the people at the top in the big corporations, banks and governments. The SWP's pamphlet can only push them towards the second, populist, alternative – "big is bad". (It also pushes towards the SWP's view of such issues as Israel-Palestine in terms of "bad" and "good" peoples, with Israel incongruously in the role of the "bad" big power).

The "new anti-capitalists" are hesitant about calling themselves socialists, for the very good reason that they abhor the Stalinism that was identified with "socialism" in common discourse for six decades. What alternative to capitalism should they pursue?

The SWP's pamphlet will push those who swallow its message towards identifying with reactionary, nihilistic anti-capitalism – not directly with Islamism, probably, but more likely with anarcho-populist anti-capitalism, a vision of overthrowing capitalism just by more and more spectacular street protests, without any particularly defined positive aims.

The "new anti-capitalists" are commonly identified by the mass media as "anti-globalisation", but many understand that to be against globalisation as such is to veer into parochialism and nationalism – a hopeless attempt to break down the world economy created by capitalism into smaller walled-off units, instead of building on it to create a socialist world.

Here again, the SWP's arguments can only push them back. If globalisation is just the megalomaniac "drive for global economic and military dominance" by the USA, the drive of which the current war is "the military wing", then who with any sense can do other than oppose it flat-out?

The SWP's pamphlet, in sum, is a primer in anarcho-populist "anti-imperialist camp" politics – or, more precisely, in the doctrine that precise political arguments do not matter so long as they seem to stir up feeling against capitalism, aka the USA. This approach, and these politics, may help build a small agitational group on the edge of the labour movement. They cannot possibly help equip young anti-capitalist militants to go into the workplaces and the labour movement, to learn to base themselves on the class struggle and to convince their fellow workers.

One further point about the pamphlet requires attention. So far as its picture of the "drive for dominance" by the USA which is inescapably driving people in the Middle East to "rage" and "despair" is based on specific political facts rather than just attributing the results of capitalist market economics to the ill-will of the US government, it is centred on Israel-Palestine.

Workers' Liberty is for the withdrawal of the Israeli military from the West Bank and Gaza, and an independent Palestinian state. But what really needs explaining here, from a working-class socialist point of view, is how rotten and chauvinist the Islamist view is, which tells workers as far away from Jerusalem as Morocco in one direction and Afghanistan or Pakistan in the other that their main enemy is not their own exploiters and rulers, but a small non-Muslim population in a small corner of the Mediterranean seaboard.

That is not how the SWP sees it. For them, Israel somehow is the key to the "stark contrast between wealth and poverty... in the Middle East". "Britain... encouraged Zionist colonists from Europe to seize land in Palestine, knowing they would be able to survive only by acting as a guard dog for Western [oil] interests. The US has taken over the dominant role from Britain since the 1940s. The methods of domination remain the same... The West backed Israel in its wars against Arab states in 1948, 1956, 1967 and

1973..." Etc. etc.

The history here is cock-eyed. While Britain ruled Palestine, the Zionists there bought land (from Arab landlords) rather than "seizing" it. Britain mostly did not "encourage" them; in fact the British government banned all land transfers after about 1940. As the persecution of Jews in Nazi Germany was escalating before World War Two, it closed the doors of Palestine to Jewish refugees. At the time Britain made its promise of aid for a "Jewish homeland" in Palestine – in 1917, as a gambit for Jewish support in World War One – the oil industry was only just starting in the region. The Jewish settlers were not then, and would never be, of any practical assistance to British (or later American) companies in maintaining their oil interests or in "pacifying" the region. On the contrary, they soon became a handicap and an embarrassment.

The west did not back Israel in 1948; it imposed an arms embargo on the Israelis, just as it did on the Bosniacs in 1992-5. British officers helped command the Arab armies against Israel, and Israel's main outside support was from the USSR (via Czechoslovakia). While Britain and France allied with Israel against Egypt in 1956, it was the USA that opposed them and forced them to back off.

The picture here of Jews and "the west" conspiring against Muslim peoples, with "the methods... the same" ever since World War One, is little better than a socialistic gloss on the anti-semitic agitation of the Islamists.

The SWP does not spell out here (or in their recent pamphlet directly on the Israel-Palestine question, *The New Intifada*) what they propose to put things right. The implications are unmistakable, though.

"Israel acts as a colonial outpost with all the arrogance pioneered by Britain and France when they ran the Middle East before the Second World War." The answer to the British and French colonial and semi-colonial domination was, quite rightly, to throw them out. But Israel remains as "the colonial outpost". (Of whom? Most Israeli Jews were born in Israel. It is not their "outpost", but their home). The answer? Throw out the remaining "colonial outpost". Destroy Israel.

The motive, for sure, is a sympathy with the Palestinians which we share. But loose demagogy has its price. Here "anti-imperialism" turns full circle, and by way of being translated into "anti-West" sentiment, becomes a desire for the crushing of a small nation – and a weaseling endorsement of bin Laden's excuse for the 11 September atrocity.

Martin Thoma

REVIEWS

The politics of Yankophobia

Rogue State: a guide to the world's only superpower, by William Blum. Zed Books

THIS is a sort of companion volume to the *Black Book of Communism* produced by a team of mostly ex-Communist-Party French writers a few years back. It is much more businesslike, brisker, and less inclined to extrapolate vast (and pre-conceived) philosophical conclusions from data partly real but partly contrived.

Blum gives a clear, matter-of-fact documentation of the US state's brutality, cynicism, and arrogance. His account is so crisp that it defies summary – every detail is as condensed and concise as it could possibly be.

The book is well worth reading, especially in these days when George W Bush and Tony Blair are crowing so loudly about the USA's supposedly unique ability to embody democracy, freedom and peace and generously to extend those virtues across the world.

It is worth reading critically, however. An uncritical reading, which would inflate the real and horrible facts of US militarist brutality into a picture of Washington and New York as the nodal points of all the world's evil, so that almost any force coming into conflict with the US government must represent at least relative progress, would produce a "Yankophobia" politically a mirror-image of the "Stalinophobia" typical of those French intellectuals who have rallied to bourgeois politics of one sort or another out of recoil against the (also real and horrible) facts of Stalinist crimes.

Blum is transparent about his own sympathies. He is a supporter of the sort of "socialism" exemplified by the old USSR. That stance, however much we would disagree with it, does not undo the facts he presents about US crimes, any more than Stalinist atrocities ceased to be atrocities because they were denounced by pro-capitalist ideologues. In fact, it makes his book easier to deal with – seeing one-sidedness where it appears – than many similar books produced by writers who are not Stalinists of any sort, but have become possessed by Yankophobia, Noam Chomsky for example, or the ideologues of the SWP.

One example will illustrate the sort of critical reservation which readers should bring to Blum's book. He claims that the CIA was involved in the attempt at a military coup in 1961 against the French government made by France's top army chiefs from their base in Algiers, where they were commanding a war to keep Algeria under French rule.

A similar coup in 1958 had succeeded, but the president brought to power by it, General De Gaulle, was (accurately) perceived by the 1961 coup-makers as having shifted decisively towards conceding independence to Algeria. The 1961 coup failed, since the vast majority of the army rank and file stayed loyal to De Gaulle, and the putschists went underground, forming a terror organisation which killed vast numbers in the remaining months before Algeria's independence (in 1962) and then, its members fleeing to France, became part of the subterranean structure of the French far right.

An ugly business! CIA support for such people must testify to utter contempt and incomprehension of the struggles for colonial liberation, racist arrogance, and disdain for democracy even in advanced and stable countries like France.

But what is the evidence? Most of Blum's statements are footnoted. This one is not. There are good reasons to doubt the statement. The USA generally supported independence for the colonies of France and Britain. It had publicly and firmly, though not militantly, supported Algerian independence since 1957 at latest. Although there were tensions between the USA and De Gaulle, France was a major American ally. Lightminded support for destabilisation of the French state made no sense for US policy.

Read the history books, and these are the facts. The USA quickly assured De Gaulle's government that if any American forces came into contact with the putschists, they would fire on them. The story about CIA support from the coup comes only from the unsupported assertions of two groupings – the putschists themselves, who wanted to convince wavering sympathisers that they were on a roll, and the French Communist Party.

The CP was highly appreciative for USSR foreign-policy reasons of De Gaulle's diplomatic sparring with the USA. It was eager to pursue any plausible gambit to sharpen conflicts between Paris and Washington, such as alleging CIA support for the coup seemed to be. Moreover, it could allow the CP to counter the coup-makers – ultra-patriots for the glory

159

of France – by being even more patriotic themselves, and presenting opposition to the coup as a stand for France against Yankee meddling. In other words, for the decaying old world power against the brash new world power.

Very Yankophobic. But very far from working-class politics.

Gerry Bates

The biography of an equation

E=mc², by David Bodanis. Pan.

DAVID Bodanis was inspired to write this book when he heard that the actor Cameron Diaz had said in an interview that she'd really like to understand what "E=mc²" means. He decided to tackle the task himself, not by explaining how the equation came to be derived, but by treating it almost as a person: he decided to write the biography of an equation.

Its birth was in the Bern Patent Office, where its immediate parent, Albert Einstein, was languishing in exile from the academic world: his irreverent attitude to his teachers meant that he got bad references when he applied for academic posts. Its ancestors were the ideas of a varied bunch of bright sparks, who often had to fight against the dead weight of established authority or prejudice.

Young, working-class, Michael Faraday was to come up with one of these ideas. He was able to see the connection between electrical and magnetic energies, hitherto thought separate, because, perhaps, of his unorthodox religious views. He then saw his mentor, the more socially accepted Humphry Davy, try to steal his discovery, a common theme in science. The key idea that came from Faraday's work was that all forms of energy are interchangeable, and the law of conservation of energy entered scientific orthodoxy. Einstein was later to overthrow this law.

The idea of mass as a theme unifying the apparently unrelated types of matter, such as gold and oxygen, or chalk and cheese, was also crucial. Newton had shown that all matter was affected by the force of gravity. Antoine Lavoisier, assisted by his wife Marie Anne, was able to show not only that, when iron burnt or rusted, it gained weight, but also that the surrounding air lost the same amount of weight. This pointed towards the existence of oxygen but also to the law of conservation of mass: Einstein was to overthrow that law, too.

By the end of the 19th century, it was apparent that mass could have energy but the idea that mass *is* energy was revolutionary. And the suggestion that the conversion factor was the speed of light squared (*c²*) was super-revolutionary. But what was the speed of light, *c*? Previous attempts to measure it had often failed because, unlike the speed of sound, the time intervals to be measured were far to short to be detectable with the available clocks, even with the longest distances possible on Earth. It only takes about one ten thousandth of a second to reach the horizon, for example. The idea that it travelled at an infinite speed became dominant.

In the late 17th century, a young Danish astronomer, Roemer, proposed that a puzzling feature of the orbit of one of Jupiter's moons could be explained by the different distances that light had to travel to Earth as Earth orbited round the Sun. He even estimated a speed for light close to the current known value. His work was rubbished by his boss, the prominent astronomer Cassini and his career stalled, another common theme in science.

In the mid-19th century, Maxwell took Faraday's discovery of the inter-relationship of changing electric and magnetic fields further, by supposing a mutually perpetuating oscillation of fields. He realised that this would travel through empty space at the speed of light and in fact was light. This idea came with the corollary that the speed of light was determined by the nature of space and was not altered by the speed of the thing sending it out.

So we have a type of energy (light and all the things that behave like it, such as radio waves, ultra-violet and X-rays) that travels at an enormous but definite speed in space. We also have matter (mass) that can travel at different speeds. Surely, it should be possible to accelerate a piece of matter to *c* or even beyond. Newton's laws did not rule this out. However, Einstein suggested that *c* was an absolute barrier beyond which nothing could go and, if you tried to expend energy accelerating some mass to *c* or beyond, what you actually succeeded in doing was increasing its mass! Einstein showed that the calculation of this increase of mass included the speed of light squared.

Now, expressions for kinetic energy (the energy of a moving object) include the factor of speed squared. Bodanis describes the role in establishing this fact of Emilie du Châtelet, a rich young woman of 18th century France who studied mathematics and the sciences and died giving birth to her child with Voltaire. She played a major part in replacing the previous notion of energy, which is what we now call momentum (including speed as a factor). The new definition explains, for instance, why the stopping distance for cars increases fourfold when the speed doubles.

Initially, after 1905, Einstein's equation, and the theory of special relativity that contained it, were ignored. Gradually, it became more widely known and accepted, perhaps because it seemed to offer explanations for phenomena like radioactivity. In this, energy changes millions of times greater than those found in chemical reactions take place. Something like $E=mc^2$ would be needed to explain these, as it would when contemplating the incredible concentration of mass in the nucleus of the atom, discovered at about the same time by Rutherford. Experimental verification of the predictions of Einstein's theories of relativity helped, too.

One of the important consequences of $E=mc^2$ was that the power source of the Sun could be explained. This could only happen after it had been shown that the Sun consists almost entirely of hydrogen and helium. Once again, discoveries by a woman (astronomer Cecilia Payne) were first dismissed and then appropriated by the established scientists. The hydrogen is in the process of being converted into helium with the loss of a little mass. The Sun is a gigantic nuclear fusion reactor converting four million tonnes of mass into energy every second.

The other important consequence was the discovery that it was possible to release locked-up energy from certain types of nuclei by splitting them. This was nuclear fission of atoms like uranium-235. Here, the prime mover was Lise Meitner, but, as a woman and as a Jew in Nazi Germany, she was forced into exile. Later, she was to see her former student and friend, the non-Jew Otto Hahn, receive the Nobel Prize for their joint work. Bodanis' discussion of the development of the atom bomb by the US — and the failure of Nazi Germany to match it — is fascinating.

The book includes accounts of the lives and fates of other people mentioned, such as Lavoisier and Heisenberg, as well as 50 pages of notes (rather interesting, actually!) and suggestions for further reading. My only complaint is the use throughout of US units, which British readers educated since the 1970s may find confusing. I hope Cameron Diaz read it.

Les Hearn

Exploitation in China

China's workers under assault, by Anita Chan. M E Sharpe.

Labour market reform in China, by Xin Meng. Cambridge University Press.

TWO books on the same subject. Both, as it happens, by Chinese-Australian academics based at the Australian National University in Canberra. Both full of facts and conscientious in their dealing with those facts. And utterly contrasting pictures of the reality.

The contrasts illustrates the truth that there is no neutral or objective vantage point for economic studies. Anita Chan writes from a viewpoint which identifies with China's 80 million or so "migrant workers". Those workers — migrants from China's countryside to its cities, not from other countries — provide the bulk of the workforce for the new factories, producing for export, owned or part-owned by foreign capitalists or Chinese private capitalists, which have mushroomed along China's coastline. Xin Meng identifies with the Chinese government officials wanting to maximise the investment, international competitiveness, and profitability of those factories. That explains the different pictures.

Chan systematically collated reports from the state-regulated Chinese press about labour abuses. Such reports exist. China's ruling bureaucracy has become less monolithic. But Chan shows that many abuses took months to get into print, suggesting that many more never get published.

The background is that from the mid 1950s until about 1978, China had state control of labour much tighter than anything achieved in the USSR even at the height of Stalinism.

China, with its huge peasant population, never had the labour shortages the Stalinist USSR faced. The rural population was banned by law from moving to the cities. In the cities, those lucky enough to "inherit" jobs in state enterprises — "inheritance" was a large part of it — got a secure wage and social provision, all organised through the workplace, but at the cost of total state direction of who worked where and on what terms.

Workers could not move to new jobs. Usually they didn't want to. The "iron rice bowl" in state enterprises was grim, but better than the chances of scraping by on the semi-legal fringes of the urban economy or being sent to the countryside.

Since 1978 state control of labour has loosened up — with the paradoxical result of extending semi-slave conditions! The state enterprises have cut lots of jobs, and worsened workers' conditions. A vast new swathe of industry, dominated by private capitalists, has emerged, and now accounts for the majority of China's industrial production. Some of the new factories are huge. One Taiwanese-run factory in Dongguan employs 40,000 workers, producing shoes for Nike, Reebok and Adidas.

The new workers, mostly young women, still have the legal status of tolerated exceptions to the rule that rural people stay in the countryside. To move to the cities they need an official permit. When their employers take their permits "for safe keeping", as they often do, the workers are tied to the factory as securely as any serf to a feudal estate.

Employers also keep control over workers by demanding from them large advance payments — up to a year's wages — before granting them a job, and paying them hugely in arrears. Workers stick to jobs in the worst conditions for the sake of a chance of getting their back wages and paying off their debts.

At the extreme, workers are literally imprisoned in dormitories within the factory compound. In one case documented by Chan, two workers were stoned to death by management thugs when they tried to escape from the compound. No official charged or prosecuted anyone for the murder, though the dead workers' families are attempting a private prosecution.

Inside the factories, sexual harassment and violence. In a Taiwanese-owned footwear factory in Guangzhou, the boss punished workers by hanging heavy iron moulds (designed for shaping shoes) round their necks, and forcing them to run round the factory grounds, or by making them stand upside down, with their hands on the ground, against a wall, for more than an hour.

The dormitories where the workers live are foul. Work conditions are unsafe. Chan cites one cutlery factory which had 142 accidents among 400 workers within three years, with 35 workers losing parts of limbs. The hours are very long. Some workers never have a day off. And the wages are low, often around US$1.50 a day.

One article in the magazine of China's official (state-run) trade unions commented, with what must have been deliberate sarcasm: "In early capitalist societies, the suppression of basic worker rights and the control of their movement was widespread. Today, such practices have almost disappeared except in socialist countries such as our own".

The workers fight back. In one chapter Chan documents "worker resistance". Strikes are becoming more common. One case cited by Chan also shows how trade unionists internationally can help — that of Chinese seafarers on a British-owned and Greek-officered ships, hideously mistreated until the ship docked in Italy and the Italian dockworkers, finding out about the seafarers' conditions, refused to service the ship until improvements were conceded.

The same facts, blurred, appear at the edges of Xin Meng's vision. For example, he knows that "a common feature of China's present labour market is that migrants get paid less than they are supposed to, do not get paid at all, or have payments delayed", and he deplores it.

But his focus is elsewhere. His concern is with measuring how much Chinese government measures since 1978 have promoted market efficiency. His method is statistical analysis on surveys done, usually by Chinese government agencies, on selected groups of factories and workers.

His conclusion is that China is moving towards market efficiency, but still has a long way to go. The big problem is "that everybody in urban China has always been looked after by the state and has an expectation that this should continue. It may, therefore, take a considerable amount of time for individuals to adjust psychologically to a new situation, particularly one which is unlikely to be as generous or caring".

He argues that China must not develop a welfare state. The country cannot afford it, and it can only slow the necessary "psychological adjustment", which "can be quick when it is a matter of survival".

Ruthlessness is better in the long run, because it will create a more efficient and thriving market economy from which, eventually, the benefits will trickle down to everyone. Xin Meng's argument is exactly like one which Marx dealt with over 100 years in *Capital*, coming from economists who held that job cuts through introduction of new machinery were really a blessing because the process generated new capitals which would create new jobs. "And this", Marx exclaimed — "and this the apologist calls a compensation for the misery, the sufferings, the possible death of the displaced labourers during the transition period".

Rhodri Evans

Trotsky in World War One

Leon Trotsky and World War One, by Ian Thatcher. Macmillan.

W HEN the great powers of Europe went to war in August 1914, Leon Trotsky was living in Vienna. Fearing arrest, he fled to Switzerland for three months. In November 1914 he moved to France as a war correspondent for *Kievskaya Mysl*, a liberal newspaper for which he had worked since 1909, including during the Balkan wars (1912-13). Trotsky was a participant in the anti-war socialist conferences of Zimmerwald (September 1915) and Kienthal (April 1916), which laid the basis for a new international. He was deported from France in October 1916, travelling through Spain, where he was briefly imprisoned, arriving in New York in January 1917. He left for Russia at the end of March 1917, and there, with Lenin, helped lead the revolution that created the world's first workers' state.

This book by Ian Thatcher is an ambivalent contribution to our understanding this period of Trotsky's life. Thatcher provides an account of the 16 articles Trotsky wrote for *Kievskaya Mysl*, and information about Trotsky's articles in socialist newspapers such as *Nashe Slovo* (published in Paris) which has not appeared in English before.

But Thatcher also claims that when Trotsky, after the Russian revolution of 1917, put together a collection of his writings against World War 1 (*War and Revolution*, 1922), he deliberately excluded most of the articles in which he polemicised with Lenin, and "falsified" other articles to make it appear that Lenin's views converged with his own. Thatcher says that an examination of the documents reveals "a story of almost continuous opposition between Trotsky and Lenin".

Whether Trotsky's editing was suspect or not − and I think Thatcher makes too much of it − could only be judged by comparing the text of *War and Revolution* with the original articles. In any case, the differences between Lenin and Trotsky are very well known even from the collections currently available − the Stalinists certainly made sure Lenin's polemics against Trotsky were widely available in print.

Trotsky did not accept Lenin's slogan of "defeatism", and promoted slogans for peace and for the United States of Europe which Lenin rejected at times during the war. Whether their views fundamentally diverged is a different matter altogether.

Lenin argued that Russia's defeat in the war would be a lesser evil for Russian socialists. It was a formula Lenin used to demarcate the Bolsheviks from other socialist opponents of the war. By contrast, Trotsky wrote that, "under no condition can I agree with your opinion, which is emphasized by a resolution, that Russia's defeat would be a 'lesser evil'. This opinion represents a fundamental connivance with the political methodology of social patriotism, a connivance for which there is no reason or justification, and which substitutes an orientation (extremely arbitrary under present conditions) along the line of a 'lesser evil' for the revolutionary struggle against war and the conditions which generate this war" − "Open Letter to the Editorial Board of Kommunist", June 1915 (Pearce 1961: p. 32).

Trotsky never came round to Lenin's view on this. When he came to write the theses *War and the Fourth International* in 1934, Trotsky omitted the slogan of "defeatism" from his first draft. Under pressure from his comrades, he then incorporated the term, with a content different from Lenin's original use but compatible with Trotsky's own old views (Joubert, 1988). He wrote that, "Lenin's formula 'defeat is the lesser evil' means not that the defeat of one's own country is the lesser evil as compared with the enemy country but that a military defeat resulting from the growth of the revolutionary movement is infinitely more beneficial to the proletariat and to the whole people than military victory assured by civil peace."

Did Lenin come round to Trotsky's opinion on "defeatism"? We know only that Lenin never again took up "defeatism" systematically after 1917; and, as Hal Draper pointed out, there is "not even a hint of any kind of the defeat slogan in any of the documents of the first four congresses of the Comintern... It played no part in the programme, policy, and principles of the Communist International under Lenin" (2001: pp. 98, 99).

We also know that during 1916, Lenin's attitude towards the slogan of peace began to change as war-weariness became more evident among the soldiers.

And the United States of Europe? Both Trotsky, in his pamphlet *War and the International*, and the Bolsheviks' first manifesto in November 1914, called for a Republican United States of Europe (p. 43). It was part of the culture of the Social Democracy before the war — Kautsky had formulated the slogan as early as 1908. At the Bern conference (1915), Lenin advocated the slogan politically, but also said it needed to be evaluated more fully from an economic point of view.

By the middle of 1915, Lenin had decided against the slogan. He wrote in *Socialism and War* that, "Either this is a demand that is unrealisable under capitalism, proposing the establishment of a regulated world economy under a share-out of colonies, spheres of influence and so on. Or this slogan is reactionary, signifying a temporary alliance of the great powers of Europe for a more successful exploitation of the colonies and for robbing the more quickly developing Japan and America." (p. 67).

Trotsky accepted Lenin's distinctions between the political and economic sides of the question, and between a bourgeois and a socialist United States of Europe. He agreed that in conditions of imperialist war, the bourgeois unification of Europe was a utopia, or it would be partial and reactionary from an economic point of view (e.g., following a German victory). Nevertheless, he argued that, "If the capitalist states of Europe succeeded in merging into an imperialist trust, this would be a step forward as compared with the existing situation, for it would first of all create a unified, all-European material base for the working class movement" — *The Peace Programme* (1916).

Trotsky also criticised Lenin's inconsistency on the political side: Lenin was willing to accept the possibility of the right of nations to self-determination (i.e., the demarcation of states) as realisable in the present epoch, and yet refusing to allow for the possibility of a democratic unification of states. He also argued that the slogan of a United States of Europe emphasised the interdependency of the European working class, and the necessity of international coordination in making a proletarian revolution. The slogan for Trotsky was a bridge between the conditions of war which divided the European working class, and the aspirations for a socialist revolution across the continent.

In 1923, during the Ruhr crisis, Trotsky raised the slogan of a United States of Europe once more (*Pravda*, June 30, 1923). Again he defined it as a transitional slogan, like the demand for a workers' government, a bridge between the crisis situation and the dictatorship of the proletariat. The Executive of the Comintern took up the political line shortly afterwards on Trotsky's proposal and in the teeth of opposition (although not from Lenin). It was not until the Seventh Plenum

of the ECCI (November-December 1926) that the slogan was finally cast out of the Comintern. Trotsky made its omission the starting point of his critique of Bukharin's draft programme at the Sixth Congress of the Comintern (1928), and included the slogan in his later major programmatic documents.

Although he admires Trotsky's foresight and appears to accept the slogan, Thatcher does not even take us as far as the Comintern discussion, and only alludes to its present day prescience. Support for the slogan does not equate with support for the organisation of the European Union, in fact it points to the limited, partial development of bourgeois institutions, and demands their democratisation. But it recognises that the EU is fundamentally a reflection of the drive by capitalism to knit the world together into larger economic units, and it points to international working class unity as the answer to capitalist integration, as opposed to the reactionary separation into national states.

I think Thatcher is fundamentally wrong on the divergence between Lenin and Trotsky. The disagreements on "defeatism", as on other matters, were revived artificially in 1924, by Zinoviev and others, as part of the campaign of the Stalinist bureaucracy to discredit Trotsky. Unfortunately the author of this book lacks any sympathy with Trotsky's rationale for subsequently seeking to minimise his wartime differences with Lenin, and writes as if the fight against Stalinism was merely an argument among epigones. Thatcher's sneers about Trotsky's delay in joining of the Bolshevik party, "What kept him so long?" (p. 213), and about why he worked for *Kievskaya Mysl* (Trotsky never enjoyed the comforts of the university chair, but still had to earn a living) are hardly in keeping with the seriousness of the subject matter. That, together with Thatcher's tendentious interpretation of Trotsky's relations with Lenin, undermines what might have been a very interesting book.

Paul Hampton

References

Draper, Hal [1953-54] 2001, "Lenin and the Myth of Revolutionary Defeatism", *Workers' Liberty* 2: 1.

Gankin, Olga and Fisher H.H. eds. 1940, *The Bolsheviks and the World War*, Stanford: Stanford University Press.

Joubert, Jean-Paul 1988, "Revolutionary Defeatism", *Revolutionary History*, Vol 1, No 3: pp. 2-7, 36.

Pearce, Brian 1961, "Lenin and Trotsky on Pacifism and Defeatism", *Labour Review*, Vol 6, No 1: pp. 29-38.